FEDERICO FELLINI

Fabrizio Borin

FEDERICO FELLINI

in conjuction with
Carla Mele

GREMESE

To Massimo… Amarcord

Books of cinema for schools and universities

Photography credits:
According to the Editor's research, the photographs in this volume are attributed to Nicola Arresto (*The Nights of Cabiria*), Domenico Cattarinich (*Fellini's Satyricon, Toby Dammit*), Ettore Pesce (*I Vitelloni, Variety Lights*), A. Piotti (*La Strada*), Pierluigi (*La Dolce Vita, Amarcord, Fellini's Casanova, I Vitelloni, Orchestra Rehearsal, City of Women, And the Ship Sails On, Ginger and Fred*), G. B. Poletto (*Il Bidone, Juliet of the Spirits, Fellini's Roma*), Paul Ronald (*The Temptations of Doctor Antonio, Eight and a Half*), Tazio Secchiaroli (*Eight and a Half, Toby Dammit, Fellini's Satyricon*). In particular the photos on pages 90, 104 (below), 105, 106, 170, 171 are by Elisabetta Catalano; those on pages 162 (below), 163-166 are by Emilio Lai.
As far as possible the Editor has tried to find the name of the photographers whose photographs are published in this volume, in order to attribute them correctly. However, this research has not always been successful and therefore the Editor apologizes for any possible errors or omissions. In the event of reprinting the Editor declares himself ready to make any necessary corrections and to recognize any rights, according to article 70, from law number 633, 1941.

Cover and back cover photographs:
Domenico Cattarinich

Original title:
Federico Fellini

Translation from Italian:
Charles Nopar, with the collaboration of Sue Jones

Cover design:
Sergio Alberini

Phototypeset:
Graphic Art 6 s.r.l. – Rome
e-mail: dva@uni.net

GREMESE EDITORE s.r.l. – Rome
© 1999

ISBN 88-7301-356-2

Index

Introduction

"*Does the shadow die?*" This is the splendidly rhetorical question that Federico Fellini poses in order to underscore the immanent character of the clown in contemporary shows. It is a superfluous question, on a par with the one asked by his last clown, Ivo-Benigni in The Voice of the Moon, about the destiny of sparks and of music when it ceases to play. And it is precisely this poetry of the useless exalting the apparently unessential that suffuses Fellini's great art: a fantastic universe that absorbs and reinterprets reality, an invented dream world that is mirrored in life, the image of the probable and the fictitious on film.

In short, the presence of an absolutely resolute persona, irreplaceable, incomparable in the artistic and cultural panorama of this century, aiming to prevent our society from losing its way. A presence that goes beyond the limits of mere cinema, which has given us heart, soul and unforgettable images. A role and significance so wide and limitless as to make one think of Fellini as an alien author, a "magician of light" who has been touched by the same fate as his characters, whether they be clowns or alter egos. The more one tries to define, decipher, classify and file them away, the more they take fright, flee, reinvent, disappear, and return to the unknowable sphere of the music of sparks.

Much has been said about Fellini, often of a contradictory nature. Each of his movies (and the context within which they were produced) has left discordant critical traces, has moved people, divided and enthused generations of viewers, has provoked negative reactions and won prestigious international awards, has marked an epoch of Italian cinema and, like few others, has influenced its language at root level, freeing its oneiric imagination, its memory, its fantasizing about reality.

Much has been said about Fellini, but still not everything. And not only because of what has not been published or the interpretations that will continue to bud like the flowers of a kaleidoscopic rainbow, but because, together with Fellini the Director (the artist of Italian genius) and Fellini the Personality (exported and known throughout the world), there is still digging to be done into Fellini the Man, Fellini the Classic, Fellini the Shadow.

Fellini the Man is certainly still continually brought to the fore, from movie reruns – truly liberating psychoanalytical sessions – as well as statements and interviews from more than forty years in the business; but there are still rich, unexplored reserves to be tapped (his dreams and writings for the screen, his private life and his designs, his story-telling and the unforeseeable qualities of a visual and evocative creativity worthy of a raconteur of the printed page). Fellini the Classic ….

And if, by chance, somebody's brow should suddenly furrow in perplexity or somebody else's nose should wrinkle, let them not fear: for the moment, there is no danger. Those like Federico Fellini who give voice to the imagination and to memory, to both pretence and reality, open up new perspectives with every fresh viewing of their work, and make minds turn somersaults and tingle with merriment and sincere emotion. They do not disturb orthodox beliefs, they are bashful and deceitful to the insensitive, fascinating and shameless to those who completely accept them. Like clowns and their melancholy human shadows, they make one laugh and cry because they are clowns and shadows, as evanescent and dense as air, cinematic phantoms and solid forms. But do shadows die?

f. b.

Fellini dressed as a waiter on the set of the high society party in La Dolce Vita

Life is a Dream

Federico Fellini was born in Rimini on the stormy night of January 20, 1920. His father, Urbano, a salesman nicknamed 'the prince of merchants', came from Gambettola, an inland market town. His mother Ida came from an established Roman family on her mother's side. He inherited a number of characteristics from each of them which would have more than a little influence on his artistic future. As he grew up, he developed a unique sensitivity that was to make him stand out from other artists of the twentieth century.

Fellini, who was a solitary child and adolescent, has this to say about his own character: "Deep down within, some people cry, whilst others laugh. I was always inclined to keep my feelings private. I was happy to share joys and laughter with others, but I did not want them to know of my sadness and fears." These simple words clarify the direction his movies would take when combined with the memories, the brilliant imagination and the mixture of true and completely fictional events they contain.

Many of these memories live on as images within his movies, whereas there are other scenarios for which Fellini cannot account, uncertain as he is whether they are memories of his own life or have been "borrowed from someone else, as is the case with many things we remember. All I know is that these memories belong to me and will exist as mine for as long as I live."

This declaration ought to clear up, once and for all, the doubts regarding the biographical truth of the things Fellini recounted during his life. In other words, in this book we shall not be looking for deeply hidden motivations, nor hazard theories or far-fetched interpretations – something that the director always abhorred even while being amused by what others dug out of his movies concerning his life.

It will be enough if one is content to enjoy the feelings which Fellini succeeds in arousing within us, those same things which allow each of his admirers, as Bernardino Zapponi says, to find affinities for himself, be it in an image or a flash, a word, a laugh; and this not for a lack of philological scruple, but rather so as not to diminish Fellini's imaginative and visionary power, his universality, his simple and, at the same time, complex way of communicating with everyone, even in his less successful works. In short, that magic which only the great can handle when, with their mysterious alchemy, they illustrate life, real or dreamed, or, more precisely, really dreamed.

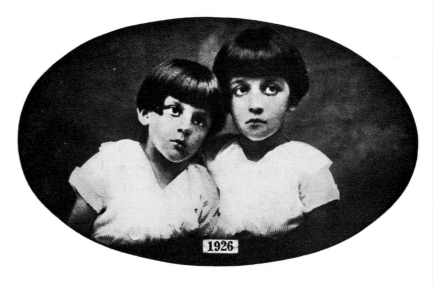

Aged six, with his brother Riccardo

"We are such stuff as dreams are made on", writes Shakespeare in Act IV of *The Tempest*. And no definition appears more appropriate than this when speaking of Fellini who, as has been said, one can easily imagine still intent on dreaming his veracious visions, his primary reality, perhaps his only reality, seeing with what rigor and insistence he has recalled those dreams ever since childhood, relived them with open eyes and presented them to us.

But Fellini the child is not only this. If his love of solitude makes him dream with eyes closed, half closed, or open, it also allows him to develop other attitudes, preferences, sudden loves, unequivocal premonitions.

9

With Riccardino in 1933, dressed in
avant-garde costume

Photograph of Rome with dedication,
1940: "To dear mum, Federico"

One example is the memory of running away with the circus, which paves the way for the future themes of travel and the love of that world which he immediately feels to be his own. It is an episode to which, in the course of time, the director adds new and sometimes incredible details, perhaps because it is a presage in which he wanted to believe and use to shape his sensibility.

On his first visit to the circus he was upset by the clowns – "I did not know if they were animals or ghosts" – but he had the distinct premonition that this was the world awaiting him. "At the time I did not know that my future was going to be in the circus… the cinema circus", but he dreamt of it by day and by night, convinced that he had discovered his rightful place. His encounter with Pierino, his first clown, is revealing: "I realized that he and I were one being. I sensed my immediate affinity with his lack of respectability. It had something to do with his carefully planned self-neglect, something that was both amusing and tragic."

And so, fascinated by that world, he 'ran away' for an entire afternoon and bound himself forever to these people by helping out with washing a depressed zebra, a feeling that he would never forget. The adventure – described for many years in a wealth of detail as a

genuine flight of varying duration – had in fact been an episode lasting just a few hours and interrupted by a family friend who brought him back home – a detail that is scarcely mentioned in the enlargement made of the story by the adult Fellini's fable-producing memory. "I recounted the story of my desires rather than my actual experience. After many years spent retelling an ever more embellished version of the same story, this appeared to me more real than reality. Exaggeration had become so familiar to me that, by then, it had become part of my memories." The memories of an honest liar, the justification of his inventions in which we have no reason not to believe.

It is a bit harder to believe in his assertion of having been a very bad student. For a quiet kid – on the surface anyway, because it is clear just how tumultuous his inner life was – to advertise himself in adulthood as having been a good-for-nothing in a world as creative, chaotic and rather extroverted as the Italian cinema, can be considered a unique thing: the innocent lie that masks banal normalcy. But, reading between the lines, one gets the true picture: surely Federico was an intelligent but rather bored student who, not finding valid motivation in a Fascist school, managed to just get by all right so as not to make his mother unhappy.

Conversations with Charlotte Chandler reveal a high school student who spent many hours doodling in class while pretending to take notes – another opportunity to live in his highly personal fantasy world which, having found expression in drawings ever since elementary school, opened up the world of comics to him and, above all, the adventures of Windsor McCay's 'Little Nemo', who was "someone like me who did fantastic things, a stimulus for my imagination", a twin brother

A classic Venetian setting in Piazza San Marco in September 1937 (from the left: Fellini, the father, and Riccardo)

who, at the end of every adventure, realized he had been dreaming.

Federico spent many happy hours drawing, encouraged by his mother who taught him the basics in spite of opposition from the very energetic Urbano. He used his imagination a great deal in his little theater, constructing marionettes like Bergman – "one of my most tenacious memories." Thus he sharpened his dramatic sensibility by writing the scripts and acting out all the parts himself, a technique which he did not abandon when, as a director, he needed to show an actor his way of seeing the character.

What else is there to add to so 'complete' a biography, even if it is based on a flood of memories rather than on the punctilious checking of dates and events? Having fled, by way of the imagination, from one's family and a repressive/regressive Catholic and Fascist education, he now needs a pretext for attempting a real flight without disappointing anyone, without causing suffering, as was his disposition. Indelible formative years that will lead him to say: "I spent my life trying to recover from my upbringing".

How to uneducate himself, to liberate himself from such limitations when the imagination no longer suffices? Only one thing remains: to leave Rimini as soon as possible, to get away from an unhappy and oppressive maternal figure, an inward-looking provincial town, a religion that operates solely on the sense of guilt, an unstimulating school, an absentee father. To find an excuse, some pretext to flee like his father – the father who remains a stranger to him "until after his death", when Federico will finally get to know him properly.

To find a motive for leaving Rimini, just like Moraldo in *I Vitelloni*. When only just twelve, Federico starts sending drawings, stories and illustrated anecdotes to several Roman and Florentine comic magazines. He uses various pseudonyms all beginning with 'F', such as Fellas, but is not taken seriously until one day he manages to place his first cartoon, and many others then follow on. The pay is laughable, but the pride in seeing himself published is boundless. By now, he is seventeen, and he finally finds a reason for leaving: he will go to Florence to work at '420', a satirical review for which he had worked as a freelancer. "I stayed there for about four months. Rome is where I really wanted to go"; and, having finished high school, the dream is about to come true.

From March 1939, Federico Fellini is officially registered as a resident of Rome, on the pretext of reading law. With him are his little sister and his mother, who has re-established the relations with her family interrupted after her marriage.

His experience of the city is wonderfully familiar. "No sooner had I arrived than I felt at home. This is the secret of

Stylish Federico with his friends in Rimini in 1937

Rome's seductiveness. It is not like being in a city, but rather like being in one's own apartment. I was very pale and romantic-looking. My shirt was always dirty, my hair long." Confident that his mother will be appeased because he had promised to enroll at the university (but not to attend classes), he busies himself with earning money in the city which "totally exceeded anything my imagination could produce, a reality that far outran any fantasy", even if he discovers for the first time what it means to go hungry.

Not knowing many people, he approaches the editors of humorous magazines, offering them stories, cartoons and vignettes, the only things in which he has considerable experience. He dreams of working for the legendary 'Marc'Aurelio', but must achieve this by working first of all for 'Il Piccolo' and 'Il Popolo di Roma', more in the role of a secretary than that of a journalist. He has a romantic concept of the latter, based on his adolescent infatuation with the tilt of Fred McMurray's hat and – a detail not to be underestimated – the fact that American newspapermen all have cars and glamorous girlfriends. "I had had no experience of the life of an Italian journalist. When I realized my dream and got a job on a daily paper, nothing was the way I had imagined it. It took quite a while before I could afford a trench coat."

Meanwhile, he is becoming more and more settled in the

capital. "Rome became my home at first sight. That was the moment of my birth. It is my real birthday. If I could remember the date, I would celebrate it." A friendly, magical city, where he begins to make his first acquaintances – with the painter Rinaldo Geleng for example, a friend from the very beginning and collaborator in many movies to come. Together they scrape a living doing portraits in restaurants and decorating shops, a job which is unsuitable for Federico, as he does not know how to use oil paints (and will never learn to).

Having got a feel for the place and experienced Roman life with other insignificant, temporary jobs, Federico finally gets the chance to work for 'Marc'Aurelio', a biweekly comic paper with a large circulation. He shows up with a portfolio of vignettes, as Stefano Vanzina, secretary of the editorial department at that time and later film director going by the pseudonym Steno, recalls. "As soon as he spread them out on my table, I realized that they were an omen – they looked like drawings by Grosz. So I had him wait for the managing editor. At that time, Fellini was the figure he later portrayed in *Fellini's Roma* – tall, lean from hunger, with a wide-brimmed hat on his head and a white scarf. On a human level, I immediately recognized him as one of ours. And he stayed with us, starting to work for the publication straight away, because the managing editor, Vito De Bellis, who has always been a great talent scout, had no hesitation in employing him."

His circle of new acquaintances widens through working at 'Marc'Aurelio', a real storehouse of humorous minds, who were already partly working in theater and, later on, were loaned to the movie industry. Fellini draws numerous vignettes and writes about seven hundred articles, from his debut column *Raccontino Pubblicitario* to *Ma tu mi stai a sentire?*, a series of political attacks that will win him the hearts of the young readers. In these first attempts, he borrows the somewhat surrealistic style of Cesare Zavattini, although he will soon abandon this for a more personal one based on autobiographical experiences.

Towards the end of 1939, and for the whole of the following year, he dedicates himself to the theater with a series of humorous sketches about vaudeville, depicting each of its components, from the comedians to the ventriloquists, dancers and magicians – all characters that he will transform into movie images in *Variety Lights* and later in the long episode dedicated to the Barafonda theater in *Fellini's Roma*.

Autobiography and self-irony make up the quintessential nature of his columns and, in essence, the secret of their success. *Seconda Liceo*, the very popular *Primo Amore* and *Oggi Sposi* introduce the figures of Cico and Bianchina – clearly they are Federico and Bianca Soriano of the unhappy Rimini affair which was cut short by the oppressive interference of his mother. When this column is adapted for radio, Bianchina will take on the name Pallina and the voice of Giulietta Masina, an excellent setting for the first encounter between the future film director and the young actress. During this time, *Il Mio Amico Pasqualino*, published as part of the 'Umoristi Moderni' series, also appears, while another album from 1945 is entitled *La Bomba Atomica*. His last article for 'Marc'Aurelio' appears in November 1942. By now, having permanently settled in Rome, Fellini is a regular contributor to radio broadcasts; and, having had considerable success as scriptwriter of Mario Bonnard's *Avanti c'è posto* with Aldo Fabrizi, he increasingly looks for more lucrative work within the movie industry.

Fabrizi and the best known variety actors drew more than a little from 'Marc'Aurelio' for their quips. Fellini begins to frequent this circle, first of all in the company of colleagues, and later on his own when writing for the weeklies 'Cineillustrato', 'Cinemagazzino' and 'Il Travaso'. For 'Cinemagazzino', he is editor of "Che cos'è l'avanspettacolo?" ("What is vaudeville?"), a series of interviews with the leading stars of the moment: Anna Magnani, Totò, the De Rege, Nino Taranto and many others, including Fabrizi, later to become his friend.

Many comedians ask for jokes, songs and character sketches (to be paid for, of course). Among these are famous and well loved figures such as Nuto Navarrini and Macario, whom Federico goes to see in their dressing rooms because "the dressing rooms, corridors and wings have always fascinated me", certainly more than the theater as seen from the auditorium. This is an attitude that he will maintain throughout his life.

At this time, light theater was divided into two main types: the luxurious reviews of Macario, Dapporto, Wanda Osiris and the Za-Bum Company; then there is variety or vaudeville with Fanfulla, the Maggio family and Fabrizi, who appears as a special guest star in the finales of other people's reviews. This latter genre, experimental and inventive, is aimed at an informal, working class public who would not accept the repetitious formulas of reviews which were the delight of the upper and lower middle classes attracted by the glittering sets. However, it is vaudeville …

Fellini first meets Fabrizi at the Cinema Corso, where he goes to hand in his new quips. He does not normally go into the auditorium, but one of the few occasions on which he decides to see the show is when the Roman comedian is appearing. The rapport between Fellini and Fabrizi is instant. Together with Ruggero Maccari, Fellini often goes to meet Fabrizi at the end of the show, and accompanies him home, walking through Rome in the hours when one feels "truly Roman". During these encounters, Fabrizi recounts stories on which Fellini will draw to create characters and situations in his work as scriptwriter, gag writer, and later film director.

Over time, numerous differences of opinion will divide the friends, but Fellini always pays tribute to the influence of "the fabulous companion of my early days in Rome. A kind of Daddy Bear, a good-natured Demon Caron, a most valuable guide. It was through him that I began to truly get to know the Roman character, the lives of the people living on the outskirts of the city."

The world of vaudeville furthermore leads him to write two reviews with his friend Maccari: *Divagando* and *Hai visto com'è?*, the rights to which he will cede to the lead

1939: a last photo before leaving his home town

Being a director means noticing even the smallest detail. Fellini arranges Melina Amour's costume (his wife, Giulietta Masina) in Variety Lights, *together with Aldo Buzzi the costume designer*

comedian, as was customary at that time. Meanwhile, he continues his radio work and pursues his relationship with Giulietta Masina which, after the usual tactic of an invitation to lunch, continues to develop, and ends in marriage after less than a year. Things are going better for him now. He is paid well for his contributions and a new, more lucrative kind of work is waiting for him: scriptwriting.

Fellini creates the comic tram conductor character for Aldo Fabrizi and puts him into the movie *Avanti c'è posto*. The actor is well-suited to the popular humor of this unlucky, comical figure who goes from one misadventure to another with the easygoing jocularity of the fat man from Rome.

This is the first script on which he works together with Piero Tellini, marking the beginning of a successful collaboration which will continue for at least ten projects.

It is not always easy to trace Fellini during these years: the scriptwriters work as a team, and their names do not always appear in the credits. On other occasions, they get credit for extremely limited contributions. Fellini's presence in Turin as part of Nicola Manzari's team for *Quarta Pagina* is highly controversial, as is the African adventure for *Gli Ultimi Tuareg* (or *I Predoni del Deserto* or *I Cavalieri del Deserto*)

where, according to him, he risks his life aboard a German plane which comes under American fire.

Apart from his marriage to Giulietta, 1943 is not an easy year for people in show business. Although Rome is occupied by the Germans, there is plenty of desire for escapism, however, and the fatalistic, courageous Romans go to the theater in the afternoons. A little clandestine filming is carried out and the Basilica of St. Paul is the location for the shooting of *La Porta del Cielo*, a movie which lasts as long as the German occupation. Another interesting fact about this "ghost movie" (because it was never publicly released) is that an incredible three thousand people worked on it, many of whom escape the transfer of Cinecittà from Rome to Venice.

With the arrival of the allies, actors and technicians alike come out of hiding, including Fellini who, having made use of a mix-up about his place of residence in order to evade the draft, had concealed himself in Giulietta's aunt's house. On one of his rare sorties from the house, he is caught by the Germans and loaded onto a truck in Piazza di Spagna, destined God knows where. But he saves himself with an imaginative ruse that is worthy of a storyteller.

After nine months of occupation – "which made one feel

Liliana (Carla Del Poggio) owes her outstanding début to her scantily dressed appearance and final walkdown in the dazzling Variety Lights

15

Four of the company stars stand between two smiling young ballerinas: top comedian Dante Maggio, aspiring soubrette Carla Del Poggio, would-be international variety artiste Peppino De Filippo, and Giulietta Masina.

Peppino suffers many misfortunes, and he is even forced to offer Liliana an expensive meal

constant terror every hour of every day, even if one were to stay in bed with closed eyes and ears stuffed with cotton" – he begins writing once more for Fabrizi, creating the movies *Campo de' Fiori* and *L'Ultima Carrozzella*, which are considered to be minor works even though they are not lacking a certain primitive and ingenuous kind of neo-realism which, according to Fellini, is nothing more than a way of looking around at things without prejudice.

And he is an excellent observer, motivated by great curiosity about the world as well as the fascination of group writing and in the human fauna that populates the movies (extras, groupies, the art of making ends meet as practiced by so many poor wretches hoping for a part). At Alleanza Cinematografica Italiana, in the offices of Vittorio Mussolini, director of the 'Cinema' magazine, Fellini meets Roberto Rossellini, who he will meet again in 1944.

Rome is invaded by American soldiers and Fellini, together with his friends from 'Marc'Aurelio', runs the profitable Funny Face Shop, where they draw caricatures of customers in ancient Roman costumes – an enormous success based on a brainstorm idea which he had already tried out on tourists in Rimini and in the caricatures of famous actors commissioned by the owner of the Fulgor Movie Theater.

In what he remembers as a kind of Wild West, made up of fights and idiotic behavior among drunken soldiers, Rossellini approaches him and asks him if he will act as a go-between with Fabrizi – easygoing as an actor, but stubborn and touchy in person – whom he wants for a short on the life of Don Morosini. The subject, written by Alberto Consiglio, is incomplete, but the participation of Sergio Amidei and of Fellini himself, whose job is to concentrate exclusively on Fabrizi's character, will make *Rome, Open City* an unequivocal masterpiece.

The relationship between the two of them continues in the co-scripting of *Paisà*, where Fellini also works as assistant director. "It was a very important experience for me. Rossellini created movies shot outdoors among people under the most unpredictable conditions. It was in accompanying him on the shooting of *Paisà* that I discovered Italy. It was from him that I got the idea of a movie as a journey, an adventure, an odyssey. For me, he was an incomparable teacher and friend. He was inimitable."

The movie turned out to be a revelation for him because it makes him realize that "film making was perhaps the most congenial form of expression for me, the most suitable one considering my laziness, my ignorance, my curiosity about life, my desire to poke my nose everywhere, to be independent, free from rules and regulations, and my incapacity for making any real sacrifices. This is the most important lesson I learned from Roberto – this humility in front of the camera and, in a certain sense, this extraordinary faith in things photographed, in the people, the faces. Up until then, I remember, when I entered a set, when I worked as a scriptwriter, I had no idea of what was going on. It seemed to me that I was wasting my time. Essentially, I was writing literature of a kind rather low in tone. There was always something ascetic about it: just me, alone with pen and paper. The thing that most struck me, and which finally made me understand, looking at things with this love, my very own profession, my trade, is this communion that you create from time to time between yourself and a face, between yourself and an object. I realized that making a movie could really fill your life; I might not have to look for anything else; it could be something so rich, so exciting, so emotional as to justify you and help you find some meaning."

With Rossellini ill, the young assistant tries his hand at directing the demijohn scene in the Florence episode, but this is purely by chance. In 1946, he meets Tullio Pinelli, with whom he writes, among other things, *Il Delitto di Giovanni Episcopo*, directed by Alberto Lattuada, with Aldo Fabrizi, now well known following his appearance in Rossellini's masterpiece. Next comes *Il miracolo*, a brief episode which, together with Jean Cocteau's *La Voce Umana*, adapted for Anna Magnani, Rossellini's companion at the time, makes up *L'Amore*. For this subject, Fellini delves into his childhood memories and comes up with the story of a pig castrator who passed through Gambettola, where it was said that he caused a woman to give birth to the devil. In this work, where Rossellini pays homage to Magnani, Fellini makes his acting debut as a St. Joseph with peroxide blond hair.

Once again with the Roman director, he collaborates in *Francesco giullare di Dio*, then writes other successful scripts like *Senza Pietà* and *Il Mulino del Po* for Lattuada, and *Il Cammino della Speranza*, *Il Brigante di Tacca del Lupo* and *La Città si Difende* for Pietro Germi. He also plays a part in writing *Persiane Chiuse,* which is supposed to mark the directing debut of Gianni Puccini. But Puccini has a breakdown and renounces the job. The producer, Rovere, suggests that Fellini direct the movie. Fellini, in turn, suggests Luigi Comencini. However, in order to keep the shooting on schedule, he directs a scene – the police finding the body in the river Po – which so favorably impresses the producer that he entrusts *The White Sheik* to Fellini's direction some years later.

By now aware that directing may be his true vocation, Fellini gives it a go with *Variety Lights* (1950), co-directing with the more experienced Alberto Lattuada. In truth, although he puts his name to the movie, he is essentially

Middle-aged Checco Dalmonte (Peppino De Filippo) goes along with the whims of his "discovery", believing he is winning her favor

involved with the script (aided by Ennio Flaiano), while also undergoing a short, intense apprenticeship in the rudiments of the technical side of film making.

Variety Lights closes the chapter on his friend-father relationship with Fabrizi, who accuses him of having drawn too heavily on his (Fabrizi's) tales of vaudeville. Fellini always denied the charge, saying that he drew upon "memories from a tour I made around Italy with a stage review". It is probable that the subject had been written at an earlier date with and for Fabrizi who, out of spite, decides to make a 'counter movie', *Vita da Cani*, which the producers Ponti and De Laurentiis immediately shoot. The situation is more or less analogous to the one that will lead to the painful break in the long-standing friendship with Ennio Flaiano many years later.

Variety Lights tells the story of Checco Dalmonte and the actors of the rag-tag 'Star Dust' theater troupe, the Neapolitan singer, the fakir Edison Will and his duck, the aging soubrette Valeria Del Sole, and the younger Melina Amour, Checco's fiancée and daughter of sor Achille, the administrator.

In a small, anonymous town, the troupe's box office takings are confiscated, and they decide to sneak out of town. While at the station, they are approached by Liliana Antonelli, a lovely young country girl and an avid reader of romantic pulp fiction, who has decided to become an actress.

The first one she approaches is Checco who, misunderstanding, courts her crudely and is rejected. When they reach their destination, Liliana gets her own back, as she is the only one who has money for a carriage. With calculated courtesy, she invites the others to share it, thus making the troupe accept her despite themselves.

Her new number in the review entitled 'Everyone to Bikini' is enjoying great success with the naïve public, who only want to see a bit of leg. The lawyer, La Rosa, has set his sights on the new girl, and invites the troupe to his large house on the outskirts of town, where they are at last able to eat their fill. During the night, Checco discovers the lawyer in Liliana's bedroom and, after a violent fight, their host throws the miserable players out of his house, and they start walking to the station as the sunrise dawns.

In Rome, the lead comedian introduces his new discovery at the Galleria Colonna, a meeting point for artists in search of employment. Counting on her beauty, he wants to stage a new show. He plans an evening at a nightclub in order to meet with the impresario Palmisano. Liliana orders lobster and champagne, creating havoc with Checco's finances, and then disappears with the impresario, leaving Checco to foot the bill. Offended, he waits for Liliana outside the house, intending to seduce her, but she outwits him.

Intoxicated with this new infatuation, Checco ignores all advice and gets Melina to lend him the money for the new show: 'Lightening Bolts and Sparks', a piece involving a black trumpet player, an American gunman and a South American guitarist who all accidentally meet, as well as a so-called Hungarian choreographer, arrogant and completely inept. But Liliana has other plans. She moves into a hotel and hangs around with Adelmo, who gets Palmisano to take her on as a soubrette in a sumptuous review.

One day, at Rome's Termini station, two trains are standing on either side of a single platform. Checco sees Liliana in a couchette on a train bound for Milan. The encounter is brief, just long enough for the merest greeting between one who is heading for success, and the other who must accept the truth. The latter returns to Melina in their third class compartment and, while he is thinking of his missed opportunity, another girl tries to attract his attention. A new fantasy begins for Checco.

Up to now, following his brief adolescent attempts at one thing and another, Fellini's early career has demonstrated a passion for design, for concise comic writing, for the humorous annotation of scripts – all of them indispensable premises for the complex creative activity of directing. An essential apprenticeship for the one who is born Fellini, but who must become a director. A collection of premonitory signs which must inevitably lead into the spectacular and artificial world of the cinema from whose grip Fellini will never be able to free himself.

Fellini Sponge

The White Sheik • I Vitelloni • Marriage Agency • La Strada • Il Bidone

" I make movies because I do not know how to do anything else, and it seems to me that events came together in a quite spontaneous and natural way in order to bring this about [...] I would never have expected to become a director, but from the very first time I shouted 'Camera! Action! Stop!', it felt like I had always been doing it, and that this was me and my life. Besides, by making movies, I am merely following my natural inclination, which is to tell stories by way of movies, stories that are congenial to me and that I enjoy telling in an inextricable tangle of truth and invention; the desire to astonish, to confess, to be absolved, the shameless desire to please, to interest, to be a moralist, a prophet, a witness, a clown... to make people laugh and to move them".

It is clearly not possible to summarize the entire life of a man with one detail; and yet, when presented with such an important detail that is somehow absolute, one can almost succeed in doing so. The movies learned this lesson once and for all from Orson Welles, and the sled called 'Rosebud' in *Citizen Kane* (1941), a crucial detail to know and hold on to, even if it does not reveal the soul of the tycoon Charles Foster Kane. The words of Federico Fellini – the grotesque Kane of the Italian cinema – will be our "guiding sled", the chosen method of travelling the entire journey we could call

The military fanfare has just completely overwhelmed Ivan Cavalli (Leopoldo Trieste), the abandoned husband in **The White Sheik**

The Journey of F. Fellini – paraphrasing the legendary, never undertaken *Journey of G. Mastorna* – around and within his unique world of fantasy. In an arbitrary manner, to be sure. In an incomplete way, certainly. In a way which will lead one to venture onto terrain that has been little explored, ignored up to now, such as the subject of his fictional personal history, the sense of his 'Roman horror', his memory, his phantasmagoric psychoanalysis and whatever else may present itself for examination in a spectacular, ordinary, gross, sublime, pathetic, decrepit or non-intellectual way.

All this while being fully aware that the contradictions and images which are shown by the distorted mirror of his cinema are the basic ingredients of a personal and artistic life, without which the architecture of the Fellini galaxy would be deprived of all function and meaning. And so, if the complete picture should, in the end, slip through one's fingers, be impossible to grasp because it is deliberately hidden in a game of hide and seek between truth and fiction, one might just as well follow the false leads, the disconnected fragments, the traps and the smoke signals. And, as there are already innumerable fascinating biographical-critical incursions, one might as well let oneself be drawn into the magical realm where that creative

Above: *The romantic fantasy of the photo story is more important than her honeymoon, and Wanda (Brunella Bovo), the "passionate doll", stares in adoration at her beloved White Sheik (Alberto Sordi)*

Left: *A framed snapshot of the magazine stars on the exotic seaside set*

The clumsy pass made by the White Sheik / Fernando Rivoli, former butcher's boy, succeeds because of his character's surprising fascination

The "lovers' lies", and Wanda's naïvety, provoke a violent outburst from Fernando's wife (Brunella Bovo, Alberto Sordi and Gina Mascetti)

presence resides, peer between the lines in order to gather the traces of an incomparable wealth of most fragile and cunning humanity.

On the other hand, how can one be suspicious of someone who declares that it is his destiny to make movies because he does not know how to do anything else; and that, prior to those preliminary efforts to create caricatures, invent short stories, gags, themes and scripts, his whirlwind, childish imagination shot movies in his mind after naming the four corners of his bed after the Rimini movie theaters? And even if it were not true, as many of his declarations are not, how would this change the imaginative content of his movie sequences, or the audience's legacy? Not in the least. Most definitely not in the least. On the contrary, to know that Fellini is one who 'tells stories' with moving pictures increases the inventive quality of the oneiric-poetic language, along with the felicitous ambiguity of his inspiration, which gives rise to the deliberate portrayal of that which is not true and the mechanisms which support it.

This inherent trait – the inclination towards 'fictional cinema' – comes to light on the very first day of shooting the first movie: "The first day of work on *The White Sheik* went badly, really badly. We were supposed to shoot outdoors. I left Rome at dawn and, as I said goodbye to Giulietta, I felt as if I were on my way to sit an examination. I had a Cinquecento, and I parked in front of a church, where I actually went in to pray. I thought I glimpsed a catafalque in the shadows, and I succumbed to the superstitious belief that this was a bad omen. But there was no catafalque, and there wasn't anybody, living or dead, in the church. There was only me, and I couldn't remember even a single prayer. I made a few vague promises of repentance and then left, feeling more than a little uneasy". In the *Intervista sul cinema*, we find an exaggerated version of events as follows: "That morning (my first morning as a director), I said goodbye to Giulietta, and left the house at dawn. I was rather agitated, and the housekeeper stood at the door and skeptically wished me luck, commenting that: 'You are going to die of heat dressed like that'. Because, in spite of the fact that it was already summer, I had dressed up like a director in a sweater, boots, leggings, tinted glasses around my neck and a whistle like a soccer referee's. Rome was deserted. I scrutinized the streets, the houses, the trees, looking for a propitious sign, a favorable omen. And, just then, a sacristan opens a church door as if he were doing it just for me. I give in to an ancient impulse, get out of the car and enter. I wanted to summon up a prayer, try an invocation, make myself worthy of help – you never know. Strangely, given the early hour, the church was all lit up and, in the center, a catafalque with

21

hundreds of candles, their flames standing straight and motionless. A bald man was kneeling in front of a casket, crying into a handkerchief. I ran back to the car, making a circle of good luck signs around myself from my feet to well above my head."

Verification that this scene did in fact take place, that events really did unfold as he relates, and that there actually was a catafalque, would be pointless and, above all, uncharacteristic. The existence of a Cinquecento in 1952 is clearly complete fabrication (perhaps in order to explain his tardiness because of a flat tire). From his earliest days, Fellini demonstrated an extraordinary capacity for description, accompanied by a haughty disregard for the boring, constrictive space-time realities which would leave any real flights of fancy dead in the water. For Fellini, past and present are interchangeable whilst navigating through the higher spheres of cinematic fantasy, and it is difficult, not to say futile and meaningless, to make the distinction between reality and imagination, between memory and its arbitrary reconstruction.

We will have to get used to his approximations of events which, he says, are always true when he himself relates them, confirming the liar's paradox: because he is a known liar, no-one ever believes him; and we never know if he is actually telling the truth, even if he solemnly swears that he is telling nothing but the truth. This is what we will discover in his movies, and is identical to what one finds with Orson Welles, another genius of the programmatic lie who is much closer to our subject than the much proclaimed affinity with Ingmar Bergman's world.

The similarities between these two superb charlatans of the screen in their mastery of cinematic forgery are almost touching in their disarming, perceptive candor. The natural habitat of the Italian is the circus and the set, while the American feels at home somewhere between the stage and the histrionic sense of tragedy which he reinvents with the camera. If Fellini moves nonchalantly through the melancholy distortion of a reality which has been restructured within the world of dreams, Orson Welles, some ten or fifteen years earlier, lays the foundations of contemporary cinema, which Fellini will also indirectly pay tribute to. Both have an intuitive gift for spectacular narrative, the ability to recount movies through film. Both make their debuts by creating a dilemma within language: Welles by means of radio, and Fellini by making use of the photo-story. These will become exemplary because, after *Citizen Kane* and *Eight and a Half,* their imitators will be countless. The cinema within the cinema and all its variations – the movie within the cinema, the cinema within the movie, movie stories within movies, the lives and dilemmas of actors, of cinéastes, producers, using a variety

of contexts and metaphors of sight, vision, reflection, etc., in all their infinite, obsessive forms – all this will become the fabric of stories, and stories in themselves. But what counts most is the predisposition to lying which neither of them (in the company of many others within the movies) intends to abandon, as it is an integral part of their artistic nature.

Welles could not have escaped it even had he wanted to, because the duplicity of the mask, of the theater actor's fantasy and the magical power of the director, will mark him for the rest of his life. One need only think of the lies of the labyrinthine Kane, of the revealing title *It's All True* (1942), of the Nazi-transformist Franz Kindler in *The Stranger* (1946), of the traps and deceptions in *The Lady from Shanghai* (1948), of the specular Shakespearean confrontations of *Macbeth* (1948) and *Othello* (1952), of the lucid madness of *Don Quixote* (1972), of Gregory Arkadin's murky, evasive past in *Mr. Arkadin* (1955) and Hank Quinlan's diabolical one in *Touch of Evil* [1958], of the tangled web of Kafka's *The Trial* (1962), of the excessive posturing in *Chimes at Midnight* (1966), of the unreal obsession of *The Immortal History* (1968) – a legend brought to life, but never realistic. And to complete the circle, *F for Fake* (1975) suffices or, to return to the beginning, the radio program *The War of the Worlds* (1938).

It was precisely during this great Martian landing in the States that an alien from Rimini landed in Rome. In this symbolic city of cinema mythology and the phantasmal immortality of the Church, he soon became known for famous caricatures – that is, distorted images – early presage of the animated caricatures in *The White Sheik*, a movie about the false illusions created by the brittle lies of the world of photo-story magazines.

Fellini's forgery (as earlier with Welles) is new and completely valid, given the absence of an original within the invention of the motion picture. Lacking that genetic humus, that aura of a non-technically reproduced work of art, the motion picture does not actually feel this absence as something which diminishes. In effect, it is not a loss, but has instead the same structure as an identical copy. So then, if the motion picture is born and reproduced as a tracing, a duplicate, a replica/imitation of itself, it will not be able to exhibit the fascinating call of the 'here and now', nor for that matter the impossible nostalgia for the 'one and only'. Instead, it will exhibit with reckless urgency the irresistible attraction for the plural, only acknowledging the transparencies of the camera and technical replicability as its 'parent'.

However – and it is here that the names Welles and Fellini become most synonymous – cinematic reality is based on methods of manipulating and falsifying its unstable foundations even while trying to convince us that it is

The shrewd editor of the photo story (Fanny Marchiò) mistakes the shy, romantic newly-wed

reproducing and portraying reality, that it is able to restore real portions of space/time.

When the falsehoods of the Dream Machine were hidden behind stories, this created what may be called a corrupt deception, where it became completely impossible to suggest taking the machine apart in order to see what was inside. As soon as the cinema starts telling lies, it is trying to fool itself (and others) into thinking that it is portraying the truth. So then, in learning from our two directors, it portrays the makeup and deceits as if they were the real origins of innovation. It is just as well, then, to open the mystery box, and to disclose the soul of the toy in order to see (as a director) and show (the spectator) what it contains. It will surely not lose any of its fascination but, on the contrary, will perpetuate the infantile magic behind the tricks of its creation. And so it will be able to portray what the technique of corrupt deception had so carefully hidden from tenacious adherence to the remains of idealism. The latter gained satisfaction from the hidden contrivances of its priest-directors, actors, producers and workers, while the spectator, an economically important player, was kept out

of the ritual, collaborating only in the role of an essential outsider.

Ever since the tricks of the cinema have been revealed, 'commendable deceit' has been in evidence, systematically creating falsity while openly declaring it at the same time, disclosing the narrative representation of that falsity. This is the true significance of Welles and of Fellini, our native deceiver, within the panorama of contemporary cinema: that of making a significant contribution to the expansion of linguistic potential and, at the same time, creating a mosaic in which the pieces are the many directors who, following the Forties and Fifties, have found an appropriate place within it, not forgetting the principal intelligence of our two 'masters of ceremony'. In their hands, falsity assumes a truly unprecedented dignity of meta-cinematographic affirmation and fascinating display. Particularly in the case of Federico Fellini, the story-telling and mendacious art of the film illusionist is summarized in the catafalque incident described above, the prologue to a long voyage he is about to undertake. The following statement,

*Wanda's private dreams
and her husbands' public
prejudices have just collided with reality*

to take a chance on a completely inexperienced director when Antonioni abandoned the project. Rovere was the last in a long line of producers who had turned him down because they were not convinced about the success of the project, refusing to give the leading role to Alberto Sordi, as they believed the public disliked him, and that he was therefore a guaranteed box office failure.

In *The White Sheik* (1952), the set plays an important role right from the first scene. The narrative setting, fundamental to Fellini's art of story-telling, had been traditionally omitted. Here it has been deliberately used as an ideal way to destroy the conventional relationship between truth and fiction, between the narrating machine and the story, by immediately putting on screen that which by definition should be behind camera. Chronologically, it is true that this was not a complete innovation, but Fellini uses it in a new way, in an anti-symbolic, meta-narrative format. Fellini works in his own down-to-earth manner: he places the set and its very human inhabitants in front of the line of demarcation ideally represented by the camera. Then, he intentionally mixes and confuses various roles, plots, settings and rhythms, giving them a very free, bi-frontal 'sponge' effect.

The liberating alienation of the 'sponge shot' will be developed to extremes during the two golden decades of Fellini's production, the Sixties and Seventies, and will be the reason for his style standing out from all the rest and becoming one of the principal phenomena of this century's art.

quoted by his biographer – Tullio Kezich – provides proof of this:

"My movies are complete inventions from the first to the last scene: they are not related to the truth. The Rimini I loved, as I have repeated ad nauseam, is the one I have reconstructed in the studio, the only true one. As for the rest, if you want to tell the truth, the word "I" is already a misguided point of view. To reveal the truth, one would have to get rid of 'I'; instead, one cannot do without it. Not even to say 'I was not there'."

Knowing then, that Fellini's 'I', as well as being the distorted mirror of a macroscopic 'Self', transferred to the celluloid figures of others, is also the vehicle for his art of escapism (is not the 'I' perhaps someone else?); and realizing that, for Fellini the producer, the visionary is the only true realist, one can confidently raise the curtain on his inner screen, once more rejoining the plot of his initiation into directing.

Amorosa Menzogna represents Fellini's professional baptism, an authentic premonition, because it is, on the one hand, the title of Michelangelo Antonioni's study of the world of photo-story magazines but, on the other, it reveals the themes and characters of *The White Sheik* and all other future obsessions.

Credit must go to Luigi Rovere for his fortuitous decision

Wanda and Ivan Cavalli are an unsophisticated couple spending their honeymoon in Rome during the Holy Year. The petit bourgeois husband, methodical and tenaciously organized, has already planned out every step of the short trip: the hotel, meeting up with his uncles, dinner with his De Pisis cousins, a visit to the Vatican and a papal audience, the archeological itinerary and even the times for relaxing.

At the hotel, Wanda, having made the excuse of going to take a bath, goes out to the editorial offices of her favorite photo-story magazine so that she can deliver a drawing in person to her dream hero, the White Sheik. Her encounter with this fascinating world sends her into such a whirl that she actually forgets all her obligations, and accompanies them down to the beach where they are shooting the new episode.

Meanwhile, her husband, awakened by the overflowing bath tub, discovers her disappearance. In the confusion, he puts a letter in his pocket and, having questioned the bell boy, rushes over to the editorial office just as their trucks are setting off in the opposite direction. The letter, addressed to 'Passionate Doll', and signed 'Your White Sheik', is evidence of a possible betrayal. Ivan is overwhelmed by the events around him, including a platoon of soldiers on the run and the hammering perseverance of his uncles from whom he tries to hide his wife's absence.

When they arrive at the beach, Wanda, realizing that she has gone off for too long, is trying to get back to Rome when she suddenly catches sight of her majestic White Sheik on a high swing. The two introduce themselves, and Rivoli (the actor who plays the part of the White Sheik), using her fascination with his character to his advantage, begins to court her in a way which is as clumsy as it is effective.

Amidst joking, problems, rowdiness, and sudden interruptions, they prepare the set, which is disrupted by a strong wind. After a few hitches, they start shooting an action-packed sequence of love and death. Wanda, her head in a spin, is made up for the part of Fatma, the sheik's faithful slave.

Meanwhile, in Rome, the farce of Ivan's restaurant meal with his uncles continues, while his wife, during lunch-break on the beach, goes off in a boat with Rivoli, who is determined to bring his conquest to fruition. They return to shore only after a small mishap, amidst the shouts of the furious director and the anger of the wife of this coarse seducer, who is really only an unemployed butcher.

Ivan becomes more and more distressed. He goes to see Don Giovanni with his uncles and, swayed by the opera's theme, decides to go to the police. His erratic and somewhat bizarre behavior cause the police not to take him seriously and Ivan, afraid that he has landed himself in trouble, runs out of the police station and wanders around the city.

Giulietta Masina playing the role of Cabiria, an unlikely prostitute, a character first introduced by Fellini in **The White Sheik**

Rivoli's wife makes a huge scene, and Wanda goes off into the pine woods, and manages to get a lift back to town. Once she gets to the hotel, however, she is afraid to go in. Meanwhile, Ivan meets two prostitutes, Silvana and Cabiria, in whom he confides his woe. He decides to spend the night with Silvana. In the meantime, Wanda, in order to make amends for her dishonorable actions, decides to drown herself in the river, but is prevented from doing so because it is too shallow!

The next morning, returning to the hotel, Ivan learns that his wife is in hospital. Determinedly ignoring his uncles, he rushes away to fetch her, as they have a rendezvous arranged with Ivan's relatives in St. Peter's Square. Having finally regained their roles of respectability, the couple hurry off for the papal audience.

This bridge between the imaginary and the real is the movie's opening motif. That childhood fantasizing is the point of suspension between real life and the future of the adult couple. The honeymoon in Rome is the ritual pretext for the start of the whole story in which the two, for different reasons, are caught up in events bigger than themselves, in the face of which Ivan's middle class mind means nothing, incapable as it is of comprehending the imaginative desires of the woman he thinks is his fragile and submissive little wife, an unremarkable woman and provincial dreamer, but who is determined to betray her husband/father for an apparently ingenuous motive which is, in reality, more subtle: to lose herself fabulously in the arms of an exotic 'lover'.

The main collaborators, Fellini, Tullio Pinelli and Ennio Flaiano, along with Bernardino Zapponi and Tonino Guerra, emphasize the contradiction between appearance and real existence by placing the protagonists in a kind of hyper-realistic limbo between duty and desire, between real things and people, and those taking a different path from normal, everyday lives. This will make their existence (in the movie) very hard for both. Ivan has to defend his honor as a Southern male, and particularly his future 'career' as a civil servant, if his uncle's connections at the Vatican work. At the same time, he must preserve the social image of his wife who, by running off, has disrupted his carefully made plans and created turmoil with regard to the extremely punctual relatives, in particular the famous De Pisis cousins. To miss their dinner party could be interpreted not only as a failure of his organizational abilities, but also as an affront almost worse than missing the papal audience. Their sharp-sounding name magnifies the importance of a family most definitely of long-standing in the town, and thus made legendary by their status, which is reflected in that long 'De Pisis'.

Ivan's experiences with social commitments, his unfortunate visit to the police station, the gloomy performance of Don Giovanni, and his rendezvous with Silvana (Cabiria's friend – a prelude to the heroine portrayed in *The Nights of Cabiria,* played by Giulietta Masina) are contrasted with the misadventures of the 'Passionate Doll', allowing the director to smirk affectionately, and increasing the genuine anguish of the characters.

This realism will have a particular impetus in *I Vitelloni* and *La Strada,* and will cause inevitable comparisons with neo-realism, the great post-war theme for which Italian movies are reknowned, esteemed and imitated throughout the world. And when one speaks of neo-realism with regard to Fellini, it is preferable, rather than mentioning De Sica, Zavattini or Visconti, to consider the way he wrote for the screen, and his relationship with Roberto Rossellini, of whom he is an admirer for three distinct reasons: for being his friend, for working with him as scriptwriter and actor, and for giving Fellini a passion for cinema – and particularly for cinema reality, entirely autonomous, 'humanistic', non-ideological and apolitical.

"It seems to me that I learned from Rossellini [...] the possibility of keeping my balance in the most adverse conditions of conflict and, at the same time, the natural ability to turn these adversities and conflicts to my favor, transform them into feelings, into emotional values, into a point of view. This is what Rossellini did: he lived the life of a movie, as a marvelous adventure to be experienced and simultaneously recounted. His self-abandonment to reality, always attentive, lucid, earnest; the way he automatically placed himself in an impalpable and unmistakable position between the indifference of detachment and the clumsiness of union allowed him to capture and fix reality in all its dimensions, to look at things from the outside and the inside at the same time, to photograph the air surrounding things, to reveal what life contains that surpasses understanding, that is arcane, magical. Is all of this not neo-realism?"

The magic of life attracts the young Fellini, together with everything that moves comically on the seaside set. What else is it that fascinates the fragile Wanda when she comes into contact with the stuff that her dreams are made of, if not an enchantment masquerading as a photo-story? She experiences it with the same unawareness as Ivan listening to Mozart's Don Giovanni. And while Wanda "would like to, but would not like to" accept the advances of her awkward seducer, she falls into a magical atmosphere when confronted with a very real world, of which she had only previously dreamed – an incongruous combination, which the director reveals as affectionate images of people in costume, speaking Roman dialect, who shout, wholeheartedly laugh, engage in repartee, eat. In short, they live and work as on any other crummy set.

With one difference: in *The White Sheik* Fellini instinctively

A series of glances, a spiked drink and dancing at the kiosk in the pine wood bewitches the young admirer, who finally realizes her dream (Alberto Sordi and Brunella Bovo)

distances himself from extra-Rossellini neo-realism, because "the neo-realist never laughs" – and serious analysis would stifle his movie – whereas he is not yet ready for the cinema-set of *Eight and a Half*. In order to create his esthetic of crisis, he will first have to experiment with the destruction / recreation of the narrative, alternating the separate stories of the couple, often for analogy and sometimes for contrast. Furthermore, he adds to the atmosphere an element that will be frequently present from now on in his director's bag of tricks, an element ostensibly removed from the visual options that movies impose: the wind.

To ride with the wind from one event to another allows one to carry the echo of the dream when it touches reality. The background to the opening titles, the deserted beach at sunset, shows the tent blown about by the wind in the foreground and, below, a kind of turret with the camera mounted on a tripod, while in the distance there is the White Sheik on a horse to complete the picture, and the wind that whistles as we hear the theme tune by Nino Rota – musical scores that form a single entity with Fellini's images. And the wind, this element that one cannot see and cannot photograph (but which can contribute to the creation of the story by disarticulating it), ensures that Rossellini's wager is achieved because, in the words of the St.

John's Gospel, and as will be remembered at Fellini's funeral: "the wind blows wherever it pleases; we hear its sound, but you cannot tell where it comes from nor where it is going". The director instinctively understands the cinematic quality of the wind, at one and the same time a threshold leading to a fantastic universe and an invisible special effect, the harbinger of the irrational and the unknowable, of a world of surprises, of subconscious invention and the undeniable texture of dreams. Fellini learns to film the wind in order to make something impalpable visible and, by showing the invisible – that is, what for him is not yet visible and may, in fact, never entirely become so – he will create his movies in a pure state, in his mind, using the imagination.

For the little provincial lady, the mischievous wind that reveals her sheik on a swing may be sufficient. An irksome wind disrupts the 'posing' on the beach, or another sudden gust thwarts Fernando Rivoli's conquest. The wind, once again, leaves the mind in a whirl, but creates a strong impression of action by the simplest of production techniques, an impression of movement, when one captures a snapshot of a false action only just hinted at by the actors' caricatured posture.

With a motley crew of workers, extras, curiosity seekers,

animals, odalisques and characters such as Felga and Oscar, the cruel Bedouin, the atmosphere surrounding the set seems to move as lightly as a camera: how can one fail to remember Rossellini and his ability to "photograph the air surrounding things"? The overpowering wind of adventure and Wanda's unconscious desire to actually participate in the events she so avidly reads about alone in her little room – while she is made up as Fatma, we enjoy imagining Ivan intently sniffing around the drawers of their dining room – bring about a 'blessed forgetfulness' that causes her to utter the excusing phrase "Oh, I am not in the least calm" with regard to an unstable situation about which Wanda ought to feel very agitated. But Fellini's wind, which will later set in motion the ghosts of memory and the dreams of time-paled phantoms, prevent the bayadère, for the moment, from continuing to live irrationally. She will return to her senses outside the hotel.

Humanized grotesqueness reaches its peak in her attempts to drown herself in a shallow stretch of water, whilst Ivan is spending the night with a prostitute. At the apex of their crises, the spouses each feel 'guilt' which, for Wanda, is a dreamy but stupidly honest folly (she reveals

the nonsense about a magic filter to Rivoli's wife, and this will steer the story towards its conclusion), while, for Ivan, who always has the initiative, it represents self-absolution for his 'little adventure', his farewell to celibacy.

In the end, it is a grotesque of physical features bathed in dazzling light, of close-ups of extras resembling ink stains, the faces of waiters, doormen, workers and all the other species of humanity which populate Fellini's movies, faces on which one can perceive the special attention he gives them, his sharp sense of the photogenic, his extraordinary ability to hit on the stories behind these faces and make them emerge, to transform them into phrases, anecdotes, stories.

It is a grotesque which is dissolved by the couple's hurried confession under the sanctification of St. Peter's cupola, and during the race to the papal audience: "Ivan, I didn't do anything bad, you know. Really, it was doomed. I am pure and innocent." "So am I, you know". Not, however, before Wanda has told her husband, who is emotional and willing to be understanding, that public proprieties and private tears are under control: "Ivan, you are my White Sheik". With which one realizes that, from the first night of their

Fellini, along with Leopoldo Trieste who is wearing a chinese mask, gives out the instructions for one of the Carnival scenes in I Vitelloni

The young people's boredom as they loaf about, set against the background of a winter sea: an expressive summary of the author's complex microcosm

marriage, and for the rest of their lives, no doubt slightly gray, she will continue to think of her cardboard sheik because, when dreams are realized, they lose their fascinating mystery.

Variety Lights, with its shabby theatrical company, and *The White Sheik,* with its ramshackle photo-story set, as well as being part of the minor show business world, both exhibit in reverse the attitudes and vices of a vast provincial Italy, where the city artistes go off to the country, and the country couple come to the capital. A round trip that allows Fellini to good-humoredly mock that world not far removed from his own origins.

I Vitelloni (1953), on the other hand, takes the provinces by the scruff of the neck and, for the first time, creates something clearly autobiographical from it, and thus clearly exposed to falsification because it is absorbed by the sponge of artistic invention and distortion.

As has been mentioned, the personal, private aspects of the director, the element that reflects on his past, is to be understood as self-reference, when put into cinematic form, only with great caution, especially as critical analysis has shed light upon what could be called, without any irony at all, 'participatory detachment', the languid disenchantment

of time revisited. One could easily fall into the trap of attributing direct autobiographical and chronological intentions to Fellini, or feelings and fears of long ago, but traceable in episodes deliberately dispersed, confused and falsified, the fruit of the development of the imagination and observation of reality.

At most, *I Vitelloni* is the beginning of a therapeutic directing process which will lead to many voluntary insights into his memory, genuine Proustian incursions among the lightening flashes of adolescence – *Amarcord*, the pre-finale of *City of Women*, some moments in *Eight and a Half* – but only after the mediation of Cinecittà, and the contemplation of artistic and private maturity with the phenomenon that was *La Dolce Vita*, the 'gospel' *Eight and a Half*, the melancholy *The Clowns* and, last but not least, *Fellini's Roma*, the most successful of the frescos of that generation. It is almost as if the direction in which his inspiration progresses were inversely proportional to the passing of time. In terms of Fellini, the 'first' comes after the movies interpreted by his alter ego. Marcello Rubini's agitation and dissatisfaction (*La Dolce Vita*), and the fires burning within film director Guido Anselmi (*Eight and a Half*) come forth only after the door of the imagination is actualized once again – could Fellini really deny that there

are no traces of himself in Wanda, the photo-story addict – and thus after the memories of the places and people of his sleepy Rimini years in *I Vitelloni*.

To get to Rome, he must leave Rimini. To descend the dream slide that is *City of Women*, he must first clamber up the steps of his obsessive origins, and pace the length and breadth of the premises of his movie world, from *La Strada* to *Satyricon*, from *Il Bidone* to *Orchestra Rehearsal*, from *The Nights of Cabiria* to *Intervista* to *The Voice of the Moon*. In saying that in order to arrive, one must depart; to slide down, one must first have climbed up, is not just to make witty remarks like the impish 'Snaporaz' (the nickname exchanged by Fellini and Mastroianni, and also a character in *City of Women*. Instead, it brings less obvious evidence into focus, the preliminary movements of an impending journey, prior to the official arrival in Rome.

Thus, before arriving, or, having arrived fourteen years earlier, Fellini now decides to tell how and why he left Rimini, to recount what happened beforehand through the portrayal of the false life of the 'vitelloni' (shirkers) of his home town. "I was never a 'vitellone', and I didn't even know that the ones I saw were shirkers. I regarded them with admiration: one because he was skillful with a billiard cue, another because he wore beautiful scarves, and yet another because women liked him. But the whole time I lived in Rimini, I never mixed with them. They would not even have deigned to greet me, they wouldn't."

The benefit of the doubt that we grant the magnificent liar cannot prevent us from pausing a moment to consider that 'they wouldn't' as if, after such a long time, he could still maintain his interest in lives so different from his, and the almost jealous pain of an ironic and affectionate eye cast over people who had already become personages.

'Vitelloni' are louts who, for as long as they can get away with it, avoid any sort of commitment to work or relationships; non-enrolled students who hang around the coffee bar or roam around in groups without being completely ostracized from society like Pasolini's *Ragazzi di Vita* or Lina Wertmüller's *I Basilischi*. The 'vitelloni' are the archetype national average, boys who will move to the city when they grow up, fill government offices and the streets of the Italian comedy, carrying with them all the stereotype qualities of their origins.

The nickname 'vitelloni', together with all the other pet names, diminutives and augmentatives that Fellini affectionately invents throughout his life, are analogical, tell their own stories and are symptomatic examples of his contradictions, ranging from the serious to the grotesque, exaggeration and subtle understatement. In short, they range from the quest for poetry to the fear of all-too-human perceptions, from conspiratorial affection to little artistic

Top: *One of the many of Fellini's portrayals of the Variety Show, affectionately ironic as always. In the foreground, Franca Gandolfi, Maja Nipora and top comedian Achille Majeroni*
Above: *Family arguments for two of the* vitelloni: *from the left, Sandra (Eleonora Ruffo), Fausto (Franco Fabrizi), Moraldo (Franco Interlenghi), Paola Borboni and Enrico Viarisio (parents of Moraldo and Sandra)*

Alberto (Sordi), drunk and depressed at the party, portrays the classic icon of a stupefying provincial tragicomedy

lessons, polite but scathing. Just consider 'Marcellino' ('little Marcello' Mastroianni) and 'Anitona' ('big Anita' Ekberg) – all the '...inos' and '...onas' added to the names of his troupe, and an incredible number of other inventions, until we get to the world famous 'Papparazzo'. It is a language entirely of his own, invented in order to ensure an exclusive complicity, but also a very precise distinction between the roles played out in his movies and his real life, which should never be forgotten: mix them together, perhaps, but always with great clarity.

The 'vitelloni' are part of the Italy of the Fifties and, just like those in *Amarcord*, are sons of his land, Romagna: "A mixture of marine adventure and Catholic church. A land with this misty, towering mountain of San Marino. A strange, arrogant and blasphemous psychology where superstition mixes with a challenging attitude toward God. Humorless, and hence defenseless people, but with a sense of mockery and a taste for swaggering. One man says: I can eat eight meters of sausage, three chickens and a candle. A candle as well. Circus stuff. Then he does it. Immediately afterwards, they take him away on a motorcycle. He has gone puce, and the whites of his eyes are showing. And everyone has a good laugh over this atrocious event, death from gluttony [...] And yet, there are also infinitely sweet

rhythms in this land, that come perhaps from the sea." A native and symbolic sea, very little loved, hostile in certain aspects, on which Fellini works progressive transformations to the point of denying it as a natural liquid element, and falsifying and circumscribing it so as to control it and thus be able to relate it.

Rimini 1953. A society evening on the terrace of the Kursaal for the 'Miss Mermaid' beauty competition is ruined by a sudden rainstorm, and the discovery that the winner, Sandra, is pregnant. The culprit is Fausto, the head and spiritual leader of a group of friends, among whom are the Roman Alberto, the intellectual Leopoldo, the young Moraldo and the robust Riccardino. Called to account, Fausto tries to flee, and only reluctantly allows himself to be persuaded to start a family by marrying Sandra and going to live with his in-laws after a honeymoon in Rome.

The friends continue to spend their evenings in the coffee bar playing billiards, joking around and recounting their unattainable dreams as they roam the deserted streets before going back to their homes. Alberto lives with his anxious mother who waits up for him every night, and his sister Olga, the family breadwinner. Riccardo lives with his parents and checks every evening how much weight he has gained, while Leopoldo, having eaten the dinner his aunts have prepared for him, spends the night writing his new play and courting the maid from the house across the way. Only Moraldo does not return

Sandra and Fausto's conciliatory celebrations. From the left in the photograph, Riccardo Fellini, Franco Interlenghi, Eleonora Ruffo, Leopoldo Trieste, Franco Fabrizi, Borboni and Viarisio, and Jean Brochard (Fausto's father)

The disturbing newcomer (Arlette Sauvage), heartbreaker of the movies, is unable to attract Fausto any more, as he is worried about what has happened to Sandra and little Moraldino

home, but always hangs around the train station. A dreamer by nature, he listens to the train whistles, looks at the stars, and follows his thoughts. Perhaps he would like to leave, but he contents himself with making friends with Guido, a juvenile railway worker.

Life continues in its lazy way when, one Sunday, as the group goes to look at the winter sea, Alberto discovers that his sister is still in a relationship with a married man.

Fausto and Sandrina, who have returned from their honeymoon with all the latest gossip from Rome, begin a turbulent married life. Fausto is now working as a clerk in the respectable habedashery owned by Michele and his wife, Giulia. Obstinately pigheaded about assuming responsibility, bored with his job and family life, he ends up picking up a woman he does not know and leaving his wife in the movie theater.

Carnival time comes along with its jovial annual fancy dress party. Moraldo accompanies Alberto home at dawn, drunk and dressed up like a woman, just in time to run into Olga, who has decided to elope with her lover.

During the festivities, Fausto makes a pass at his boss's wife, and begins to flirt with her outrageously the following day, thus getting himself fired. He decides to wreak revenge and, pretending that he is just the victim of a tyrannical boss, he gets Moraldo to help him steal a carved wooden angel which he says is just about worth part of what he is owed as severance pay. The two of them, together with the idiot Giudizio, try in vain to sell it to various religious institutions and get caught. Sandra is frantic because of her husband's infidelity, but allows herself to be reconciled once more, because their child, Moraldino, has just been born.

The evenings become more balmy, Moraldo continues to meet the little railway worker, and spends an evening with his friends at the theater, where Leopoldo is going to meet the great actor, Sergio Natali, who has been reading his last play.

After the show, the 'vitelloni' are enjoying themselves in a restaurant with the dancers, while the intellectual reads his play to Natali who, just to make him stop, and possibly with other, more ambiguous motives, invites him out to the dark, wind-swept beach. Fausto is unfaithful to his wife once again with the soubrette. This time, however, Sandra is not inclined to forgive him, and she runs away to her father-in-law's house. He is a simple working man and a widower, who lives alone with his little daughter in a dignified manner.

Desperate, Fausto and his friends look for her everywhere. On returning to town in the car, they encounter some road repairers, whom Alberto offends and taunts, making the others laugh. Suddenly, the car runs out of gas and stops, and the road workers come after them, determined to wreak revenge. Fausto finally finds Sandra at his father's house, where he is given a sound lesson with blows from his father's belt.

The next day, at dawn, Moraldo gets on a train without telling anyone, possibly without even having an exact destination in mind. Little Guido sees him and, after a brief goodbye, he walks off, balancing himself along the railway track.

In this movie, too, the wind has a fundamental, evocative role. Gusts of wind accompany the changes of scene, and bring with them the spirit of unseen places beyond the horizon; sudden breezes emphasize the lazy awareness that those regions of infancy are not going to be abandoned,

As he is waiting to leave, abandoning his friends to their vain existence, Moraldo makes the acquaintance of a small railway boy, who is mature for his age (Franco Interlenghi and Guido Martufi)

and caress the ears of the characters, making them dream of, and awaken to, unforeseen events. From the very start, the ordinary pleasures of the party are interrupted by a summer storm brought on by a change of weather that, just in a few shots, sets the action, and Fausto's anxiety, into motion. Like the circus director he always dreamed of being, Fellini precipitates a static action, augments the rhythm of the characters' movements, alternates up and back in the shots, in the music, in the commotion of the gestures, the dialog, and the acceleration of the editing. It is a way of conveying confusion and uncertainty, creating passages and impressions of interlinking fade-outs, which are often present within his vision of the real and the cinematic imaginary. These circus sequences, reproducing the spectacular dilation of the simultaneous presence of two apparently opposing contexts, aim to dislocate and surprise. In the realism of the opening shots of *I Vitelloni,* one already recognizes, for example, the finale of *The Nights of Cabiria,* the aristocrats' party in *La Dolce Vita,* and the memorable line dance at the end of *Eight and a Half.*

Equally involved is the famous shot of the friends standing before a winter sea agitated by a cold breeze, lazily hinting at the suggestion of the summer months lurking beyond the horizon, which will change the face of that

sleepy Rimini. Riccardino keeps his hand on his hat, Leopoldo's bohemian scarf blows in the wind, and the motionless profiles, stark against the gray of the lowering sky and the sucking sound of the surf, just barely work as a counterpoint to Riccardino's typical 'vitellone' comment: "If someone came along and offered you 10,000 lire, would you go in for a dip? I would!" Meanwhile, they continue walking along apathetically until Alberto's chance meeting with his sister.

Once again, the metaphysical wind blows change into the carnival sequences, along with the music, costumes, and the characters, all captured in moments of ephemeral gaiety, which will soon leave a bitter taste in the mouth of those who do not know how to restrict the amount of enjoyment – such as Fausto who, dazzled by Giulia's unusual vivaciousness, deludes himself into thinking that he can exploit the spirit of misbehavior of Mardi Gras in order to make a new conquest, without understanding that, on Ash Wednesday, there is to be no more joking around in the devout haberdashery.

And, in fact, Giulia's husband, Michele, does not joke around. Before firing Fausto, he gives him a lesson about contented conjugal love that Fausto will hardly be able to share with Sandra, considering the squalls of betrayal he

34

slyly commits (one example will suffice: the case of the unknown woman in the movie theater, an episode connected to the emotional wind of Sandra's fear as she waits for her husband out in the cold until the end of the movie).

Masks and disguises, as in The White Sheik, anticipate a change of direction in behavior: Leopoldo courts the maid, but goes off with another girl; Fausto is ashamed of his wife because she eats a sandwich; Alberto, drunk as a lord, in fancy dress, carrying an enormous papier-mâché head, is caused to reflect on his life by the repulsive greeting of the carnival puppets, and also the lack of a woman. Compelled by Moraldo and the morning air, he goes to the real women in his life. The exhortation of the impenitent bachelor – "we must get married" – is obliterated by the storm that is about to break over his head when Olga goes off with her lover. The drunkenness and the careless gaiety of the festivities give way to inherent melancholy and the first ever verbal acceptance of responsibility when he tearfully tells his mother: "I'll stay with you, I won't go away. But you'll see that she'll come back. And if she doesn't, better still! What does she think? For the lousy pittance she provided us… let her go, let her go away! I'll find a job… I'll find…" And the mother, with hope even in her pain: "Really Alberto? Have you found something?" He: "No…!" And so, the dramatic, bitterly ironic lines are

The vitelloni search in vain for Sandrina in an expensive car, but they have no petrol

In order to take revenge for his dismissal, Fausto gets Moraldo and idiotic Giudizio (Silvio Bagolini) involved in the pointless theft of the angel statue

resolved in just a few words, almost an anticipation of the mockery against the 'Workers!'.

Events and people mature in unforeseeable ways, in which solitude plays various roles. Fausto is terrified of it, whereas Moraldo reacts by deciding to leave so that, in solitude, he can find the courage to make the big leap. *Moraldo in Città* (Moraldo in the City) will be the title of this subject, written in 1954 with Flaiano and Pinelli. And, even if it was never shot, it became the indirect inspiration for *La Dolce Vita*. Nocturnal meanderings, in the style of Cesare Pavese, through deserted streets or to the railway station, at a time when everyone else is already back home and there is nothing to do other than the nothing they have already been doing, conclude with the friendly soughing of the little railway worker, who starts his job when Moraldo goes to bed.

The accumulation of memories etched in his mind, and the premonitory whistle of the unseen train impel this hero, in some positive way, to leave his boring adolescence behind. "Where are you going?" the railway kid asks him. "How come? Didn't you like it here?" And Moraldo/Fellini replies: "I don't know. I'm leaving, I don't know. I have to go. I'm going away".

In Marriage Agency, the fourth imaginative episode of Love in the City, a girl replies to a fake advert, and is actually prepared to marry a werewolf in order to try and escape her miserable life

The definitive question about his departure should not be played down, as Fellini himself has always tended to do, nor over-generalized: "I don't seem to have anything to say: I was born in Rimini, I came to Rome, I got married, I got into Cinecittà." Nor should it be mythicized in relation to the countless cinematic 'departures': "Making a movie is like going on a trip, but what interests me about travel is the departure, not the arrival. My dream is to take a trip without knowing where to go, maybe even without arriving anyplace, but it is difficult to convince banks and producers of this idea". The departure, an answer to loneliness and monotony, is the impetus for getting us on the move, setting things in motion, for discovering and recognizing something we have carried inside ourselves for a long time and that, even including the waiting, manages to overcome it.

From one season to the next – as in *Amarcord* – one expects, who knows what, perhaps nothing in particular; one lives, one sees oneself living in an intrepid, but squalid, adventure, in the vindictive theft of a sculpture, in an actor's wind-swept homosexual/theatrical joke, or in the rebellious lesson of Sandra and the working class father. But also in the piercing work of a director countering the risk of making an entirely male friendship too sentimental, as when Alberto, more concerned about eating than about Sandra's disappearance, makes light of it, saying: "Listen, Fausto, Sandra is at home. Sandra is at home, I'll bet you anything she has come back", and Fausto (impatiently), ready to go looking for her on his bicycle, says: "Let me go, come on". Alberto: "Now you are letting yourself get scared. You should have thought of it sooner". And here, as in Olga's departure, comes the strong part. Fausto (pushing Alberto roughly aside and starting to pedal): "Come on, let me go, idiot! Worry about your sister who never came back". A dialog displaying realistic cynicism about existence, which Fellini follows up with the farm woman's invitation to taste a bacon omelet.

"They always talked about going away, but only one of them, one morning, without saying anything to anybody, actually left." And so, for the time being, the parable of the 'vitelloni' comes to an end: the off-screen voice that had marked the narrative sections, functioning as the watershed between representation and reality, is, like the wind, the invisible sixth 'vitellone' – possibly the director himself. It departs with Moraldo, leaving the other four to stay put and to grow old in a deep sleep of expectation and remorse, of time lost and never regained, except as figures in the little world of *Amarcord*.

In the meantime, Fellini's sponge has given back a part of his consuming vital juices, and the director has, in truth, put his film world into motion: fantastic images and intuitions, prophetic openings based on a minimal and eccentric reality, decisively non-political in the banal, traditional sense. An exercise in 'clairvoyance of the ordinary', the product of an acute eye focused on the present and the future in order to disappoint all those who want, now and forever, a Fellini outside of society and its collective and cultural implications.

Fellini enters into society, in his own way of course, with the *Marriage Agency* episode of the movie *Love in the City* (1953). After *I Vitelloni*, which had won the Leone d'Argento prize at the Venice Film Festival, he is secure in the knowledge that his career, endangered by the failure (from the producers' point of view) of his first two movies, has now been safeguarded,.

Cesare Zavattini, the man who discovered the film-inquest and the device of 'spying', asks him to shoot this episode in "the most journalistic way possible", in order to increase the realism of dramatic documentaries that were, in actuality, complete inventions. "Because Zavattini gave me this opportunity, I decided to shoot a short in the most neo-realistic way possible, with a story that could in no way be real, not even 'neo-real'. I asked myself: 'What would James Whale or Tod Browning do if they had to shoot Frankenstein or Dracula in a neo-realistic style?' And thus *Marriage Agency* was created."

To recount "the incredible in a straightforward way" was also a real and exciting challenge for Tullio Pinelli, and the two authors, probably with a great deal of fun, sat down to write the story of a girl so keen to get married that she even accepts a werewolf.

A journalist, in order to get a story, goes to a matrimonial agency in the working class district of town and, concealing his true identity, asks the proprietor to find a wife for his friend, who suffers from lycanthropy. The woman, not at all dumfounded by this, suggests Rossana who, in order to escape from a large, poverty-stricken family, accepts: all things considered, a werewolf might give her less trouble than her terrible relatives.

The neo-realistic intentions found at the start of the movie, and entrusted to the popular actor, Antonio Cifariello, soon mutate during this short story, and reveal *Marriage Agency* to be not in the least neo-realistic, but simply a true horror story. Ironically, the critics accepted it as neo-realism – but one does not know to what extent – thus allowing Fellini a perfidious revenge for the misunderstood realism of his previous movies. Apart from the already dated misunderstanding between modern gothic and neo-realism, there remains the fact that even this little *divertissement* contains hints of things that the director will later transfer to the character of Gelsomina. In fact, Rossana

The owner of the Marriage Agency describes the qualities of an ideal candidate to a journalist (Antonio Cifariello)

The reporter and Rossana in conversation in the car: the marriage is not going to happen even if she never finds out that she has been the subject of a journalistic scam

37

can adapt to anything, even to a werewolf, because she is someone who "gets fond of people". And, with this, the director proves that his sponge has not dried out at all, but is ready to piece together the fragments of another story.

"Why am I shooting this movie, this one rather than another? I don't want to know the reason why. Reasons are obscure, inextricable, confused. The only reason that one can honestly cite is that I have signed a contract to make it, have received an advance, and so, since I don't want to give the money back, I am obliged to make the movie. And I am trying to make it in the way that I believe the movie wants to be made."

The declarations in inverted commas, taken from statements made in *Fare un film*, a true mine of contradictory information, inadvertently provide an essential clue for any study of Fellini's cinema. A lead that is relevant to his destiny because, as Tullio Kezich writes, "*La Strada* is the project in which Federico Fellini's cinematic vocation emerges, his 'kinematische Sendung'"– the visual-poetic predestination that is etched into his very existence.

Zampanò, a gypsy street entertainer, arrives at Gelsomin's house in order to take her on as his assistant in place of her sister Rosa, who died. Gelsomina is a young girl who lives in poverty with her mother and four younger sisters.

As they travel along in his caravan, Gelsomina watches his strongman act in amazement as he breaks an iron bar in half with his bare chest. Then, under duress, she gradually begins to learn the spiel for his miserable show by heart, and to put up with sleeping in the back of the wagon with this brusque, rude man without making a fuss.

Made up as a clown, funny little Gelsomina begins to practise, playing a drum and reciting farcical, disjointed pieces about sunny squares in isolated villages. She imitates his every little gesture, keen to learn everything. When Zampanò goes off with a prostitute and leaves her all alone after a hearty meal at a *trattoria*, Gelsomina is bitterly disappointed, and sits on the pavement and sadly waits for him all night long. She finally finds him in a drunken sleep on the outskirts of the village. While she patiently waits for him to wake up, she discovers the possibilities within the surrounding terrain, and plants some tomatoes, in an unspoken desire to settle down somewhere.

Her destiny, however, is a vagabond life, wandering the world with an ill-tempered, taciturn master, which leads them into discourse with guests at a rural wedding banquet organized by a tireless widow. While Zampanò goes off with her under the pretext of fetching the clothes belonging to her deceased first husband, the chilren take Gelsomina to the bedroom of little Osvaldo, who is ill and bedridden, so that she can make him laugh with some funny faces.

An insensitive, habitual creature who lives only for the moment, Zampanò does not understand how the poetic soul of his assistant can be moved to emotion by a short burst of song heard from an open window. Hurt by such an unfeeling response, she decides to leave. She puts on her threadbare cape and canvas shoes, and leaves the stable

Federico Fellini and Giulietta Masina happily accept the Oscar award in 1955 for La Strada

where they are bedded down to follow the lure of three 'magic pipers' heading for the fair in the next town.

After following the procession, Gelsomina assists il Matto ('the Fool'), a strange tightrope walker who performs forty feet up in the air, with his acrobatic act, in the midst of a large crowd who are all looking up at him. After the entertainment is over, she finds herself alone once again. Zampanò finds her at two o' clock in the morning and, with hefty slaps, takes her back to their caravan.

And so to the Giraffa circus on the outskirts of Rome, where Zampanò can perform his act. Here, Gelsomina sees il Matto once again, playing her favorite tune on his fiddle. The latter, for some unknown reason, pokes fun at Zampanò once he is dressed again, who, completely impervious to jesting and interruptions, chases him among the caravans. But the mischievous acrobat manages to make himself scarce.

The vendetta continues the following day when Zampanò catches him trying out a new act with Gelsomina. Zampanò objects to this, and il Matto throws a bucket of water over his head. The gypsy runs after him with a knife to kill him. Rescued by the police, the acrobat confides in Gelsomina and reveals that he no longer wants to wander around after the circus. He takes her in his van back to the barracks, where Zampanò is released the following morning.

The two of them resume their wandering. They offer a lift to a nun returning to the convent, and are offered a bed for the night. In the middle of the night, the strongman steals some former offerings of gold, after Gelsomina refuses to do so.

Zampanò (Anthony Quinn) has arrived, and innocent little Gelsomina (Giulietta Masina) delightedly learns to play the trumpet

In the morning, the girl cries as she takes leave of the sisters with whom they are staying, but sets off again, believing that there is no-one else who could possibly put up with Zampanò, as il Matto so correctly perceived when he confided in her.

An accidental meeting with the acrobat, who had pulled over because of a flat tyre, turns into tragedy as Zampanò lays into him with powerful fists. He punches him in the head and il Matto, after a short fit, dies. As Gelsomina watches on in terrified horror, Zampanò hides the body and tries to make it look like an accident by trashing the acrobat's vehicle.

Nobody witnessed this incident, but Gelsomina, still in shock, feels that she is to blame. During the cold winter months, she becomes delirious, falls ill and seems to lose all reason, not wanting her master to sleep anywhere near her in the wagon. After ten days or so, on one sunny morning, Gelsomina goes out into the snow, apparently better, but still thinking that il Matto is hurt... then she lays down on a blanket and goes to sleep. Zampanò doesn't know what to do for the best. He covers her up and quietly departs, leaving her some money and her beloved trumpet.

Some time passes, at least four or five years. It is summertime, and Zampanò has a new assistant, and is performing in a small circus near the coast. He goes for a short walk before the show and, whilst eating an ice cream, he hears a female voice singing Gelsomina's song. When questioned, the girl confirms that Gelsomina was there: a stranger who played the trumpet, sat out in the sun, and just didn't wake up one morning.

Shaken, Zampanò goes through his act like a zombie. That evening, he gets drunk and is thrown out of the tavern. He goes to the beach, and walks into the sea. He washes his face, goes back to the shoreline and appears to be dazed. He looks up at the sky and, for the first time, he bursts into sobs as he stands there alone.

"At the beginning of *La Strada,* I only had a muddled perception of the movie, a sustained note that filled me with an undefined melancholy, a diffused sense of guilt like a shadow, vague and consuming, made up of memories and portents. This feeling insistently suggested a journey taken by two creatures who are fatally united without knowing why."

The feelings that move Fellini come from the desire of the two characters to establish a relationship where there is real communication, a true problem of modern society. Fellini and Pinelli had already talked about making a movie about ramblers, and Pinelli had begun to write a piece while Fellini was still completing *The White Sheik.* They present it in vain to Luigi Rovere who, too devastated by the previous disaster, passes it from person to person in the so-called "dance of the producers", skeptical about the choice of Masina as the leading role. The piece ends up on the desk of Lorenzo Pegoraro, who provides financial backing only in exchange for more scripts (one of which is *Moraldo in Città,* the other *I Vitelloni,* the only one to be actually filmed).

It is a never-ending story, the first of so many of Fellini's never-ending stories involving producers, beginning in 1951 and concluding in 1953 (the movie will be released in 1954), because Fellini holds fast to his conviction that this movie has to be made with these particular actors and, more specifically, with that particular beginning and that melancholy ending. Two years go by since its initial conception, a period of maturation that, together with Flaiano's valuable contribution, was of great benefit to the final result. An excellent example of the exhausting refinements and modifications, the passing of the work from person to person that invariably happens with all his projects, and which he seems determined to mention during interviews and statements.

With so exhaustive a background contributing to the project, the incommensurable sum of thoughts and feelings coalesces first into a series of drawings for Gelsomina – his old habit of drawing pictures of the characters before going on to the written text. The synthesizing of the character of Gelsomina is connected to an appreciation of the expressive medium and accuracy of the direction, attained from editing *The White Sheik.* The director probably had to go

Closely watched by the amused villagers, Zampanò performs his strongman act

through that suspended dimension and that same 'metacinematographic' involvement, the intentional fusion of some aspects of reality with 'vulgar' manifestations of the false – in that way so entirely his own, affectionate and relentless, bringing the fabulous component down after having created it so lovingly, giving the impression of 'poetic abdication', which was transferred with the same intensity up to, and beyond, *The Nights of Cabiria*.

Perhaps it is being too rhetorical to recall to mind that Fellini is both the amazed Wanda and the wrathful photo-story director of *The White Sheik*. Now he is preparing to be Gelsomina and Zampanò and also, in his own way, 'il Matto' ('the Fool'). In the final analysis, it would be enough to get up onto the precarious turret mounted on the beach in *The White Sheik* and look down in order to recognize the final shot of *La Strada*, where Zampanò cries for the first time in his life as the camera pulls back. And so Fellini does away with the initial image, and closes the circle by returning to the opening, with Gelsomina among the sand dunes.

Created for Giulietta Masina, Gelsomina is a "creature who lives in a world too hard and brutal for her temperament". An allegory of the victim of violence, she loves and wants to be loved with that unnatural candor that the world reveals to her when causing her to suddenly discover that she, too, is of some use.

"If I don't stay with you, who else is going to?" she repeats, somewhere between comedy and tragedy, adopting the Fool's opinion: "But… if you don't stay with him, who else is going to?" And she says it with conviction to that brutal and distracted great beast of a Zampanò, that creature who, like dogs, "look at us, and it seems they want to speak, but instead they only bark."

The Fool's reasoning strikes home with the little clown lady. Even if he did compare her to an inert pebble, he gave her the courage to defend, in a fit of anger, her role and, above all, her woman's reasons for continuing to love even in the midst of brutishness. "I'm going to burn everything, mattresses, blankets – everything. That will teach you. I never said I didn't want to go with him. He paid 10,000 lire, and I'll knuckle down to work. And he beats me." Vengeance and rage give rise to feelings: "Is that how to behave? He doesn't use his head (she taps her forehead). I tell him, and what does he care? So what's the use? So, I'm finally going to put poison in his soup. You think I won't? And I'm going to burn everything. If I don't stay with him, who else is going to?"

And the last time this simple truth is spoken, Zampanò "doesn't really understand it, and that frightens him even more. He scrutinizes her silently for an instant, then exclaims aggressively, with genuine, subconscious despair: "But I can't

The crowd enjoy the improvised "comic farce" performed by the clown couple

For the wandering artistes in this Fellini masterpiece, the big top of the Giraffa Circus is not only a magical place, but a focal point for tension and argument. This is revealed by the worried looks of the director (Aldo Silvani, in the centre) and Gelsomina in the background, as Zampanò threatens the Fool (Richard Basehart)

The title La Strada was not translated, thus retaining its aura of pointless love and desperate hope, portrayed by the expressive intensity of Masina, the "female Chaplin" of Fellini's circus

go on like this! I have to earn a living! You are sick... You are sick here! (and he strikes his forehead furiously). Gelsomina turns to stare at him in silence, strangely; then, slowly, calmly, she starts to arrange her rags as if she intended to lie down and sleep against the wall." We are at the conclusion. The Fool is dead; Gelsomina, even though she is ill, has remained with Zampanò and, in spite of the anguish which has caused her to lose control of herself over a guilt which is not hers, she saves her man's life by making him abandon her in the snow; and the little warmth found between the stones of the wall and the tiny pebbles on the ground, serves as a basis for the end of the movie, before the epilogue: "It feels good in the sun... We need a little wood. The fire is going out..."

The fire, primary element of nature and of a child's amazement, is no longer burning; it is slowly going out before our eyes, just like the life of the heroine, as the small truck rolls away with the motor switched off. Zampanò, the brave Zampanò, is an emotional coward. Only a summer sea breeze will accompany his memories, bringing with it the notes of the clown lady's sad song – notes which will cause his remorseful tears on the beach, in the loneliness of his human condition.

"La colpa è del bajon", or how to earn a living at a country wedding (Masina in a bowler hat and Quinn on the drum)

It almost seems to be a paradox, but *La Strada*, which will have more than a little influence on some American 'road movies' (which mark the departure from Hollywood studios), is based not only on the phenomenon of nomadism, but on the visceral element in considering 'off beat' types like Zamapanò, rather than normal people. A double-edged concept/journey already seen in the figure of the railway kid: when Moraldo, leaving for an imaginary future, observes with us what the poet Andrea Zanzotto calls Fellini's continuous creation: "something that is simultaneously magical and commonplace."

The overwhelming effect of the movie lies precisely in the conflicting co-existence it creates between hard reality and ferocious fable, the cruel magic of an existence without ideas (Zampanò) and an artistic idea without real existence (Gelsomina and the Fool). Ever since she left her mother and her numerous siblings, Gelsomina is content to take the place of her sister Rosa and go wandering as she learns her 'art' of singing and dancing. But, unexpectedly, she becomes sad. Zampanò's only solo act is one using his 'pectoral muscles or chest'; while she, seated in the truck, looks on in amazement. It is one of the few times we will see Gelsomina inside the mobile home, and Zampanò will be seen there even less often.

It is a tunnel, an open double window from which one can look out in two different directions. Two privileged observation points which, by connecting the two sides of the truck, allows Gelsomina to comfortably watch the road

Gelsomina's gypsy training even takes place at the tavern, where she accompanies the "brutish" Zampanò

behind (the past, the farewell to the family, etc.) and Zampanò who, driving, is obliged to look ahead (but without awareness). This emphasizes the two opposite directions in which the characters can see their world.

The cinema, which is to say the camera, by focusing on the two open ends of the truck, lifts that lurid curtain, reduces the lack of communication and is able to rely on the camera's movements without having to cut very often. An good example would be the first notable narrowing of the field. The gypsy, having eaten the soup "fit for pigs", forces Gelsomina to lie down with him. The two sub-frames reduce the volume of physical space therein practically to zero, and allow the director to show the characters as if, somehow, they were always inside the vehicle, prisoners of that rickety truck, even when they are on the outside.

The difference between the two of them is made clear. Gelsomina has to beat the drum in a certain way, and solemnly announce that "Zampanò is here". But, having decided to have fun whilst she is learning, she makes her boss angry, because he is opposed to the playful side of life, and has the right to impose his will because he bought that damned 'scatter brain'.

Gelsomina, however, just like her creator/husband, is naturally talented, a born artist, and she has fun playing the part of a clown, because the instinct for clowning is within her like song is in a bird. Only for this reason does she fail to obey orders, and Zampanò trains her by cracking the whip. The Fool, for his part, will lose his life for having indulged in the sheer pleasure of seeing Zampanò angry. Incurably inharmonious by nature, Zampanò fears spontaneous harmony, observes how irrational it is and defends himself through brute force, while the two congenial imps are unaware that they have asked the impossible of him. Zampanò's truck is not the circus, but the symbol of a creative block, as Via Veneto will be in *La Dolce Vita*, the spa in *Eight and a Half*, the concert hall in *Orchestra Rehearsal*, the television studio in *Ginger and Fred* and *The Voice of the Moon*…

When Gelsomina discovers the little treasure trove of the charlatan's art, she puts on the derby hat and the makeup, and takes up the trumpet and the drum, which make her euphoric in a way she must hide from her intolerant, gloomy mate. And so the apprentice clown girl learns by imitation, performs according to orders and quickly finds her place in the theater of the road, achieving great personal success among both children and adults, who instinctively love her. And, in the *trattoria*, it is equally marvelous when, following orders "to learn to keep her mouth shut", she opens it with great gravity and amusement, only to stick a toothpick into it in imitation of her barbarous Pygmalion.

During the journey undertaken by 'these two creatures who stay together without knowing why', Gelsomina appears to Fellini "in the guise of a clown, with a massive dark shadow – Zampanò – right alongside her for contrast." She is a character who is modeled, as has been said, on Giulietta Masina, who her husband finds "singularly gifted to express the astonishment, the dismay, the frenetic gaiety and the sudden comical gloom of a clown, [because] the clowning talent of an actor is his most precious gift and the sign of an aristocratic vocation for the theater."

Gelsomina sees what she has left behind her, but she can also see, wide eyed, that which never even crosses Zampanò's mind. And, above all, she thinks. She thinks about the future, of filling the emptiness within a violent man with a horde of feelings she believes she can just glimpse. The source of her optimism lies in the art of masquerade, honest fiction, the opposite of Zampanò's way, which is to act just as he lives, entirely without taking the soul into account. Someone who asks himself no questions, perhaps because he does not think it possible to do so, he lives by his instincts, using what nature has provided him with: healthy lungs, muscles of iron and a voracious physical and sexual appetite.

But on this shared journey among the villages, countryside and valleys of the Apennines, these two lives cannot be joined, and in the pre-finale, the protagonists, each accusing the other of not thinking (the one because she is mentally ill, the other because he is instinctive), both use the same gesture: the gypsy furiously beats his forehead with the impossibility of becoming human as long as there is this 'dog-like' attachment for his clown who, in turn, puts her hand to her forehead and, with all the strength she can muster in light of her physical weakness, expresses her feelings by caressing him in her mind.

As the drama moves towards its conclusion, the switching of strong and weak roles is more evident than at the beginning or middle of the movie. Gelsomina's progressive growth has, as a counterpoint, the primitive mediocrity of Zampanò, satisfied at having taught everything to an assistant "who didn't even know how to open her mouth." Obedient fidelity, the only way of being accepted, comes to the surface the first time she is briefly abandoned, when Zampanò goes off with a redhead. Gelsomina waits on the sidewalk like an abandoned dog, and does not even eat until a woman tells her where the truck and her man have gone. Her apparent dependence masks an act of emancipation, the readiness to wait without being resigned, and to enjoy the little things. Gelsomina plants tomato seeds even if she will never see them grow because the trip will continue into uncharted areas where not even the unfortunate itinerants of *Variety Lights* had ever set foot.

The unfortunate viciousness of the street entertainer results in the death of the frail Fool, and hastens Gelsomina's demise

And this might suffice, if destiny had not set new traps in an attempt to break her fragile equilibrium. One of these is the show put on for a country wedding party. To the tune of *La colpa è del bajon*, the rooms and corridors of a farmhouse open up before us, the places of a childhood memory which has been offered several times before. Rooms, stairs, hiding places inhabited by strange, sequestered, phantasmatic creatures, both the old and the ill, like the little macrocephalous Osvaldo, from whom Gelsomina tries to wrest a smile.

This sequence contains a truly typical element of Fellini's cinema: a suspension of time between the certainty of the narration and the uncertainty of which direction to take, almost a fear of opening the next door. It is a gay and melancholy mood, similar to the carnival festivities in *I Vitelloni,* and the finale of *Amarcord.* A moment that is just barely sketched, but with the same bitter taste of so many collective ritual occasions: fiestas, dinners, processions, pilgrimages, automobile and motorcycle parades, people coming and going in compromising places, when the laden tables are full of leftovers, the light fades, it sometimes rains and the usual latecomer fills the screen. What is it, if not the valuing of something which has been and is about to end? The world gets on track, the sudden agitated pressure of Fellini's action is in the hands of diverse characters who come on and go off camera, to create confusion with the intention of re-establishing order, and allowing their director time to think.

Within such a context, her first attempt to leave Zampanò takes place – "not because of the work, because I like it, I like being an artiste. It's you I don't like" – either because he does not answer her questions, or because he "goes with women". The man, with the excuse of fetching some costumes, goes off with the widow. And it is these costumes which mark the beginning of a new phase: when she reappears in a double-breasted jacket, wearing white makeup and the derby hat, Gelsomina once again, conversely, puts on the military cloak of the first encounter. Having returned to the initial stage, she is once again prey to her infantile curiosity and, as in all fairy tales, follows the piper to the town square, where the tight-rope walker is performing. The wind shaking the rope is the same wind, only worse, that surrounds her when Zampanò goes to fetch her after her rebellious gesture. It is her first encounter with the Fool, someone like herself, whom she will find again at the Giraffa Circus camped outside the walls of Rome.

With Fellini, one always goes to Rome; and should one already be there, one stays put. In this story about the great emarginated, one necessarily remains on the outskirts of the city. While the Fool plays Gelsomina's song, the wind, messenger and shaper of events, shakes the tent and creates sparks between the mocking of the spiteful acrobat and the violent outbursts of his rival.

In the circus ring, there are strong men, animal tamers, trapeze artists, acrobats, tight-rope walkers with wings, clowns, the Fool and Gelsomina – a sharp contrast between two realities that, in *La Strada* show themselves only in a few images. The distinction between the gypsy and the Fool/Gelsomina comes to the fore when, in Zampanò's absence, they rehearse a new comic number. Zampanò opposes it and, not being able to come up with any good reason, capriciously says "because that's how I want it, that's the way I want it." And when his rival reacts yet again by throwing water in his face, he goes after him with a knife. The night he spends in a cell will seal the friendship between the two 'angels of the circus', who sit on the pebbled beach and discuss, semi-seriously, the universe and Gelsomina's role in life.

The movie takes a dramatic turn with the incident involving the pail of water, an object analogous to the tools used for Gelsomina's first lesson as a clown. Both incidents come about because of the unexpressed jealousy felt by instinctive Zampanò, not so much for the woman – she is no use for taking to bed, she makes no gifts of clothes, she has no *ex votos* to steal – but for himself, his intense ego. Gelsomina is his, and he wants no changes to his one and only, monotonous number; but most of all, he does not want her to work with the Fool, because the Fool mocks him. Being someone like Gelsomina, the Fool does what she does not want and cannot ethically do: he takes revenge. First with the water, and then dying a senseless death that

Two villagers get taken in by the buried treasure scam of the crafty swinders in Il Bidone. *From the left, Richard Basehart (the priest), Franco Fabrizi (the driver) and Broderick Crawford (the Monsignor)*

paves the way for Gelsomina's madness and death, a necessary condition for the sense of the ridiculous to be transformed into the liberating tears of the finale.

"If I don't stay with you, who else is going to?" is not a distracted repetition dictated by a liking for one of the loveliest lines in Fellini's poetic output. It is that the movies – sometimes an industrial bull in a china shop – can also move with the lightness of a butterfly in a flowering field, and is full of lines which have become proverbial. The sensational visual emblem of *La Strada* is a high point of the potency of feelings of union between two halves of a world, overturned yet repairable. It is an invitation to look into the other levels of the movie, and what it has inspired in broader, more symbolic and actual terms.

In short, the comic figure, the benefactor of humanity, is presented in the guise of a Fellini clown, one of acting's highest and most difficult expressions that, on the occasion of the Oscar award for *La Strada*, won for Giulietta Masini the accolade of 'female Chaplin', because she is, in Fellini's words: "singularly gifted to express the astonishment, the dismay, the frenetic gaiety and the sudden comical gloom of a clown. That's exactly what Giulietta is – an clown actress, an authentic 'clownesse'. This definition, a magnificent one in my eyes, irritates other actors, who suspect it may diminish them, mar their dignity, indicate something crude. They are mistaken: to my mind, the clowning talent of an actor is his most precious gift and the sign of an aristocratic vocation for the theater." An art which can only express itself in the circus, in street theater at country fairs and fiestas. As he had already done in *The White Sheik*, the director continues his exploration into the noble, plebeian ancestry of the cinema, which he has already discovered – in its spectacular embryonic forms – in his first love, the circus.

Finally, in that 'you', there is hospitality to be found for the alter ego, still a little concealed, a self in development – Zampanò, and also Federico – in whose womb a conflict is established, an insidious fight for identity which can only be opposed by Fellini the artist, the only one adapted to coexist with the many facets of the other Fellini, the one who, three weeks before finishing the movie, will be struck by a sudden depression, a kind of 'psychic Chernobyl'. But that plural 'you' is also that which can accommodate future characters, who only have to emerge one at a time, or else in a closely knit cortège.

"The cinema of truth? I am more in favor of the cinema of lies. Lies are always more interesting than the truth. The lie is the heart and soul of a show, and I love a show." A useful remark to use as a Dantesque device to introduce *Il Bidone*, a highly falsified work, inasmuch as it deals with

In the struggle for existence in Italy in the Fifties, two completely opposing characters square up to each other: Iris (Giulietta Masini), Picasso's wife; and cynical, elderly Augusto (Broderick Crawford), not wearing a cassock

trickery and swindle. In fact, to tell of trickery, of falsification, is an upside-down device, an alibi for the desire to intensively practice, not so much the small deceits of the plot, as the scenic tricks which are perfected in all Fellini's subsequent work. The end of the director's declaration now states: "It is not necessary that the things one shows be authentic. In general, it is better if they are not. What must be authentic are the feelings one has in seeing and giving expression." And what else are his shows,

The gang drink a toast to celebrate the umpteenth successful trick at the expense of the poor locals (Richard Basehart, Franco Fabrizi, Broderick Crawford)

other than the glorification of the Fellini Lie, of which *Il Bidone* (1955) is the dress rehearsal?

'Baron' Vargas is awaiting the trio of swindlers, Augusto, Picasso and Roberto, in order to give them final instructions with regard to the buried treasure swindle. Disguised as priests, Augusto and Picasso, with Roberto's help, easily manage to cheat two ingenuous peasants who, in exchange for a treasure-trove of rubbish, obtain a wad of banknotes which, according to them, are intended as payment for masses for the dead. Another successful ruse is the false assignment of public housing to the Roman hut dwellers. The three go to the outskirts of the city, where whole families of poor wretches, invalids, and unemployed struggle to pay the 'quota', without once suspecting anything from the nonchalant behavior of the three pretending to be officials from the institution.

The reality of their private lives is altogether a different thing. The angel face, Picasso, is a painter, possibly a forger. In order to keep his wife, Iris, and his daughter, he has given up his art and joined with Augusto, the elder of the three. Roberto, who has the ideal countenance for the role, with a perfect cynical, insensitive scoundrel's face, aims to break into the big time, and is just learning the trade whilst waiting for his big break.

During a New Year's Eve party at Rinaldo's house, a con man who has made it big, Augusto offers his services to the host, but is rudely put down, while Roberto is publicly exposed and humiliated when he tries to steal a gold cigarette case. For his part, Picasso cannot keep his wife from discovering the source of the dirty money he earns.

After one of numerous trips into the countryside to sell old, reconditioned overcoats, the squalor and distress of that unpredictable life cause a crisis for the painter, who gets drunk and finds the courage to give it all up and return to his painting and tranquil family life. By chance, Augusto meets his daughter, Patrizia, who is living with her mother, from whom he separated in order to be free for his new job. Augusto invites her to spend a whole day with him. During lunch, the girl explains her plans to her father, and he promises her the security money she needs in order to get a job as a cashier, which will in turn allow her to pay for her university studies. Father and daughter go to the movie theater, but a former victim recognizes Augusto, and he is arrested.

When he is released from prison, he learns that Roberto has set himself up well in Milan, and he goes back to work for Vargas in the old buried treasure gambit, at the expense of a peasant with a paralyzed daughter. As usual, Augusto is very credible, perhaps too credible, because the handicapped girl thinks he really is a monsignor, and asks to speak with him. The conversation bothers him, partly because of the girl's ingenuous faith in him, but also because the loot corresponds to the amount of money he has promised to give Patrizia.

After the swindle, when the two fake priests are changing their clothes, Augusto confesses that he has given the money back to the girl because he was touched by her situation. When the rest of the gang do not believe him, he runs away, but the others throw stones at him.

One strikes him and he falls, breaking his back, and his accomplices find the money hidden in his shoe. At daybreak, after a night of agony, Augusto tries in vain to find help, and dies alone just as he has almost reached the roadside.

After *La Strada*'s touching journey through the contradictions of the soul, the study of human nature in Fellini's movies is reflected in the story of the *bidonisti* (con men), and the character of Augusto, played by the American actor Broderick Crawford. Whereas Zampanò was the bulky, evil shadow lurking over Gelsomina who, not fearing him as a man, was animated by an innate *pietas*, a new kind of fear manifests itself in *Il Bidone,* which fluctuates between the tender anxieties of Wanda, the immaturity of the *vitellone* Fausto, and the faltering uneasiness of Moraldo as he leaves his provincial Heimat.

Here the fear is always present, tangible – if one gets caught, one ends up in prison – but also metaphysical, associated with the uncertainty of a future based on risk.

The anguish and ambience are underscored by the music of Nino Rota, a composer who established a very special relationship with Fellini. The musical theme of *La Strada*, one of the most memorable motifs, full of "menacing, heart-breaking music", and the other works – perhaps the most famous and catchy being the motifs from *La Dolce Vita*, *Eight and a Half*, *Amarcord*, *Orchestra Rehearsal*, and *Casanova* – have created a completely inseparable intertwining of music and image within the public's imagination.

Successful collaborations between director and composer are not frequent in the history of the movies, either because of a hidden contempt on the composer's part for the movie, or because the medium of film itself inevitably draws

The fake priest begins to feel some remorse when faced with the calm acceptance and realism shown by the young cripple (Sue Ellen Blake)

When indifference is replaced by the loving unselfishness of a father, it is inevitable that Augusto will end up in jail, because a swindler cannot give in to tenderness

attention to the stronger element, the shot and the sequence, adapting the contribution of the music to that of following the narrative. But, in the case of Rota and Fellini, a magical interplay takes place, an enveloping hypnosis which allows the maestro at the piano to extract from the keyboard – on the basis of the director's confused, or vague, or quite precise solicitations – a little motif, possibly only just glimpsed, but immediately accentuated, with no direct connection to the story, the characters, the narrative blocks or even the overall theme. In short, Rota had the miraculous gift of being the reflection, if not the unique image, of that moment, that episode, that character, even

while having no direct cognition (despite the minutely timed notations that exist in his tightly-packed notebooks). The underscored insistence of that intuition, and no other, coincides with the incomprehensible and magnetic attraction of these two 'great distracted ones' of the artistic imagination. The result is an enrichment of Fellini's movies with unforgettable melodies which, in turn, are nourished by the identification/memory which the impact on the eye can impose on the ear, until the 'cinemusical' pendulum moves from mental vision to 'visual listening' in a continuous interchange.

In this regard, Nicola Piovani, who wrote the scores for *Ginger and Fred*, *Intervista* and *The Voice of the Moon*, recalls: "What we might call the poetics of the Memory of the Motif presides over the whole span of the sixteen works of genius that Fellini and Rota produced. A constantly displacing sound montage, music that rarely presents itself with real and true comments, but as echoes of fragments-become-objects, and brought back into an otherwhere that, little by little, is shocking, consuming, pungent, demystifying or mystifying, but always strongly involved in a dialectic with the editing of the images, thanks, of course, to the genius of a musician capable of infusing sublime soul into whatever the current material, the basic clay used may be."

Let Fellini himself describe Nino Rota: "Between the two of us there was immediately a complete, a total understanding beginning with *The White Sheik*, our first movie collaboration. We did not need any breaking in to understand each other. I had decided to become a director and Nino was there as a premise for my continuing to do so. He had a geometric imagination, a celestial musical vision, which made it unnecessary for him to see the film images. When I asked him what motifs he had in mind as musical comments for this or that sequence, I clearly saw that the images did not concern him. His was an inner world to which reality had scarce possibilities of access. He lived music with the liberty and spontaneity of a creature in its natural element. He was a creature with a rare quality, that precious quality which belongs to intuition. This was the gift that kept him so innocent, so light-footed, so happy. But don't misunderstand me. When the occasion presented itself, or even when it did not present itself, he made very acute comments, deep and impressively precise on people and things. Like children, like simple people, like some psychics, like certain innocent and candid people, he suddenly said things of dazzling brilliance."

If one should try to understand his working "method" in these musical collaborations, one would be astonished to discover that contrary to what usually happens, Rota composed *on* the scenes already shot. Certainly there were no questions of "priority" inasmuch as Rota neither wanted to or was supposed to "illustrate" anything, but rather to *create* a twin musical and harmonic world that was yet different, united but independent, a sound track that was yet a supporting *column* co-original with properly cinematic phrases and narrative phrases. And all this without ever making Fellini realize that he was doing something other than what Fellini had *asked for*.

Here is how the director explains the procedure which, furthermore, is implicitly indicated by the composer in his notebooks filled with tempos, episodes and visual scansions: "When I am working on my movies I am in the habit of playing certain records as background music. [...] Obviously then, when the shooting is finished I have become fond of that improvised sound track and do not want it changed. Nino immediately agreed with me, saying that the tunes were beautiful (even if they were the most sugary trumpery),

were just the right thing and that he would not have been able to do better. Then, suddenly, the discrete and crafty miracle arrived in two stages. The first stage was that as he said this, he tinkled on the piano. 'What was that?' I asked after a few moments. 'What were you playing?' 'Playing when?' Nino asked with a distracted air. 'Just now,' I insisted. 'while you were talking you were playing something'. 'Was I?' Nino replied. 'I don't know, I can't remember.'"

Thus it was only in the second "trance" stage that the genuine and deep invention of the exchange of parallel artistic sensibilities took place, which could only be integrated in the impenetrable, highly personal musical feeling: "I took my place there beside the piano to describe the movie to him, to explain what it was I had tried to suggest with one image or another, one sequence or

Augusto's initial dramatic plan following his final, fated trick at the expense of his colleagues

The tragic destiny of a professional trickster unfolds: having been discovered, Augusto will die alone just moments away from safety

another. But he did not listen, he was distracted even if he nodded or said yes with broad gestures of assent. In reality he was establishing contact with himself, with the musical motifs inside himself. And when he had made contact he did not follow you anymore, did not listen. He put his hands on the keyboard and started off in a kind of trance like a true artist. When he had finished I said: 'That's beautiful!' But he replied: 'I have forgotten it already'. These were disasters which we remedied by t he use of tape recorders, but it was necessary to turn them on without his noticing or else the contact with the celestial sphere was broken…"

In his "diary" of *La Dolce Vita*, Rota himself, asked by Tullio Kezich, summarized better than any paraphrase could do the essential aspects of that alchemy between music and image: "We go to the piano and make music, as always. I give him the gist of some theme, serve it up to him if I have something ready. At times we actually compose together. Fellini gives me a hint, not as a musician would, but always with a firm rhythmic idea and maybe with a snatch of melody. In short he suggests a musical expression in an embryonic form. Perhaps this time too, as for *The Nights of Cabiria*, we will look at the moviola and sketch out a musical comment to the silent images, once we have established the 'contacts'. [Fellini] is not a director that the

musician has to worry about. He gives more importance to the music than I would myself. It often happens that he irks the sound technicians by eliminating all the natural sounds, all the realism of the scene that carries a musical comment". And he ends with a compliment to his friend's sensibility who "believes that the cinema has not yet expressed everything it is capable of expressing. He has the true director's sensibility that coordinates all the elements into a whole. He is not a man of letters, but he knows how to make use of a literary expression with the utmost security. He does the same with music. This is a gift that other directors, who may be very fine musical connoisseurs or even good musicians, do not have at all."

Thus with Rota's music Fellini's films become something really special in artistic and evocative memory, doubtless more than either of the two would have been able to do without the other. (Naturally this does not refer to music apart from films). Something light and phantasmagorical while at the same time melancholy, grotesque or even downright gloomy. An ambiguity and a premonitory duplicity that could easily have delighted Luigi Pirandello when at the end of the Twenties he hoped for "cinematography, the pure expression of the two major senses, the eye and the ear, tuned onto the cinematography of the double, of the musical mask where one might find a little march or a few languid notes of the violin, a joyous merry-go-round or else, as in *Il Bidone*, for example, an anguishing fear in black and white.

Il Bidone is an Italian story and the Italian is always accommodating, insincere and likeable, a polite swindler, often constrained by necessity. The war had favored the development of every kind of activity to make ends meet and the movies had amply those little edifying but justified aspects of an art of getting by that was typically Italian. The bicycle thieves had become a part of this history on a level with the multitudes of small-time crooks and swindlers that had crowded the Italian comedy of the Fifties and Sixties when they had adjusted themselves to the economic boom. Fellini's "bidonisti" (swindlers) present themselves as a connecting link between the illegality caused by sheer misery and the kind connected to the reconstruction from the rubble (physical and moral) of the war.

The most fearful of the *bidonisti* is Carlo, called Picasso. With his angel face he can con anyone, perhaps because he has about him the aura of the Fool. He can be dressed as a priest, the secretary of Monsignor Augusto, or as a simple layman pretending to allocate government housing. After the episode of the cigarette case and the scene made by Iris, this painter who has "lent himself" to the illicit because he "has a family to support" does not hesitate to return to the trade with the overcoat trick, his last excursion into crime that ends with the wild drinking bout that confronts him with a simple truth: that life of subterfuge is not for him and his real fear is less of the police than of being discovered by his wife. And then, he does not want to end up like Augusto. Picasso is a loser where money is concerned. "You don't even know how to say 'a million'," Augusto reproves him, "and do you know why? Because you can't even imagine millions". Perceiving this, if only in a confused way, he decides to go back to his old love of art and nature to which the others are completely indifferent.

On the contrary, Roberto, who repeats the character of Fausto in *I Vitelloni*, is a city fish with ambitions to swim in the great sea of the Roman underworld. Unlike the time-wasters of the provincial Romagna town who are together assiduously, he only meets with his accomplices on business and to work out the little preliminary maneuvers. He is more evolved than Fausto because less ingenuous. Both these shady personages, like the master of ceremonies in *Ginger and Fred,* are beautifully interpreted by Franco Fabrizi, an actor who in real life was quite the opposite of the immoral, cowardly and ambitious types he played in the movies. Roberto is the *vitellone* who is studying to be a con man, a simple pawn and an aspiring singer ("I have already bought all Johnny Ray's records – all of them. That's

just my style"). He aims to get set in the world of easy money even if he needs to let women keep him. Like Picasso, he does not want to end up like Augusto and in his way aspires to an artistic career (in music) by cultivating false illusions.

In Fellini's perspective *Il Bidone* represents a passing moment of an Italy undergoing change and the script allows the two youths, just because they are young, to be the first to understand that there was change in the air. And if Picasso decides to go back to painting, Roberto, without family responsibilities and although remaining in the "trade", will go to Milan where, at the precise time that Augusto is in prison, will set himself up in a big way, just like Rinaldo: "Boy, he really has it made. I saw him with an Aurelio Sport… Yes, Yes, an Aurelio Sport" Riccardo, another con man, will say.

But before setting himself up well, he will go quickly through all the phases of an initiation into crime: from a chauffeur to a hole digger in the "Monsignor Bidone" gambit. He will be the one to sift through the crowds of slum dwellers and end up as a petty thief in Rinaldo's house. During that New Year's Eve party he will finally learn his lesson and when he is found out he will submit with a smile to the man of the house's comment: "You have a long row to hoe before coming to fool around in here. Thus, Roberto begins hoeing his row by keeping the too-ordinary Picasso at a distance as well as Augusto who is too out of date. At best he might serve to help him link up with his real role model, Rinaldo with his vast business turn over, a white convertible, wife and children in Switzerland, a lover and apartment in Parioli, the rich man's quarter. At his parties figure the representatives of the (false) *dolce vita* of Roman nights that Fellini will soon be telling us about.

Augusto is as much at home in a nightclub at dawn as Zampanò is in a tavern. He is a vagabond gypsy, a lone wolf who has "always screwed everyone because the world is full of dupes", and because he wants to get out of that microcosm of two-bit crooks who want to prove to themselves how smart they are by pawning off old overcoats as new ones. The money is never enough for them because they spend it all trying to fill the vacuum of boredom that occurs after every job. This is why Augusto wants to exchange his liberty for a quieter job as manager of the Texas Club, a night spot he knows well because it is here – another prototype of the onrushing *dolce vita* – that he spends his nights when he has the cash. But Rinaldo does not accept his offer, because he now moves in higher, inaccessible spheres.

Between champagne and girls, the years slip by for Augusto, and he pays the price for neglected relationships with a painful and nostalgic loneliness. His chance encounter with his daughter arouses feelings within him – a luxury that a real swindler cannot afford. In fact, with the peasants and the hut dwellers, his criminal technique is undeniable; his placid, hound-dog face conveys confidence, security and honesty. He easily extorts the credulity of others because – unlike Picasso – he believes in his work of instilling in his feeble-minded victims a sense of security and decency that make them trust his appearance as a "big, elegant bishop" – to use Pasolini's description of Fellini – and hand over the savings of a lifetime. The meeting with Patrizia, after years of silence, puts chinks in his armor and, at the movie theater, a very Fellini-like narrative location, the director adds an artistic touch to his movie.

Augusto's parabola begins a downward turn as soon as the first deceits begin to come apart. Sitting beside his daughter, he feels like a true father for the first time ("If you want to continue your studies… I will take care of the security money. Two or three hundred thousand is nothing to me. I can get it whenever I like."), while the usher has mistaken them for an engaged couple. And it is right there at the movie theater that a former victim recognizes him and sends him to prison. But not before he has put on his tough-guy face again to ward off his daughter. The disguise for swindling the father of the paralyzed young girl will be the final pretext for the big one, the swindle courageously carried out alone, to the detriment of his greedy accomplices. Being predators of the same ilk, they will destroy him.

The scene in the movie theater could appear to be a cynical choice on the director's part if we were not dealing here with the question of the contradictions of falsity, and if,

therefore, it were not necessary to balance the pretence with a more realistic anti-moralistic denigration. The effect has to be a strong one, particularly in the two interacting moments that explicitly refer to the cinema itself: the music of the comic strip bunch in *The White Sheik* brings to mind the set at Ostia and, immediately afterwards, the father's arrest in the presence of his daughter recalls the end of *Bicycle Thief*. And so, in place of the appearance, there comes the clash with reality, a mixture of impulses so as to create a current – Fellini's wind – which will implacably lead the false monsignor to the encounter with a quasi-daughter, the sunny Susanna who is compelled to drag herself around on crutches.

Overcome by that encounter, and by the fact that he has just swindled the amount of money Patrizia needs, Augusto comforts the lame girl and decides to carry out the final swindle of his life. He does a pretty convincing acting job until his accomplices find the money in his shoe. If he had used that money for the nightclub, he would most certainly have maintained his position in that unscrupulous world; but the anomalous act of the egoist that he basically is puts Augusto in a weak position, and exposes him to the vengeance of those who, like himself, know only the law of money.

His death, in the self-punishment that he has procured for himself, is casual, like that of the Fool in the clash with Zampanò: Augusto will fall and break his back in a way that prevents him from saving himself. He dies alone and in terror, with the false ring of the false monsignor still on his finger.

The Prostitute, the Innocent, the City and Love

The Nights of Cabiria • La Dolce Vita • The Temptations of Doctor Antonio

Sometimes they seem like coincidences, and yet the seeds contained in the early work reveal themselves as a mine to be exploited in the future. This is the case with *The White Sheik* which, as with many first works of great authors, contains much, if not all, of the Fellini poetry. These seeds bore fruit in the early Fellini movies, and constituted the humus in which the mature ones grew. One need only remember Via Veneto and, in particular, the heroine of *The Nights of Cabiria* (1957), the definitive proof of the human and clownish qualities of Giulietta Masina who was already cherished in the public's memory with her interpretation of Gelsomina. Cabiria, however, is something more.

The kind, demoralized prostitute, cheerful consoler to the despairing Ivan, finds a place in one of the most typical milieus of Fellini's film world: a baroque, nocturnal Rome, a fountain in a deserted piazza, lights that pick out the shapes of the sleeping buildings, the narrow alleys paved with cobblestones which seem to give off an expressionistic gleam. A quiet and rather magical atmosphere with an airy kind of enchantment, the ideal setting for a non-threatening appointment. Two women suddenly appear in this bewitching stage set, "one as wide as the façade of the church in the little piazza, the other very petite, wearing rubber boots, a chicken-feather bolero jacket, an umbrella which she brandishes like a sword, wide-eyed with the perpetual and joyous wonder of a nocturnal sprite. As I was shooting this scene, I gave a name to this character who, in the script, had none: Cabiria."

Because of "that outburst by the bridegroom, her tears, her despair, noted and expressed in the miming of extreme astonishment, innocent grins, unhinged emotions, Cabiria's silent grimaces of solidarity or mockery acquired such a pathetic and comical cadence and dilation, that I began to think that a little personage was born that night who might have the same strength and arouse the same empathy and feelings as Gelsomina in *La Strada*. In fact, Cabiria began to keep me company, and I thought of her often. To keep her quiet I promised her a movie all of her own."

In this way, Fellini lives and converses with his little characters who have been only just barely sketched out, and are already in search of a definitive identity, using the same words as he used in his pre-cinema works. For example, *Il Mio Amico Pasqualino (My Friend Pasqualino)*, a likable little man who talks with the furniture, with invented characters and names, and who, in the seventh chapter (*The sun sets and our likable vagabond begins to get some strange ideas which force us to give this chapter a rather vague title: '7:30 p.m.: Pasqualino At Times'*) even pays a visit to the prostitute Carmen, one who has "a sweet expression on her face" and may already be a foreshadowing of Cabiria. This name entered the history of Italian cinema as the title of the second national 'epic', filmed by Giovanni Pastrone in 1914, with its suggestions of ancient Roman grandeur filtered through an improvised and minimal inventiveness.

While walking with Giorgio along the banks of the Tiber on the outskirts of Rome (the precise spot being near Acilia), the eccentric Cabiria, a street walker, is robbed of her purse, pushed into the water, and almost drowns. She is saved by a group of people, and comforted by her best friend and 'colleague', Wanda. She blocks out the memory of her lover/protector, and goes back to the profession as a 'freelancer', amidst heated discussions, derision and quarreling.

After a fierce quarrel with an older colleague, Cabiria tells Marisa take her to Via Veneto, where the high class prostitutes work, in order to give Marisa's new car a run.

There, in front of a nightclub, she witnesses a quarrel between the famous actor, Alberto Lazzari, and his elegant girlfriend, Jessy. Out of spite, and because he does not want to be alone, Lazzari invites Cabiria into his car, takes her first to the Piccadilly, and then to his beautiful villa where, for the first time in her life, the girl experiences the pleasures of a rich life, amidst impressive staircases, mirrors, huge rooms and 'white telephones', all of which increase her admiration for the screen idol. The arrival of the jealous Jessy interrupts the enchantment. Lazzari makes her hide quickly in a bathroom, and only lets her out at dawn, with a substantial amount of money for her trouble. Returning to her usual milieu, Cabiria recounts each little detail of her fabulous adventure.

One night, a religious procession passes by, heading for the Madonna del Divino Amore sanctuary. This arouses the faith and curiosity of the street walkers and their pimps, including Amleto's lame

Among the ancient ruins, Cabiria flaunts the symbols of her profession: a striped jersey and chicken feather bolero jacket. With no-one to guide her, she admires her colleague's small car, a real working class status symbol at that time

uncle, who wants to be cured. Wanda and Cabiria join the group, and the latter, greatly moved, implores the Virgin Mary to help her change her life. Like the lame man, her request is not answered and, during a picnic on the grass, she drinks and picks arguments because she is unwilling to resign herself to her circumstances. A group of orphans who pass by marks the moment of change in her very human story.

A few evenings later, Cabiria goes to the Lux movie theater where, prior to the screening of the movie *Processo alla Città*, there is a variety show starring a diabolical magician. Sighting his prey, the latter calls Cabiria onto the stage, and hypnotizes her, involving her in a romantic encounter with Oscar, an invisible prince charming, to the jeers of the audience.

At the end of the show, she is still feeling a little woozy, and an accountant, Oscar D'Onofrio, who is gentle, polite and persuasive, insists on making a date with her because he has been struck by the coincidence of the names and the girl's sweet nature.

The two of them see each other regularly. Oscar tells her about many things, brings her presents, asks for nothing in exchange. When Cabiria realizes how futile the relationship is, however pleasant, and decides to break it off, Oscar asks her to marry him. She happily sells her little shack and draws her savings out of the bank in order to begin a normal life.

After having lunch near Lake Albano, the couple go for a walk in the woods in order to admire the view from up high. Oscar, nervous and uneasy, manages to lead his fiancée to the edge of the cliff. Here, Cabiria finally realizes what is actually happening: the man robs her and leaves her lying, devastated, on the ground.

Later that night, leaving the woods, Cabiria reaches the road and encounters a group of young people singing and playing. As she walks among them, her sad expression changes into a smile.

In this play of coincidences, two of the less important, but critically revealing, details contained within this story, which had problems with the censor because of the subject matter, are a piece of clothing and a gesture in a frame towards the end of the movie. The item of clothing, the famous 'chicken-feather bolero jacket', which Giulietta Masina had already worn in *The White Sheik*, together with the pathetic socks, becomes the uniform, the identifying mark of Cabiria's clownish, common character, just as the cape and striped shirt denoted the misery of Gelsomina's vagabond existence. But Cabiria tries to evolve, pursues liberation from a reality in which exterior events play a determining role, in order to leave that world of the humiliated and the offended.

The context of the first insult to her person, decisively Pasolinian in kind, reveals itself as a determining factor right from the first images of the sunny shingled shore of the River Tiber at Acilia, a spurious agglomeration between Ostia and an unreachable Rome beyond the line of the high-rise buildings on the outskirts of town. Pasolini, whom the director called "most likable with that dusty mason's face of his, a proletarian face, the face of a bantam weight boxer from the slums" – plays an important part in the movie as a linguistic expert for the expressions in Roman dialect, and for his knowledge of characters from the proletariat masses, of whom he wrote in *Ragazzi di Vita*. Fellini and Pasolini go for long car journeys together, looking for locations, images and visions, which, due to the sponge effect (characteristic of his creativity), will end up recurring in subsequent works: "I went around with him visiting various parts of town immersed in a disquieting silence and with evocative names like medieval China, Infernetto, Tiburtino III, and Cessati Spiriti. He guided me like Vergil and Charon combined, both of whom he resembled; but he was also like a sheriff, a modest sheriff who went around keeping a check on familiar places." As well as locations, the two of them were really on the look out – possibly just a pretext – for an old whore, the 'Bomba Atomica', whom Fellini had seen during his early years in Rome. When leaving the offices of the daily *Messaggero* at one in the morning on one occasion, walking towards Piazza Barberini, he saw her, a "kind of dirigible dressed all in white coming down the street – not on either sidewalk, but down the very middle of the street." An incredible vision that "gave rise to the various *Saraghine* in my movies."

There is unquestionably a great physical chasm between Cabiria and the 'Bomba'. But it is all put to good use in the continuous internal working out and the prodigious capacity for recollection which, with no explicit motivations, utilizes memories at certain moments in incongruous contexts, as part of his accumulation of stylistic/inventive elements. Every fragment, quotation, remark, creates connections, links, recollections and ignites suggestions for present and future narrative passages.

The contradictions in the human affairs of Cabiria are many. Particularly in the representation of non-returned feelings in a dehumanized reality, for which Fellini is careful not to hazard sociological justifications which would be entirely unsuitable to his narrator's sensibility, which is why he ends up showing – inventing – the dual soul, good and bad, of that reality.

An example of this is Cabiria's monologue when she is feeling disconcerted by the theft and humiliation that Giorgio inflicted on her. She anticipates the sense of the movie, talking to herself, giving in to feelings and the enormous need for sincere affection: "But why? Why did he need to do it? I would have given him everything, I would… Everything he asked of me. So why did he have to do it?" These are the very same words she might have used of Oscar at the end of the movie, if it were not for the fact that the men she encounters in this circular story must first be individually portrayed in their negativity, which results in revealing the feminine positiveness of Cabiria, Gelsomina, and thus Giulietta herself.

Giorgio, "this dirty *vitellone*," who has to return to "selling balloons at San Pietro", is first portrayed in the figure of Amleto, Marisa's protector and nephew of the lame man (played by Mario Passante, one of Fellini's regulars, here playing the part of a cocaine pusher), a linking figure with the Divino Amore sanctuary episode, which they all experience with equal stupor, except for the brief parenthesis of religious excitement, decidedly unsuitable for bringing change to a parasitic existence.

Lazzari, played by Amedeo Nazzari in the self-ironical role of a movie idol, makes professional use of Cabiria at the most convenient time to resolve the problem at the nightclub, and for relieving boredom before his girlfriend, Jessy, arrives. In the morning, after keeping her locked up all night, he pays Cabiria off, who is almost ashamed of taking the money: she does not feel she has earned it and, anyway, just having been in that house with that man would be sufficient compensation. Creeping quietly past, she looks at the half-covered body of the sleeping Jessy, perhaps imagining herself in her place. This is a conclusion which would have satisfied Anna Magnani, for whom the scene had been conceived, but which is more moving and human in Giulietta Masina's interpretation.

Quietly leaving the villa, and adjusting her pathetic white socks, Cabiria might ideally have run into the bag man, a character who was cut in the final version of the movie. In this regard, Fellini recalls that there was very active censorship during this time and, fearing it, "following the advice of an intelligent and perhaps somewhat liberal Jesuit friend, Father Arpa, I went to see a famous cardinal in Genoa who was considered papal material and, perhaps for that reason, very powerful, in order to ask him to view the movie. […] The movie was saved, but with one strange condition:

The Nights of Cabiria *begins with our heroine's first misfortune, as she is rescued from drowning in the River Tiber, having been pushed in by her former lover*

the cutting of the scene with the bag man [...] part philanthropist and a bit of a magician, who, after having a vision, dedicated himself to a particular mission: he went to the strangest parts of town, finding the disinherited and distributing food and clothing, which he carried around in a bag, to them all. In the scene that was cut, Cabiria met him on Via Appia Antica, and went with him to the ghastly grotto of the 'Bomba Atomica'. There followed several little stories about that world of the disinherited. "It was a moving sequence that I was forced to cut. Evidently, those in certain Catholic circles found it disturbing that the movie should pay homage to that entirely anomalous philanthropist enfranchised by ecclesiastical mediation.

Another significant male character, prior to the appearance of the con man Oscar, is the illusionist, played by Aldo Silvani, who had already appeared in a vaguely similar role: the director of the Giraffa Circus in *La Strada*. Magician and hypnotist, he calls Cabiria to the stage and makes her exhibit that ingenuousness which will later make her easy prey for Oscar. But not before unwittingly exposing himself to the coarse mass of people making up the zoo-like audience, as well as the hurried interruptions after the show by the barman and the bus conductor.

And finally there is Oscar, with a sharp nose for the fragility and feelings hidden beneath the chicken-feather bolero jacket, and under the apparent self-assurance that allowed Cabiria to hold her own against the catcalls of the audience. The revulsion towards street life – similar to Marcello's disgust in *La Dolce Vita* – a feeling taken for granted, allows Fellini to avoid the danger of easy sentimentality and, worse yet, cheap moralizing. Just as it is implicit that living the 'low life' excludes one from divine grace. In the end, Cabiria is condemnable anyway, and condemned to live in sin and loneliness, which she confesses to the garrulous little *frate* Giovanni (it is no accident that this part is played by the clown Polidor, someone who unites aspiration, joy and a pervasive melancholy).

And so, using the lever of ethics on the contradiction between the pursuit of happiness and the sense of guilt, the director grafts the magical/fatalistic element onto the story which, repeating itself, returns to the opening message: experience is useless when the subconscious and love both go to work. And when the word love is used with reference to these characters, a special kind of love is intended – perhaps more a form of affection, deriving from the need to

The nightclub on Via Veneto – privileged setting for the dolce vita *– used to play host to such stars as Alberto Lazzari (Amedeo Nazzari), and bold Cabiria, in contrast to the elegant location, shamelessly exhibits herself, heedless of her pathetic white socks*

Greatly changed, the romantic ex-street walker falls recklessly in love with the trickster Oscar (François Périer), while the foreboding overhanging ledge at the lake foretells yet another tragic ending

at the precise moment immediately preceding the transformation. Cabiria has dressed like a 'normal' person, replacing the bolero jacket with a respectable little checked coat and a bizarre hat. Oscar, who has abandoned his office worker's briefcase and raincoat, looks like Giorgio without a jacket. Cabiria is saying that she wants to pay because, up until now, Oscar (like a good con man) has always paid for everything. She reminds him: "By now, everything I have is yours, isn't it?"

The director fixes this moment, unpredictable and yet already caught up in the looming fatality, before the shiver, and he does this with a simple movement of the woman's hand, which she places on Oscar's right hand: the hand of marital faith placed on the hand of a thief. The two look at each other, but the spectator does not see their eyes because Cabiria is seen from the back and Oscar is wearing dark glasses. After a brief pause, still shot in mid-range, Oscar removes his hand and places it on Cabiria's: the moment has come to bring the plan to its conclusion and, in the way that con men looked at each other or quickly changed their gestures, he moves his right hand to the wine bottle and pours. The switch to Cabiria reveals the packet of money tightly held in her right hand. In the subsequent passage, Oscar finally removes his sunglasses – an almost 'disinterested' moment for one who appears to be anticipating the joy of victory – then puts them on again, becoming evasive and nervous, as a close-up shot reveals his murky, malignant eyes in the disquieting light of sunset – a light that, together with the wind, reveals to Cabiria's mind the true face of her man, "one of those who takes money from women", one who has never loved her but only been after her savings.

All this is there between the folds of the images present in the scene showing the settling of the bill. It is a narrative and visual anticipation contained within an elliptical form of narration, which concludes the sordid business of the emotional swindle, of the fear of death, of the re-emergence from the inner bartering into which Cabiria suddenly sinks, rather than physically falling into the lake. The author suggests the ambiguity in advance, without depriving the epilogue of its tension, which is to be seen, less in order to find out how it ends, but rather to get a just confirmation of it.

This procedure is developed in putting Fellini's characters into motion when they must surprisingly enter or exit from an incongruous situation. The light breeze and those kids on a spree once again blow away Cabiria's illusions and her feigned cynicism – "one does everything for love," she had said – impelling her back on to the road again with an unforgettable smile: not onto her beat, for the time being, but towards her indestructible faith in an unjust life.

have faith in the next fellow, a lay grace conceded only due to the fact of living and sharing a life together. Cabiria's for Oscar and, earlier, for Giorgio, is the same forced attachment of Gelsomina for Zampanò. And when Oscar's trap is set, Cabiria will no longer believe that she is destined to grow old miserably on the beat, and she will unhesitatingly turn to Wanda with the same mockery as Alberto for the road workers: "Take that!" – I've screwed you: you're staying here and I'm leaving – "Hey, Wa' [Wanda], I'm getting spliced!"

But this will not be the case, because the second detail insinuates itself into the picture, another meaningful gesture of apparently little import. A barely perceived action, because our attention is entirely concentrated on the dialogue. At the end of the lunch by the lake, Fellini frames Cabiria in a mid-range shot. She is about to pay for the lunch when Oscar, wearing sunglasses and a cigarette in his mouth, picks up the bill, pulls out some money and puts it on the plate, in the small space on the left of the screen that is not occupied by the characters. The situation is captured

The last frame of *The Nights of Cabiria*, considered by André Bazin to be "at one and the same time the most audacious and the strongest of all Fellini's work", is the image of a fragile and sincere woman's desperate need for love, a hunger for affection that is also felt in varying degrees by the *vitelloni*, by Zampanò, by Augusto and by Marcello Rubini, the hero of *La Dolce Vita*: an epic movie that, since the death of the director, is only now beginning to take on more normal proportions, after having been excessively exalted and denigrated. A movie whose unusual length (at that time) demanded an enormous effort by its producers and makers, and which constituted Fellini's first sumptuous 'artistic lump', a story constructed upon reality, interlaced with the tragic and the fabulous, a truly authentic fake such as *Eight and a Half* and *Casanova*.

As occasionally happens to certain great movies, and not always the loveliest ones, *La Dolce Vita* (1960) was destined to remain forever young and, with its bitter, astute prophetic confession, it was immediately interpreted as a prophecy of social disaster. A totem movie that expressed an idea and its antithesis, and, in the end, a movie-event because it marked the end of the cinema of the Fifties and its language, its customs, its socio-political complications, its polemics, its critiques, and much more. From a distance of almost fifty years, it is not easy to conjure up the provincial, curia-communist and 'vulgar' climate of those years, into which the movie came crashing like a meteor, yet it is still valid today, even if in a less intense way. Even if the rites and myths have changed, there has been no real change, except for the worse, in the ideology and the soul condition of that class of Fellini's *bon viveurs*.

To introduce this story, articulated into various episodes, and particularly in order to understand its true impact, it would not be a digression to refer to another Italian movie,

Cabiria, an innocent Gelsomina in a world of vice betrayed by her own feelings, wants to die after the final devastating disappointment. And yet, her infallible optimism and trust cause her to smile once again

winner of the 1961 Oscar for its screenplay. It is Pietro Germi's *Divorce Italian Style*, the bittersweet story of a crime of honor, a sarcastic comedy in which Baron Cefalù, in order to free himself of a petulant wife, plans to carry out his crime during the showing of *La Dolce Vita* at the town's movie theater. Under the rubric of a movie event valid even in a remote Sicilian village, Germi caustically plays with the leading actor of both movies, Marcello Mastroianni. In fact, the voice of the actor coming from the screen showing Fellini's movie creates a duet with the voice of the same actor in the guise of Baron Cefalù: "Preceded by huge public scandal, echoes of polemics, protests, denunciations and hosannas, a sensational movie came to the small town. The parish priest of San Firmino had launched his thunderbolts against the licentious movie and admonished his parishioners to boycott it, but with little result. Nothing of the kind had ever been seen before. Not even the chairs borrowed from the Central Bar and squeezed into the theater were sufficient to cater for the crush of spectators. They had even come in from the countryside, travelling ten kilometers on horseback."

Alternating between the hicks on the main floor, transfixed by the exuberant beauty of Anita Ekberg letting herself go at 'Caracalla's', and the well-bred bourgeoisie seated in the boxes, our curiosity is focused entirely on the 'handsome actor', ready to set his delicate criminal apparatus in motion, confident of finding his wife with her lover, and finally having a motive for killing her while in the grip, as it were, of his wrath. With acumen, Germi uses the pretext of the showing of the scandalous movie, thus bringing to the fore the ironic paradox of the organized improvisation: "the plan must proceed without the slightest hitch, it's success (and the alibi) will entirely depend upon this movie about the lustfulness and vices of Rome." What better thing is there than mass hypnosis in the face of an unapproachable world of bright lights and voluptuousness? Nothing. But the baron had counted his chickens before they hatched. He had not considered that his wife Rosalia would follow his own line of reasoning, and arrange an elopement with her peasant lover to coincide with the 'desert' effect created by Fellini's movie.

Using this tactic, Germi obtains the full consensus of an audience that can be found in cinemas everywhere, guaranteed to participate because its morbid curiosity has already been attracted by counter-attacks widely disseminated in the popular scandal sheets and weeklies. Accused by politicians of having "thrown a defaming shadow over the Roman people and the dignity of the Italian capital itself, as well as Catholicism", *La Dolce Vita* is threatened with censorship and even more bitterly opposed by the Church, except for the enlightened views of Father Arpa. By recognizing the movie's moral qualities as well as its unquestionable cinematic merits, his own life will be anything but *dolce* for a long time to come.

Marcello Rubini, having come to Rome from the provinces in order to work in the field of socially committed literature, is working as a journalist for a scandal sheet. For one week, he witnesses and participates in the daily life, and the even more lively nightly events, in Via Veneto, populated by the famous and the rich.

On board a helicopter with the photographer Paparazzo, he follows a statue of Christ that is crossing Rome from the Felice Aqueduct to St. Peter's, without missing the opportunity of making an advance to a group of pretty women who are sunbathing.

In the evening, while on the hunt for some spicy happening on Via Veneto, he meets Maddalena, a rich, bored heiress, with whom he goes for a car ride. In Piazza del Popolo, the couple offer a lift to a prostitute, who lives on the outskirts of town at Cessati Spiriti. In her squalid apartment, they spend the night making love.

Returning home at dawn, Marcello discovers that his jealous companion, Emma, has tried to kill herself. He takes her to the hospital and, after vainly trying to call Maddalena, he rushes to the airport to witness the arrival of Sylvia, a famous American screen star, eagerly awaited by a crowd of photographers, journalists and curiosity seekers. The actress is holding her first press conference in Italy at the Hotel Excelsior, but Marcello cannot attend because he must look after Emma who has been released from the hospital.

Sylvia, dressed like a priest for a promotional tour of the city, climbs to the top of St. Peter's dome, and is joined by a breathless Marcello who, fascinated by her natural beauty, will see her again at 'Caracalla's' nightclub, surrounded by the usual crowd of photographers. Sylvia lets herself go in a sensual, erotic rock dance. She gets into an argument with her husband Robert, who is constantly drunk, and then rushes away from the nightclub in a rage, followed by Marcello.

Sitting in the car in Via Appia Antica, they talk very little because of the language barrier, and Marcello, not knowing what to do, drives to Rome, after having phoned Maddalena. Whilst they are near the Trevi fountain, Sylvia falls in love with a kitten, and asks Marcello to find some milk for it. When he returns, the journalist finds that Sylvia has jumped into the fountain, fully clothed, and he is unable to refuse when she asks him to join her, dazzled as he is by that vision of pure beauty. Upon returning to the hotel, they discover Robert, who, awakened by the *paparazzi*, slaps Sylvia and punches Marcello, while the flash bulbs go wild.

The following day, while covering a fashion show at EUR, Marcello runs into Steiner, whose refinement and austerity he admires. They talk for a while in a church, but when Steiner goes to the organ and begins to play Bach, Marcello leaves in embarrassment.

Accompanied by the trustworthy Paparazzo and Emma, Marcello visits a place near Terni, where two children claim to have had a vision of the Madonna. Naturally, it is pure fabrication, but, exploited by the media, the news is creating mass hysteria among the crowd. Emma, drawn in by the atmosphere, prays to the Virgin to let her marry her man. A violent rainstorm and a sudden death conclude the long day.

An evening spent with Steiner and his intellectual friends brings to a head Marcello's dissatisfaction with the mediocre life he has forced himself to live, compared with his friend. Spurred on by these thoughts, he decides to radically change his way of life, and goes to a *trattoria* by the sea in search of tranquillity in order to write something decent. Here, between phone calls to Emma, he meets a waitress called Paola, a simple, natural young Umbrian girl.

As always, he spends the evening in Via Veneto. But this time, there is a surprise visit from his father, who has arrived from the provinces. The journalist arranges an evening at the 'Kit-Kat', an old-fashioned night club, which his old man appears to appreciate, living it up with Fanny, a dancer friend of Marcello's. When the club closes, the woman suggests that they go back to her place to make themselves some spaghetti. When Marcello arrives sometime later, he learns that his father has been taken ill and intends to return home on the first train.

The following evening, Marcello is among the party guests at the great castle of Bassano di Sutri, where he once again encounters Maddalena, with whom he shares a moment of ambiguous intimacy, and also makes new acquaintances, visits the old villa, participates in a seance and finds himself in Jane's company when the bell signifying first mass summons all the male descendants of that noble family to follow the princess mother to the chapel.

Another of the endless violent quarrels between Marcello and Emma ends up with a reconciliation in bed, following a series of violent reciprocal accusations – a prelude to the tragedy which is about to take place. Steiner, for no apparent reason, has killed his children and then taken his own life. Along with the police commissioner, Marcello waits in the street for Steiner's wife to return, while the *paparazzi* ruthlessly take flash photographs of the woman's emotionless face.

A pathetic orgy in a villa at Fregene, amidst crude undercurrents and improvised strip-teases, saturates the final scenario of our hero's week in Rome with cruel boredom. In the morning, a monster of a fish, dragged to shore by the fishermen, seems to be staring right at Marcello. In the distance, Paola, the young waitress from the *trattoria*, beckons him to join her, but Marcello vanishes in the opposite direction.

In *La Dolce Vita*, the highly mobile camera is at one and the same time the mover and the mirror of events which highlight solitude, cynicism, disgust and love. These are

La Dolce Vita *as seen from the dome in* St. Peter's Square: *the journalist Marcello Rubini (Marcello Mastroianni) and the striking American movie star Sylvia (Anita Ekberg)*

Emma (Yvonne Fourneaux), dramatically on her own, gives in to excessive maternal jealousy over her lover Marcello

breaks up the story into a stylistically and thematically efficacious solution, wherein Fellini is better able to move than he could do within a rigid narrative context. Whereas the author, any twentieth century author, can only grab at confused scraps of reality, his alter-ego, Marcello, gathers up these fragments, 'pieces' of life, bits of a discontinuous mosaic, heterogeneous, unstable, completed by what the other eyes of the movie see, the camera lenses and the director himself.

This discreet stalker of the *dolce vita romana*, without any strong motivations, is another portrayal of the worn-out hero of literary tradition, the one who ought to realize his destiny, if only he did not have that small amount of humanity dedicated to others like Moraldo, Gelsomina or Cabiria. His contradictions are the image of his weakness, as well as that of a sick society, inasmuch as *La Dolce Vita* represents the sum of those single moments of crisis gathered together into the form of a movie that does not refer so much to itself, as to the idea of cinema, of 'movie-cinema'.

In contrast to 'movie-movie', which is to say movies that completely exhaust their text within the story, a 'movie-cinema', such as *La Dolce Vita,* is furnished with an inexhaustible 'classic' inner energy, having to broaden its range of action in an absolute expressive enrichment, unlike *Il Bidone*, a typical 'movie-movie', which, *after* the death of Augusto, has nothing more to say. Instead, a simple reading of the script of *Il Viaggio di G. Mastorna*, the movie that was never made, conveys the feelings that cinema imparts in a very intense way, because it communicates a particular form of pathos, bound to the written word, due to the world of the author and his personage. With *La Dolce Vita,* one gets more or less this same strange elevating experience of participation: the story of the spiritual journey of Marcello and his *deus ex machina* which, the more personal and suffered it is, the more it unfolds, on the one hand, in the direction of Cinema, and on the other, towards a sense of Death, light but present, ready to dig silently among Fellini's obsessions.

For this reason, the word *dolce,* as it is understood in a pagan and voluptuous sense, is another of the not few equivocal points of the movie. Starting from the optimistic idea that life may not necessarily be 'bitter', the message was misunderstood to mean unbridled pleasure-taking in the hedonistic individualism of the newly rich, up to the point of post-modern exhibitions of empty and ignorant television esthetics.

Loneliness. Cynicism. Disgust. Love. Four soul states with which one can walk arm-in-arm in the *dolce vita* of the southern dream of an inner Rome suspended between the crumbling vestiges of a great Empire and the comprehensive embrace of Christianity.

classic Fellini themes, sometimes amply represented within several figures, and other times subsumed in a single character, such as the uneasy Marcello in the grip of a malignant freedom, a kind of eye that does nothing but record, more passive than a determining element in the story's development as he pursues the trends of the reveling city. He lives, looks, and describes the things and the people from a constantly changing viewpoint – along with Fellini's observations – subject to neither the realistic balance nor the composite distortion. In this movie, Alberto Moravia writes, "Fellini appears to change his manner according to the subject matter of the episodes within a spectrum of portrayal that ranges from expressionistic caricature to the most sober realism. In general, one notes an inclination to deforming caricature whenever the moral judgment becomes more cruel and more disdainful, not, however, without a pinch of satisfaction and complicity, as in the extremely vivacious scene of the final orgy, or that of the aristocratic party, which is admirable in its descriptive sagacity and narrative rhythm."

The restlessness in the movements of the curious camera, placing itself at the side of, on top of, and even *inside* the heart of events, is sometimes frozen into snapshots, not unlike the photos of the *paparazzi,* while, at other times, it

Marcello is lonely. He lives with Emma, suffocated by her possessiveness, her scenes, and her wild extremes. Emma, myopic and superficial enough not to notice her man's torment, cannot look at things with reason: all she sees is the outward appearance of the intellectual world, and she allows herself to be hypnotized by religion in its simplest sense, the fruit of excitement over a (false) miracle. She loves in an obtuse way, and despairs because her man disdains even her most ordinary attentions. Marcello is lonely even when by himself, because he wants to be what he is not, a writer, possibly left-wing, sent on extraordinary trips to important meetings, whereas his ignorance has turned him into an expert scandal reporter. All he does is concern himself with petty local news by day, and roam Via Veneto by night, accompanied by Paparazzo – the name that became a worldwide synonym for a society photographer – in order to inform his avid readers about what the VIPs eat, their love affairs and betrayals. In this sense, the reconstruction of Via Veneto at Cinecittà, confirming Fellini's bigger-than-life falsification, magnifies the ephemeral society that populates that street, a microcosm of fearful moths that warm up their spirits around the lamp of incommunicability and anxiety.

Maddalena's loneliness complements this. Stimulated only by new experiences, she is happy with Marcello – who is made of the same stuff, only poor – both in the prostitute's bed, and at the Sutri castle where, even when sincerely conversing at a distance with him, she cannot resist giving herself to another man, cannot bear the loneliness that, just for one instant, has encountered that of her friend/lover.

Marcello is isolated when he is with just one other person, or in a group, when he accompanies the beautiful Sylvia to St. Peter's, is with her at a nightclub, or at the sacred icon of the Trevi Fountain, convinced that he has found "*everything, the first woman of the first day of creation, mother, sister, lover, friend, angel, home.*" And instead, in his confused and mystical search, he is frustrated by a blast of wind, by the cry of an American actor, by the dogs and the uninterrupted flow of the fountain, moments which accentuate his alienation.

Front page: Captivated by Sylvia's radiant beauty, Marcello seems to be poised between reality and indifference, finally revealing all the signs of his personal existential crises
Top: In the Via Veneto recreated at Cinecittà, we even see the Spider, one of the bikers' badges of the boom years. Marcello is teetering between memory (his father, Annibale Ninchi) and the present (Paparazzo, Walter Santesso)
Right: Steiner (Alain Cuny), a destructive, unattainable model, completely fascinates Marcello, who, hoping one day to be a writer, must instead concern himself only with newspaper scandal

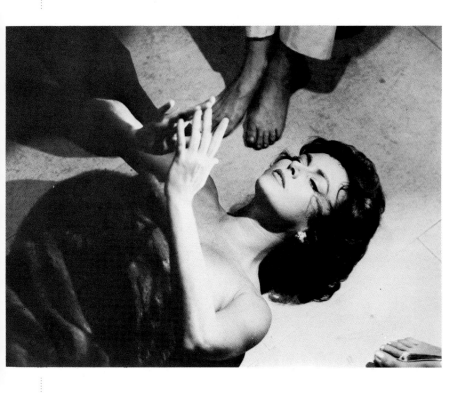

Even the 'provincial' parenthesis of his father's visit reveals his isolation in the pathetic attempt to renew a bond that has not existed since he was a child. He looks for company among the guests at the party and at the orgy, with perturbed women already suffering for their own reasons, when refusing the Paola's invitation on the beach, a presage of his loneliness, cynically experienced.

In fact, Marcello is cynical. As someone who is completely disillusioned, having to adapt to the society of appearances, he must necessarily pretend to be insensitive. With Maddalena, he speaks about Rome, and then throws her wealth in her face: "I like Rome very much. It's a kind of jungle. Warm and calm, where one can easily hide. […] Do you know what your problem is? Too much money. Listen, you don't have to worry, with all that money you've got, you'll always land on your feet if you fall."

He acts the part of the innocent representative of public opinion, even when invading the privacy of a pair of adulterers: gets angry with Emma for her blackmailing suicide attempt; during the pandemonium of Sylvia's arrival, he removes himself from the collective enthusiasm

Above: Even Nadia's striptease (Nadia Gray) during the final orgy sours Fellini's dolce vita and the pointless customs of all the social classes portrayed Right: The fake miracle, a set created in order to portray how people's gullibility is exploited by the cynicism of the Press Front page: Anitona's pagan beauty against the mythical setting of the Trevi Fountain bestows on the movies an unmistakable moment of change which proves to be epochal

The dolce vita *for Marcello's father (the actor Ninchi bearing a remarkable similarity to Urbano Fellini) comes to a head at the Kit-kat, an old style nightclub, with Fanny (Magali Noël), Paparazzo and his son*

and chats a while with the flight attendants; he takes a caustic dig at the photographer at EUR; like Paparazzo, he does not believe in miracles, but rather in the realism of an existence he does not know how to change; he is rude to Paola because the juke-box disturbs him, but is actually angry with himself because he does not know what to write; he gets into quarrels at the castle, and demonstrates his cruel cynicism during the orgiastic games at Fregene. Here the cynical behavior of Marcello is synthesized. Is it the unveiling of his true character, helped along by the influence of alcohol, or is it his despairing reaction to Steiner's tragic death? Perhaps it is both. In any case, the common denominator is his anxiety due to the fact that the much-admired Steiner has renounced his life because there was *too much* order in it.

Directly connected to the motifs of anxiety and cynicism, is that of disgust which, in Fellini, is not detached from the acceptance of the state of things. Accentuated above all in the orgy episode, where we see how deeply Marcello, not being able to withdraw, ineptly immerses himself in the subject and physical acts which nauseate him, and wallows in his aversion for hypocrisy, pretended modesty, repressed impulses. Less a moral disgust than an esthetic one for that *dolce vita* and its disorder which, though not feeling himself responsible, he cannot do without, considering that this

confusion and chaotic frenzy is what earns him his daily, or more correctly, nightly bread. When all is said and done, except for certain private episodes, he is the man who, observing, noting, and even while having to accept the rules of the information profession, often disapproves of the *paparazzi* intrusions, and ignores their requests for a photographic scoop of Steiner's corpse.

In the end, Marcello seeks love, and looks for it in women. He needs to be considered a contradictory human being, fragile and needy of affection. He seeks, and rejects, this affection in Emma, the Italian mother: "I cannot spend my life loving you. [I'm afraid] of you, your egoism, the desolating squalor of your ideals. Can't you see that you are offering me the life of a worm? You cannot talk of anything but food and bed! But don't you understand, a man who accepts that kind of life is finished, has truly become a worm? I don't believe in this aggressive, ruinous, maternal love of yours. I don't want it! It's no use to me! This is not love, it's stultification." Emma will never be on a par with the women artists of Steiner's circle, but no-one knows as well as she does how to heal, in bed, the wounds left by her man's insecurities and cowardly actions.

The female American star, a more complete version of the tiny Gelsomina, is big, exaggerated, phosphorescent, possesses something more 'mystic', some astral difference from the usual 'good-looker', is full of an instinctive love for life, but not for Marcello. She, on the rare occasions when he tries to kiss her – not understanding that she is only an ideal, a Dream Woman – is regularly frustrated by a sudden obstacle.

For their part, Maddalena and Jane represent the taste for danger, the novelty that excites, in contrast to the foreseeable present and future, the sexual surrogate for Emma's cloying love. For this reason too, Marcello, half immersed in the Trevi Fountain, barely allows himself to touch Sylvia's wondrous, distant face. The drops of water that she lets fall onto his head symbolize the return, the inner rebirth of a lay, existential nature. Perhaps one will exit from the disgust for the *dolce vita* with a new taste for the elementary things in life which, however, continue to keep some surprises in store.

The other love to which Marcello aspires is found in Steiner's house, where his gentle, smiling wife introduces him to a serenity that is interrupted only by the stormy wind – heard on the wire recorder – and the children waking up. In its satisfying tranquility, however, that love leads to suicide, a warning, or confirmation, of the fact that one must react in order to combat fear. Equally pointless was the brutish orgy, and the rising back from the depths of nastiness that occurs with the walk in the pine woods at Fregene, before the hideous disgust takes form as a mysterious marine monster that, in absorbing the negative human factors, allows the 'soap-and-water' girl to be the one to take leave of the spectator.

It is certainly no coincidence that the locations and symbols of the movie, Via Veneto and the enormous marine creature, are *false*, only truly existing in the invented representation of a miserable world of lights that comes to life by reflection when the natural light of day disappears. It is a world like that of the cinema, taken from the reality of the years when the so-called Hollywood-on-the-Tiber existed, when the American cinema came to Cinecittà to shoot its epics, attracted by the low cost and high quality of the crews. Without that having happened, the mythicized Via Veneto would never have existed, and *La Dolce Vita*, the meeting point of two decades, is the documentation of an epoch from this point of view as well. Marcello's love is derived from Cabiria's: when his disgust for the degradation of feelings is transformed into a look that is almost inside the camera, we have arrived at the final frames of *La Dolce Vita*, with an innocent act to redeem the orgy, by the simple

Fellini on the set of The Temptations of Doctor Antonio, *second episode of* Boccaccio '70

Troubled, Doctor Antonio Mazzuolo scrutinizes the gigantic advertisement for milk (Peppino De Filippo and, on the poster, Anita Ekberg)

fact of existing. And if the endings of the two movies, despite having strong similarities in their optimism, do not coincide, it is because the buds of Fellini-style deformation are already beginning to turn into the psychoanalytic larvae of *Eight and a Half*.

Before shooting *Eight and a Half*, the second cruel emblem of 'movie-cinema', Fellini completes *La Dolce Vita* with *The Temptations of Doctor Antonio*, an episode in *Boccaccio '70*, directed in 1962 and featuring Peppino De Filippo and Anita Ekberg. The Fellini episode is the second part of a joke in four acts thought up by Cesare Zavattini, which also includes Mario Monicelli's *Renzo and Luciana*, Luchino Visconti's *The Job*, and Vittorio De Sica's *The Raffle*.

A grotesque reprisal on the bigots who had censored *La Dolce Vita*, the nocturnal adventure of the moralist Antonio Mazzuolo allows Fellini to play around a little more with the ambivalent mental fresco of Rome by night, alternating the small and the large, the true and the false, night and day and, to a large degree, prudery and the obtuseness of

censorship. *The Temptations of Doctor Antonio* is, on the one hand, a Fellini *divertissement* about the movies and, on the other hand, the tempered oppositions of his hyper-realistic humor, similar in tone to the long list of things he likes and hates contained in *Intervista sul Cinema*. "I don't like parties, holidays, tripe, interviews, round table discussions, requests for my autograph, snails, travel, standing in line, the mountains, boats, radios playing, music in restaurants, music in general (submitting to it), jokes, soccer fans, ballet, Christmas cribs, gorgonzola, award ceremonies, hearing people talk about Brecht, Brecht, official lunches, toasts, discourses, invitations to places, requests for my opinion, Humphrey Bogart, quiz programs, Magritte, being invited to art exhibitions, theater opening nights, typescripts, tea, camomile tea, caviar, previews of anything at all, the Maddalena Theater, quotations, real men, movies for young people, theatricality, temperament, questions, Pirandello, *crêpes Suzettes*, beautiful landscapes, political movies, historical movies, psychological movies, windows without blinds, commitment, non-commitment, ketchup."

Mazzuolo, both moralistic and bigoted, enjoys making people aware of his views, and closes the curtains against the "scandalous" dancers

In his solitary crusade against an imaginary decline in standards, gloomy Doctor Antonio even looks for support from the authorities

There is no danger of using the list to interpret the reasons how and why it is that a certain person detests snails with ketchup, or eats caviar and gorgonzola – possibly before going to see a Pirandello play – but certainly the list of preferences, with its well-balanced combinations, is revealing. "I like: train stations, Matisse, airports, risotto, oak trees, Rossini, roses, the Marx Brothers, tigers, waiting to meet someone while hoping they will no longer be coming (even if it is a very beautiful woman), Totò, having missed being somewhere, Piero della Francesca, everything beautiful about a beautiful woman, Homer, Joan Blondell, September, *torroncino* ice-cream, cherries, Brunello di Montalcino wine, big butts on bicycles, trains and lunch baskets on trains, Ariosto, cocker spaniels and dogs in general, the smell of damp earth, the scent of hay, crushed bay leaves, cypress trees, the sea in winter, people who speak little, James Bond, the One Step, empty shops,

deserted restaurants, squalor, empty churches, silence, Ostia, Torvajanica, the sound of bells, finding myself alone in Urbino on a Sunday, sweet basil, Bologna, Venice, all of Italy, Chandler, women concierges, Simenon, Dickens, Kafka, London, roasted chestnuts, subways, taking buses, high beds, Vienna (but I have never been there), waking up, going to sleep, stationery shops, Faber No. 2, pencils, vaudeville shows, bitter chocolate, secrets, the dawn, the night, spirits, Wimpy, Laurel and Hardy, Turner, Leda Gloria, but Greta Gonda I also liked a lot, soubrettes, but also ballerinas."

It is hard to avoid the temptation of remembering the winter sea in *I Vitelloni*, of the big bottom of the peasant woman on the bicycle in *Amarcord*, of the subway in *Roma* and *Fellini: a Director's Notebook*, of the high beds in *Eight and a Half* and *City of Women*, not to mention the vaudeville shows (*Variety Lights, The Nights of Cabiria, Fellini's Roma*), and the Venice of *Casanova,* along with a Poe-inspired project that never came off. Also, the predilection for Georges Simenon, his great and good friend, located somewhere between Chandler (plot) and Kafka (the hallucinatory and the absurd), or else between the concierges and roast chestnuts – images of Maigret's Paris and Fellini's Rome and provinces. The points of contact between Fellini and Simenon are surprisingly many – one need only remember the richness of fantasy and invention, the great rigor of their working methods, alternating between a furor of imagination and sudden 'vacuities', the alter-egos Maigret and Mastroianni who, in the simultaneousness of different lives, somehow make reference to Jungian synchronicity understood as acausality. These are questions to be taken up elsewhere, because they would lead us away from the fixations of Doctor Antonio who, far from being *The Man Who Watched the Trains Pass*, limited himself to watching, and while watching with prejudice, fell into temptation.

Doctor Antonio Mazzuolo, the impeccable moralist who wears lugubrious black suits on hot Roman nights, has a fixation: the battle against the spread of immorality. He follows couples in solitary places and hates women in bikinis, as well as all other exhibitions of the female body. His iconoclastic furor is expressed in fervid rhetorical outbursts to boy scouts, nocturnal blitz raids, and the interruption of shows he considers indecent, up until the attack on a woman in a low-cut top.

One day, an enormous billboard is pasted up directly in front of his window, with a provocative blonde inviting people to drink more milk, causing Doctor Antonio to start his anti-vice crusade. First of all, he tries to prevent the pasting up of the poster, and then he goes to the pro-morality association, while the people of the neighborhood, unperturbed by his rage, merrily welcome the billboard with an outdoor party.

One morning, intent on shaving, he thinks he sees in the mirror the gloved arm of the woman on the billboard and, by now determined to provoke a scandal, gets himself arrested after splattering it with ink. He accomplishes his purpose: the billboard is covered over, to the great joy of his unmarried sister, given to nocturnal ecstasies under a false name.

While playing the piano during a party with the friends of the association, Mazzuolo sees that diabolical blonde appear, a 'plausible' thing since a sudden rainstorm has removed the covering. In the moonlight, he discovers that the photo has changed position, and is winking at him and teasing him. When it finally stops raining, Doctor Antonio dreams that he has gone under the billboard but, while the great glass of milk has moved onto the grass, the body of the temptress has left the billboard.

"I have finally driven you away from the world of decent people", he says with satisfaction when the giant woman appears in the flesh. But the temptation continues and, although occasionally giving way a little, the Lilliputian enemy does not give up his fight for the spiritual well-being of the entire city.

When the girl takes on human proportions, and tries to reach a compromise, Doctor Antonio decides to try to redeem her, even if he is conscious that he has fallen into serious temptation. So he reacts by chasing her away. She responds by stripping. Mazzuolo defends himself even to the point of covering the camera lens and, armed as a medieval knight, breaks a lance against the woman who, having returned to the billboard, closes her eyes in death.

The night concludes with a funeral cortege following the gigantic coffin of the temptress, and Mazzuolo, realizing that he will never see her again, rebels, by now totally in the grip of sinfulness.

The light of day finds him clinging to the border of the billboard, and only by injecting him with a tranquilizer do they manage to take him away to the hospital, while the tune of the advertising jingle plays ("Drink more milk") and cupid laughs to himself.

In 1961, Sergio Corbucci's movie, *Totò, Peppino e la Dolce Vita,* appears on Italian screens, aiming at profiting from the scandal provoked by Fellini's movie while the iron is hot. A strong parody in which Totò and Peppino De Filippo carry out their archetypal shady dealings in the nightclubs of Via Veneto with a large group of pseudo foreigners. In *The Temptations of Doctor Antonio*, Peppino De Filippo – whom Fellini always preferred to his more famous brother Eduardo – continues partly in the role of the character of that parody. In Fellini's work, Antonio really takes on the ironic contours of the hypocrite disguised as a respectable crusader, who represents the director's answer to the wretched criticisms that greeted the appearance of *La Dolce Vita*.

In the opening minutes of the movie, following the pattern of the old comedians, Doctor Antonio reproaches a lady for her supposedly shameless way of dressing and, when she reacts, he gives her a couple of slaps, thus defending decency and recalling an episode which actually happened involving the censor, the Italian politician Oscar Luigi Scalfaro.

The middle part is devoted to promoting the joy of living,

as expressed in the femininity of Anita Ekberg playing the part of the corrupting demon of the upright male Italian. This characteristic is put in evidence by the agitated reactions of the moralist, who awards ridiculous little diplomas to boy scouts. Fellini has fun giving these big fat kids the names of movie people such as Rodolfo Sonego (scriptwriter of many Italian comedies, for Alberto Sordi in particular) and Otello Martelli, the movie's director of photography.

The anti-sex sermons he preaches to these big kids in short pants are totally pointless, as life goes on and the workers are already there to erect the billboard. The director uses this to return to the question of the relationship between true and false, this time in connection with the alternating of big and small. Thus, no longer just the false resembling a dream-like state, but the false in a real dream on a reduced scale, with the result of confounding the eye and the character. In fact, the leading man engages in an unequal battle against Love and feminine Charm, only to be conquered by them under the amused eye of Cupid, the only one able to make the expression on a poster figure change and cause it to descend and do a strip-tease, before the final seduction when the clock strikes midnight, the 'non-hour', suspended between the old day and the new.

The billboard figure enters and exits from that particular screen, on which the director creates, somewhere between cinema and comic strip, an enormous cartoon for magnifying the most desirable features, nothing less than the incarnation of the exaggerated perception that the male lead has of feminine sensuality. With an unerring and sensual aim, his lance pierces her right breast, thus repressing even more the already suppressed appetites of the attacker. The problem of the reduced reconstruction of reality fuses with the 'very large', which always analogically completes Fellini's fascination, more than the proportions of the feminine temptation, which neutralize her dangerousness with one stroke, ridiculing whoever considered them obscene.

Antonio Mazzuolo would like that image to be invisible, as it were, to the spectator, because we are part of the farcical nightmare or repression, and so it is necessary to cover the camera lens – with one's pants if necessary.

If he were to abandon himself to real life, the temptations would vanish, and he too would be able to go out on the grass without worrying. Once again, here is a finale in line with the preceding ones: it is useless to look for the message of *hope*, but one must become aware that one is dealing with an author who does not like either 'commitment' or lack of it. Rather he prefers 'waking up' and 'going to sleep' – which is to say, to dream. In fact, it is now the right moment for the dislocations of *Eight and a Half*.

In Eight and a Half, *director Guido Anselmi (Marcello Mastroianni, Fellini's alter ego) looks to the religious authorities, the Cardinal (Tino Masini), for answers to his questions*

Nothing is Known. Everything is Imagined

Eight and a Half • Juliet of the Spirits • Toby Dammit •
Fellini: a Director's Notebook • Fellini's Satyricon

Right in the middle of a traffic bottleneck, in a silence illuminated by a blinding white light, a man in a dark suit tries spasmodically to get out of the car in which he is trapped. People in the cars around him stare at him. Others look like distant mannequins.

Finally, the man manages to free himself and climb on top of the car. He is floating high in space like a kite as an unknown person tries to pull him down to earth, and another figure arrives on horseback. That descent corresponds to the falling sensation the protagonist feels: he was dreaming, and a person in a white coat enters at the very moment of that perception.

In fact, it is the team of doctors at the Chianciano Thermal Baths, arriving to administer a tonic to the famous film director, Guido Anselmi, who is spending a restful holiday there in order to plan his next movie.

On a sunny spring morning, the guests of the spa promenade in the park and drink the medicinal waters. Guido imagines he sees a girl dressed all in white offering him a glass of water, but in fact it is merely the woman who works at the spring.

Daumier, the French intellectual who is working as an adviser on the movie, is waiting for Guido, who exchanges some thoughts with him. The writer assails him with an outburst of reservations about the philosophy of the movie and the way it is being handled. Impatient, the director jumps at the chance of an interruption – a meeting with a friend of his, Mario Mezzabotta. Mezzabotta, who is with his young English fiancée, Gloria, an aspiring actress and university student, is waiting for his marriage to be annulled.

Guido goes to the station to meet his current lover, Carla. With a high-society sojourn in mind, the woman is laden with luggage, and Guido has put her up at a hotel near the railway station, embarrassed by her vulgarity.

After lunch, the lovers retire to their room and excite themselves with a little fooling around, in which Carla, dressed only in a sheet and heavily made-up, pretends she has got the wrong room. After having sex, while Carla is reading a comic book, Guido dreams of his dead parents in a strange cemetery where his producer, Pace, and production director, Conocchia, are also present. Still as part of the dream, Guido puts on his college uniform and says goodbye to his parents. As he embraces his mother, she turns into his wife Luisa. Back at the hotel, he runs into some religious types who are attending to His Eminence, who has come to take the waters.

Other events follow which introduce us to the various characters who form part of Guido's movie: the collaborators, the production crew, the little old men vying for the part of the father, Claudia's agent, the French actress to whom Guido does not want to reveal the character of the role, the American newspaperman and wife who is always hunting for news, the fleeting vision of a beautiful hotel guest, and finally the arrival of the producer (with a horde of secretaries and a goose of a mistress) who regales his director with a gold watch.

After dinner, there is an open-air dance. Pace checks the estimates proposed by the discontented Conocchia, the foreign newspaperman persists with his questions, and Carla has sat at a table far away from the movie crowd.

Private affairs and gossip about the wealthy Mezzabotta alternate with comments about the movie, until the atmosphere is livened up with Maurice's display of telepathy, together with his partner Maya. The woman, blindfolded, guesses the contents of one woman's purse, and then the thoughts of a mature lady ("I would like to live another hundred years"), before going after Carla who, embarrassed, plays for time, and finally on to Gloria, who brusquely declines to participate in the experiment. When Maurice tries to transmit the director's secret thoughts, Maya is unable to pronounce the words and writes them in capital letters on a blackboard instead: ASA, NISI, MASA. At this point, the action switches to Guido's private childhood memories of the playfulness of baby's bath with mother, of the aunt, of other women in the house and of the grandmother who talks to herself in Romagnolo dialect about her life. In the house, there is a stairway leading to the rooms on the upper floor where the children are lovingly put to bed while, just before going to sleep, a little girl repeats the words "ASA, NISI, MASA" several times to Guido.

Late at night in the hotel foyer, the French actress, Mezzabotta and Gloria arrive just before the director's telephone call to his wife asking her to join him at the spa. Passing through the rooms used by the production crew, Guido, in spite of the lateness of the hour, has a quarrel with Conocchia, who reproaches him for not giving clear directions.

In his room, the director is assailed by existential and artistic doubts. Not even knowing what the movie's plot is going to be, he abandons himself to his imagination. Claudia appears, moving around the room, caressing him and lying down on the bed… The ringing of the telephone brings Guido back to reality: Carla, alarmed because she feels unwell, asks him questions about their relationship. But Guido is distracted with thoughts about the next day's meeting with the cardinal. This meeting turns out to be nothing but a polite formality, because the priest is preoccupied with the sobbing intonation of the albatross – the bird that sang the funeral song for the death of Diomedus.

Disappointed, Guido loses himself in the memory of Saraghina, and the time he went with his friends to see her dance the rumba for a few pennies, and was caught and severely punished by the priests at his school. Guido will return to the woman at the end of the episode.

While at lunch, Daumier continues to take apart the movie's poetic/thematic structure, and the mention of Suetonius and the Caesars impels the action into the spa's steam baths, where the guests, swathed in white sheets, are immersed in salutary vapors. It is time for the second discussion with the religious authorities, which everyone expects to come up with a solution to their problems. But Guido only learns that the Church is everything, and that no salvation is possible outside of it.

Meanwhile, Luisa arrives with her sister, her friend Rosella and Enrico, a rejected suitor. All of them visit the spacecraft set, an impressive science fiction construction where the main scene of the mysterious movie is going to be shot. As some of them mount the scaffolding, Rosella, a clairvoyant, tells Guido that it is time for him to make up his mind. The evening ends with an argument in bed between husband and wife, who is wild with jealousy.

The following morning, at the coffee bar, Guido denies that he still has a relationship with Carla (seated close by), but Luisa is more and more bitter about the betrayal and the vulgarity of her rival. The director imagines that his wife, his mistress, Saraghina, the French actress, Gloria, the charming lady, Rosella and all the other women in

his life and in the movie can live together in the great house, surrounding him with attentiveness. One sees how the older ladies of that harem, the focal point of this scene of jealousy, love, gratitude and also of rebellion, must leave the field to the younger ones, and retire to the floor above.

The conclusion of the harem episode coincides with the beginning of the showing of the rushes. Guido imagines he has Daumier hanged. Although it is late to be choosing the actresses for the women's roles, Guido cannot make up his mind. He seems incapable of continuing with the movie. He is in crisis, exacerbated by the fight with Luisa, who can no longer stand his hypocrisy.

Meanwhile, Claudia arrives, the girl he imagined at the spring, which allows him to remain vague with Pace. Together in his car, he talks about the movie with her, of his fears and feelings, of love. They stop near the spring and, after a preview of the scene, Claudia realizes that there is no part for her.

Just when everything seems to be lost, the movie-machine goes into action: the movie is going to be shot. Pace has already called a press conference for the following afternoon.

At the spacecraft set, which is crowded with photographers, radio and television newsmen and foreign journalists, the producer pressurizes the director into finally revealing something about the movie. Guido, not knowing what to say, hides under the table. His failure is complete, just like his confusion between the figures in the movie and those in real life. Perhaps he would like commit suicide: one pistol shot and his mother's voice calling him, and the fiasco is over.

At this point, the movie is called off. The scaffolding is dismantled, while Daumier draws his own rational, consoling conclusions. Guido is about to leave the set when Maurice approaches him and announces that everything is ready, they are about to start. As Daumier continues talking, Guido sees the characters in the movie, together with those from his life, appear, all dressed in white: Claudia, the women from his childhood, Saraghina, his mother and father, Carla, the prelates, the lady of the spa, Luisa and all the others. They form a line…

They have come for him, the filming can start. Four clowns and a boy wearing his old school uniform enter the scene. Playing instruments, they welcome the characters who, under Guido's direction, form a circle, joined by all the faces Guido has dreamed of and met right up until that moment. Guido closes the circle, asking Luisa to take his hand once more.

Night has fallen. The musicians leave the illuminated track. The last one to leave the scene is the boy, as the lights begin to dim, and then go out completely.

If one called *La Dolce Vita* an epic, one can say that *Eight and a Half* (1963) is an extraordinary vision of memory turned into fable, the autobiography of a crisis overcome through the power of imagination and a freedom of expression never before seen on screen.

As Pierre Kast has noted, "everything that one can say against this movie is already in the movie", in confirmation of its uniqueness and the inimitable power of its visual narrative. One certainly need not go back as far as *Hamlet* to find examples of a play within a play – the illustrious antecedent of a movie within a movie – and it would be just as unproductive to go back to André Gide's *The Counterfeiters*, with its writer *manqué*, even if Gide stands in relation to Edouard as Fellini does to Guido. Moreover, Guido is the materialization of dream autobiography, which is to say, the fantastic conjunction of Fellini's kind of realism, subsuming as much of the real and the invented as can be embodied there.

Guido's experience is almost exclusively passive: he is continually summoned, chased after, greeted, interviewed, besieged, surprised, advised, accused, flattered, derided, punished, stimulated, loved and remembered because he is

The procession of characters and figures from Fellini's oneiric world proceeds towards the unforgettable encirclement at the end of the movie

Fellini and
Marcello
Mastroianni sort
out how a truck
is going to run
during the
resumption of
filming for Eight
and a Half

so much at the disposition of life and other people as to be caught in a spider-web from which he does not know how to free himself. He runs away and everyone runs after him, calling Guido, Guido, Guido, and naturally Guidino (the producer) and Guidone (Mezzabotta). *Eight and a Half* is the exaltation of this name, whose echoes make us think of *Viaggio con Anita* (Journey with Anita), or *Viaggio d'Amore* (Journey of Love), and its hero Guido a project, originating in the memory of his father's death, that Fellini wanted to realize ever since 1957, in order to tell about the trip home of a writer with his lover, directed by Mario Monicelli. The movie came out in 1979 with the same title – *Viaggio con Anita* – but with specific changes. In the meantime, Fellini will disseminate many of his ideas up until the time of *Amarcord.*

In any case, Guido (derived from the Germanic *widu-* wood, woods, forest; or *wida-* distant) reveals spaces and contexts analogous to inner labyrinths in which the personage is lost as if in a dark and menacing forest. Not only that, but in a movie in which the *meta* aspect, so to speak, is essential – *meta*narrative, *meta*phorical, *meta*cinematographic, *meta*catholic, *meta*psychoanalytic, and one could even reach the point of saying *meta*neo-realistic and *meta*lic, like the great spaceship set – it is interesting to interpret the etymology of Anselmi: it is composed of *ansa-* (god, divinity) and *helma-* (protection, helmet, magic hood), and its original meaning could be 'divine protection' or 'helmet, magic hood, given by the gods'. Se we have a *god* (the director), equipped with a magic hood (Fellini's well-known hat, black and wide-brimmed, a kind of Faustian *Narrenkappe*) who, for some reason or other, has gone astray from the road of realism (of protection) which his earlier movies have followed. He has gone astray in a *forest* of symbols, in a dense mass of faces and situations which straddle and mix into each other within his two realities. At a certain point in the movie, Guido explicitly asks himself where he has gone wrong, and finds himself facing a menacing, futuristic forest of metal scaffolding – a return to the structure in *The Temptations of Doctor Antonio,* and a presage of the opening silhouettes of *Fellini: a Director's Notebook.*

The self-analysis of *Eight and a Half* clearly makes it a therapeutic movie, like *La Dolce Vita*. However, if the latter was an open accusation, a society on trial, the story of Guido is a confession. In other words, that which before moved outwards, here is introjected with an implosive dynamic because the protagonists of the mind and reality demand a precise place within the director's body and spirit.

Among the many ideas that one can follow within the narrative of the movie, *mutatis mutandis*, a set-up analogous to the experience of the hero in revisiting chosen tableaux,

not necessarily in chronological order, but according to the logic of the dreams and psychic associations that permeate the whole movie.

The creator-creation motif, even if nothing new, is treated in an original way due to the lucid description of that relationship, and because of the switching that happens to the memory/fear equation. This latter is a *mis en abyme*, which is to say, that practice in heraldic science that consists of placing, within a coat-of-arms, another smaller version of the first one, and a third identical coat-of-arms that is smaller still, and so on. In this study of artistic creation oscillating between private life and psychoanalytic cinema, Fellini, in the guise of Guido, seems truly to refer to the phrase in Gide's *The Counterfeiters*: "I am very fond of the fact that, within a work of art, one can find the subject of that work again, transposed to the list of characters."

The human types in *Eight and a Half* are not on a Pirandellian search for their author, but it is rather the latter who calls them, and is himself called. When reality is going nowhere, boring, or slowed down with fatigue, it is then that Guido/Fellini, always eager for the unforeseeable, looks around in search of an antidote to the fear of the vacuum, and ends up invaded by visual or inexplicable pretexts that trigger memory and, along with it, the people, events or places of childhood.

The 'there' comes from Claudia's vision, the girl at the spring. In an overexposed photo – and so, for the whole movie, this will be the chromatic solution for the black and white 'fear and memory' color – the young Claudia Cardinale, with her deep, hoarse voice, triggers the stream-of-consciousness, the flow of a man's consciousness, in teetering balance between the possible and the illusory. The past only exists in being rendered anew, and memory does not express itself as something always the same, something filed away once and for all; and so Fellini's *art of memory* is the imaginary recreation of traces of the past. All of this, while igniting the joy of those who consider Fellini to be a great visionary outside the freedom of pre-packaged time, helps to confirm, if it were necessary, the false character of his cinema, expressed in the arbitrary invention of memories and of the past, among which live the true data of reality and the equally true ones of imagination: in *Eight and a Half*, memory enriches even more the artifices of his poetic imagination.

Guido's second dream episode comes after the love affair with Carla. The mother's gesticulations introduce the cemetery dream, where his father (once more played by Annibale Ninchi of *La Dolce Vita*) awaits him. The two are expecting the producer and Conocchia – both figures incarnating for Fellini 'sane and reciprocal diffidence' – and the substitution of Luisa for the figure of his mother.

Guido (Mastroianni) carries gifts through the snow for the women in his ideal harem, a set based on Fellini's memories of the country house in Romagna where they used to go on holiday when he was a child

The space-time inconsistencies, with the wadded, extremely white elements which obliterate the coordinates of metropolitan modernity and, above all, the flashback and flash forward, splendidly 'unessential', are incoherences that come close to *Last Year at Marienbad* (1961), but less cerebral, simpler and more Mediterranean. This is illustrated by the elements of the blocked film director's private life as well as the regressive episode of Saraghina, subsequent to the second vision of the girl at the spring, and the useless encounter with the priest. Guido/Fellini knows very well – unlike the wager of the exponents of the *nouveau roman* Resnais and Robbe-Grillet – that the characters' prison is not spatial (the great hotel or the spa) but mental, interior and, having to decide that it is finally a good idea to do so with a little *coup de théatre*, astute and moving. That is why both Guido and Fellini need Saraghina: by now, the autobiographical is introjected in order to make clear how and why a Catholic education interacts with an interior monologue, with the impulses, the fascination with the Prohibited, Sin, Woman.

In this film-essay so full of poetry and *bravura* – an excellent example of that kind of 'umbilical cinema' so frequently attacked because of the propensity of certain directors to "vomit out everything all over themselves" – there are other important problems. Above all else, the question of grace, bound to that of happiness. When enveloped in steam, the cardinal reminds Guido: "Why should you be happy? That is not your business. Who told you that you came into the world to be happy?"; during the first conversation, Guido had explained: "The hero of my story had a Catholic upbringing, like everyone else for that matter, which gave him certain complexes, certain needs... no longer possible to suppress. A prince of the Church appears to him like a holder of a Truth which he can no longer accept even though it fascinates him. And so he seeks a contact, help, maybe a stroke of lightening..." And if the 'cinematographer' is "too nonchalant about mixing sacred and profane love together", the question of revelation and ritual leads the problem back to Guido the man, his weaknesses and his confusions, with which he has to live. After the night-time discussion with Conocchia, he wonders if his is not "a crisis of *inspiration*? And what if it were not one that passes, my dear man? What if it were the final collapse of a huge liar who no longer has any flair or talent?", concluding with 'Sgulp!', a trivializing comment lifted straight from the comics.

The problem of doubt is related with that of chaos, to which the girl at the spring uselessly tries to provide a solution: "I have come for good and all. I want to create order, clean things up. I want to create order. I want to clean...", maybe through love, while erotic love breaks the

Conversely, the episode with the mind-readers, Maurice and Maya, is one of voluntary memory stimulated by the gibberish "ASA, NISI, MASA", which can be the word 'anima' (soul), that which is continually threatened in Guido's mind by the difficulty of accepting reality for what it is. If the future, which is to say, the movie that is to be shot, is full of inner disquiet, a little peace can be found by the flight into childhood, the collective bath, the women of the big house and the high beds, before the three words which serve to make the images slide in the direction of present time.

circle. Conjugal love (Luisa) and sex (Carla, also shot in the rushes) cannot, by themselves, oppose the disorder of life in which one carries the weight of one's own contradictions.

On two occasions, confession is the key to the meaning: in the upshot, after the unproductive conversation with Claudia, and before the blocking of the narrative that leads up to the finale, when Guido will admit: "I don't feel like telling a story that will be another lie." And once again on the visit to the spacecraft set, when speaking with Rossella, he gives voice to his fears: "I thought I saw things so clearly. I wanted to make an honest movie without telling lies of any kind. I thought I had something so simple, so simple to say. A movie that could be of a little use to everyone. Something that could help us bury for good everything dead that we carry within ourselves. And instead, I am the first to lack the courage to bury anything whatsoever. Now my head is all confused and I have this tower on my back… Who knows why things took this turn? When did I go off track? I have absolutely nothing to say, but I want to say it all the same."

It goes without saying that this limitation, transformed into an attribute, into decidedly artistic imperiousness, carries with it a 'guiding spirit' which will make it possible to make the movie within a movie. Air, like water, is dynamic, expresses movement, the unknown, cinema, and that tender and timorous wind will bring Guido, together with his waves of memory, the inevitable, languid childhood conditionings, the first experiences of erotic curiosity and the mystique of punishment in the Saraghina episode, the authentic prototype of the Fellini woman, "the terrible, splendid dragon that represents the first traumatic vision of sex in the life of the protagonist."

This is how Fellini recalls it in *Fare un film* ('Making a movie'): "Saraghina was a gigantic prostitute, the first one I ever saw in my life on the beach at Fano, where I spent the summer vacation with the Salesian boarding school. She was called that because the fishermen obtained her favors in exchange for a few pounds of the cheapest kind of fish – *saraghine* (white bream). From us children, she was content to take small change, or even roast chestnuts [is this why roast chestnuts appear in Fellini's list of 'things I like'? It is likely, mainly because, within his process of falsification,

Guido as a child (Marco Gemini) at school, dominated by the stern, frowning portraits of former religious instructors

Two meta-Fellinian portrayals of our hero in the harem scene

roast chestnuts in summertime are perfectly plausible], and the golden buttons of our uniforms might suffice, or the candles that we stole from church. She lived in a little fortress on a high rock from the time of the great war, a kind of den that smelled of tar, rotting wood and fish. For two cents, she would let us see her rear, which entirely blocked out the heavens. For one cent more she moved it a little, and for four cents she turned face forward. What an immense belly! And under that hairy part, what was it, a cat? It is true, in my movies there is often the image of an abundantly formed woman, big, potent… But Saraghina is an infantile representation of a woman, one of the many and varied expressions of the thousand ways in which a woman can personify herself. It is a woman rich in animal femininity, immense and impossible to seize, but at the same time nutritive, just as an adolescent, hungering for life and sex, perceives her; an Italian adolescent obstructed and thwarted by priests, the church, family and a failed upbringing; an adolescent who, seeking a woman, imagines and wants her to be 'a big hunk of woman'. Like a poor man who, thinking about money, talks and raves, not about thousands of lire, but of millions, even billions."

And there is no continuity between all these women of the world and those of Guido's movie. Woman, as she is presented in the cinematic image, is gigantically enlarged, connected to the symbolism of the protagonist, who sees himself and his childish world in macroscopic dimensions. We are dealing with Fellini's *esthetics of memory* in an invented past revisited (and not its photocopy). A *dialectic of memory* that, without special effects, mixes items from personal life with those about the making of the movie, the harem episode, the finale. Let us look briefly at them in this running order.

At the spa, because he is physically a bit run down, Guido has nightmares about the movie, which does not satisfy him. He hides, he flees. This flight is impossible in reality, as in the opening dream, he is tied to a metal structure, which may be a symbol of the spacecraft set. And then, while taking the waters, not being able to avoid seeing the girl at the spring, he begins to experience real and evanescent phenomena, which come and spontaneously impose themselves, as in an alternated montage.

Mezzabotta is the first person in real life to call him 'old Snaporaz'. He does not talk to him about movies, but about his new love situation, in which he does not feel ridiculous even though he knows people are saying catty things about Gloria being with him because of his money. Guido, unfortunately, does not feel this kind of indifference, does not want to be seen with Carla, and, when Luisa throws his relationship with 'that cow' in his face, he claims, without convincing her, that he put an end to that episode years ago.

With regard to his private life, the figure of Maurice takes on great importance, a character who is the opposite of Daumier, the only one to really read his soul and thus be able to set the production of the movie in motion.

Daumier, in turn, displays Fellini's antinomy between reason and feeling, and remarks on the heavy impediments culture places in the way of the free manifestation of naturalness, passion, art. Throughout the whole movie, this French 'oracle' warns Guido about improvising, about the non-essentials of the script, thus offering Fellini a formidable critical and self-critical escape hatch – a total and ferocious shield against the possible limitations of *Eight and a Half,* and an ideal final commentary on Fellini's *opera omnia*, but also capable of really pushing Guido towards the completely fascinating border with the indefinite and the magical.

Daumier begins right at the heart of the matter, as if, by questioning the script, he wanted to block the girl's action: "Look, even at a first reading, it is obvious that the lack of a problematic idea or, if you will, a philosophical premise, turns the movie into a succession of absolutely gratuitous episodes… even if they could be amusing to the degree that they are realistically ambiguous. One asks oneself, what are the authors really after? Are they trying to make us think? Do they want to scare us? From the very start, the project reveals its poverty of poetic inspiration… Excuse me, but this could be the most pitiful demonstration of the fact that the cinema is fifty years hopelessly behind all the other arts. Then there is the narrative, which is not even up to the level of an avant-garde movie, while having all the deficiencies of the kind."

A little later, almost in a kind of juncture between the beginning and the arrival of Carla at the station: "And the willful apparitions of this girl at the spring, what are they supposed to mean? An offer of purity, of warmth to the hero? Of all the symbols with which the movie abounds, this one is the worst." And then, in commenting on the Saraghina episode: "What does this mean? This is a character from the memories of his childhood! It has nothing to do with a true critical conscience. No. If you really want to mount a polemical attack on the Catholic conscience in Italy, well then, my dear friend, in that case, believe me, the first thing absolutely required is a much higher cultural level, as well as inexorable logic and lucidity. Excuse me, but… your *tender ignorance* is entirely negative. Your little memories bathed in nostalgia, your inoffensive and fundamentally emotional evocations are the actions of an accomplice… The Catholic conscience… but just think for a moment of what Suetonius was during the time of the Caesars! No, you begin with an ambition to denounce, and end up aiding and abetting like an accomplice! Don't you see all the confusion, the ambiguity…?"

The writer's arguments gain the upper hand in the indecision of the artist. This advantage is interrupted – in the imagination – when the concrete movie gets moving ahead of the meandering of mental cinema, with the occasion of the rushes. Daumier says: "Frankly, I would like to be useful with some kind of advice. This evening, I think I perceive that you are called upon to resolve a problem that, in my opinion, has no solution. That is, to put a precise, definitive face on a mob of characters that, to judge by the script, are approximative, generic, non-existent. […] Listen to this: 'The solitary I that turns upon its own axis and feeds entirely on itself ends up being choked by a great sob or a great laugh.' These are Stendhal's words, written during his Italian sojourn. If, rather than throwing them away, one read the messages contained within chocolate wrappings from time to time, one would avoid many illusions." And with these words, the director imagines that the intellectual has hung himself and freed him once and for all from cold logic and cultural rigor.

Daumier's leave-taking sanctions the chaos and incontinence of the project. That chaos which the producer had tried to exploit in order not to allow the press conference be a failure: "Talk, answer. I bought this mess of yours. I have been paying for it all for months. If you don't make

Another childhood memory in his paternal grandmother's house, with the smell of laundry, the sound of the Romagna dialect and disturbing shadows

this movie, I will ruin you." It is a caustic representation of those whom Fellini fought all his life in order for his movie titles and endings not to be changed and, in the final analysis, to defend tooth and nail his dignity and identity as an artist. Certainly the part of the producer Pace, played by Guido Alberti, does not speak like the 'legendary' Peppino Amato, who once said apropos of *La Dolce Vita* that "there is *sporadic* interest in the arrival of this movie", or who maintained that, with the title *Via Veneto,* the movie would remain a 'millstone' in cinematic history.

It is Daumier again who thinks he can sum it all up with the following words: "You have done very well. Believe me, this is a great day for you. Decisions are hard to make, I know, but we intellectuals – I say that because I consider you to be one – have the duty to remain lucid to the end. There are already so many superfluous things in the world, one ought not to add more disorder to disorder. In the final analysis, losing money is part of a producer's job. My compliments, there was nothing else that could have been

done, and he has got what he deserves for having gone so capriciously into such a frivolous venture. No, believe me, do not be nostalgic or remorseful. It is better to destroy than create when one does not create those few necessary things. And then too, is there anything so pure and righteous in the world that it has the right to live? A wrong movie for him is just an economic matter, but for you, at the point where you are now, it could be the end. Better to let everything collapse and strew salt as the ancients did to purify the battlefields. All we really need is a little hygiene, cleaning up, disinfectant. We are drowning in words, images, sounds that have no reason to exist, which come out of a vacuum and return to a vacuum. All one can ask of an artist truly worthy of the name is this one loyal act: train himself to silence. Do you remember Mallarmé's praise of the blank page? [...] If you cannot have everything, nothing is true perfection. Forgive me for this excess of quotations, but we critics do what we can. Our true mission is to sweep away the thousands of abortions that everyday obscenely try to be born. And what you want is nothing less than to leave

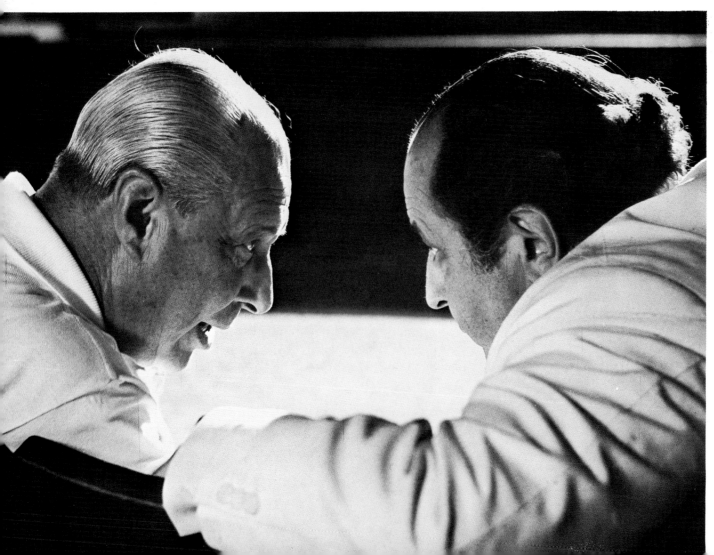

Movie folk in discussion: Conocchia (Mario Conocchia), the production director, reports to the worried producer Pace (Guido Alberti) about the expensive creative ineffectiveness of the director Guido

behind an entire movie like a cripple leaves his deformed footprint behind him. What monstrous presumption to imagine that others would profit from the squalid catalogue of your errors. And why does it matter to you to sew together the tatters of your life, your various memories or the faces of people whom you were never capable of loving?"

During this eulogy of silence, which we will come across again in *The Voice of the Moon*, the director and Daumier are once again in a car, in the same location where the opening dream occurred. Now, however, reality no longer intrudes on the dream, but just the opposite, as the wind of the unforeseeable has begun to blow again, causing the abandonment of reason in favor of Maurice, the personification of show business, of pretence, the vocation of the imaginary.

Other phases of the narrative also see the fusion of existential segments with those relating to work: the phone call to the wife is placed between the French actress and the production rooms; the visit to Carla, who is sick, is shoved into the space between the creation of the figure of the girl

at the spring and the distraction caused by the cardinal's visit; not to mention the steam baths into which the prelate's visit is immersed in anticipation of the creative mist that enshrouds Guido on the visit to the set.

The height of the confusion and panic comes with the press conference, a necessary step in the overcoming of the cinematic and real dreams contained in the harem episode, the personal place of Guido the man, just as the set will be his artistic place. In effect the two *narrative locations* are one and the same: the place where all the women of his lives are gathered in a harem without jealousy or lies so that his desire for Woman can finally be realized. Before Women and Characters can unite in a complete festive circle, the characters will first have to go through a screen test. Here cinema demands his attention, requires clear ideas and no more embarrassing and metaphorical playing around, analogous to what it will demand at the press conference where the two worlds of the director reach the deepest pit of negativity, total defeat.

But it is the world of feelings which creates a crisis for that man of the cinema. In fact, no sooner does Guido, freed from a sense of guilt, feel a new sensation that makes him tremble with happiness than the Cinema, as a character within the movie, which has up to then been frozen by the paralysis of insincere feelings, spreads its imaginative wings and, with a touch of Maurice's magic baton, without fakery or conniving – which is to say, with all the blessed bag of tricks and deceptions of the director Fellini – gets down to work.

The fable-making effect of those remembered is white – white clothes, veils, hair and white surroundings – at the moment when they are 'grafted' with the movie people. Guido's ghosts crowd around his collaborators in a final regenerating bath after the purifying immersions (holy water, infants' baths, bath in the harem with hat on head) while the angels of the circus, the clowns, give the musical rhythm and the melancholy atmosphere necessary to spur Fellini's self-awareness towards its epilogue. Here the whip of the harem has become the megaphone, and the clown with the black director's hat can set up the final celebration of life, the last turn on the merry-go-round. Afterwards, the movie might even truly begin.

For us, meanwhile, *Eight and a Half* remains an inimitable *recherche*, a psychoanalytic journey in which the couch is replaced by the trolley, and mounted on it a movie camera that 'speaks' *sotto voce*, fluttering in the entrancing wind. An experiment in deciphering the individual and his feelings, beyond which, however, there lies a mysterious territory which one cannot clarify either in life or in the cinema. And this problematic aspect of *Eight and a Half* refers one to something *behind* it, which refers to another *Eight and a Half,* and then another still. There remains the initiatory itinerary on three levels, the projected film, the existence of the director/individual, and the ranks of the phantomlike characters of his imaginary universe. It is a little as if, paradoxically, Guido Anselmi, alias Federico Fellini, were in himself a kind of 'collective imagination', a fantasy of the singular, secretly hidden in the intimacy of his inner but intolerant eye under that magic cap given him by the gods of the seventh art which is the cinema.

Nearly ten years had passed since Giulietta Masina had last worked with her husband. The imprinting of the legendary Gelsomina, her strong characterization, the wide-open eyes and the clownish expression on her face, which had merged in the 'bufoonery' of Cabiria, had really left their mark. The ten year break, a very long period for the actress, had only partially succeeded in making the public forget the expression and the humanity which had decreed her international success. Ten years before finally being able to recount a different reality, almost as if Fellini, too, had wanted to dig into the universe of his 'unfamiliar' woman

in order to render it in dream images probably referring to a delicate phase of their lives.

Not that there was a lack of other projects: before *Juliet* and her spirits had delineated themselves, Fellini had thought of having his wife act the role of a nun (after the discovery of an ancient diary in the convent of *La Strada*), a famous medium (Eileen Garrett, a personal acquaintance), a fortune-teller and other characters. All of these subjects were never realized, partly because the director feared being accused of mysticism and magic, but perhaps mostly because they were roles that may have been unsuitable for Masina's personality. All of them, however, ideas dispersed into underground rivulets, as often happens with Fellini, only to reappear in the construction of the interpretation.

Juliet of the Spirits (1965) "was born of Giulietta and for Giulietta. It had a long, long gestation that went back to the time of *La Strada*. I wanted to do another movie with Giulietta, but above all I had the feeling that my desire to use cinema as an instrument to penetrate certain manifestations of reality could find its best guide in Giulietta."

His experience of Jung's theories by way of long conversations with Ernest Bernhard not only deepened Fellini's ideas about the importance and meaning of dreams, but stimulated his interest in magic and the occult, convincing him that there existed a 'terrain of the unknown', and fascinating him with the 'promise of the arcane', the contact with dimensions that go beyond the senses.

The discovery of Jung also helped him have more confidence in fantasy and to better understand its importance. His visit to the Room of the Small Memories in Switzerland enlightens him with regard to the deep influence of dreams on the understanding of oneself. "It was as if Jung had written specifically for me [...] I managed to apply what I found there to my way of being and to shake off the sense of inferiority or guilt that had remained since the days of my childhood, the recriminations of my parents and teachers, the mockery of the other kids for whom being different meant being inferior. To follow Jung is like going through a door already opened, that of 'the other' black and white reality of *Eight and a Half*. That reading taught him that mystery can be assimilated perfectly well by reason, and suggested a point of contact between the real and the imaginary, like the inner life of *Juliet of the Spirits,* torn between dream-like visions and hard, depressing reality. Such a balance requires the conservation of that sensory perception within which every individual's life is wrapped and which, if it is suppressed or not acknowledged, tips the balance of the unconscious towards the prevalence of fantasies and, as Jung once again teaches, of ghosts.

Juliet's life is really quite unstable. We encounter her, a bourgeois woman on the threshold of middle age, as she is preparing a candle-lit dinner to celebrate her fifteenth wedding anniversary. Giorgio, her brilliant, worldly husband (very much like Mezzabotta in *Eight and a Half,* and played by the same actor, Mario Pisu), appears in the company of many friends: Val, the lawyer; the sculptress and medium, Genius, who subjects Juliet to her experiments.

During a seance, Iris is evoked, and interrupted by Olaf, an evil spirit who speaks to Juliet, telling her that she is a nobody and of no account. Juliet faints with emotion, while a telephone call with no one on the line interrupts the proceedings.

The next day, as soon as Giorgio leaves, Juliet believes she sees a monster emerging from the fountain. In reality, it is just the gardener. On the beach with her nieces, she describes her childhood visions to a doctor friend. She closes her eyes and believes she is seeing Iris. In reality, it is Susy, her exuberant neighbor who lives in the next villa. Juliet dozes off and sees an old man pulling on a rope which he passes to her. She also pulls and, from the sea, emerges a raft with several dead horses, a crude amphibian laden with obscene figures, and a second with barbaric ones. On the way home, Juliet meets the sisters Adele and Sylva with their beautiful mother, all three sophisticated, gaudy, talkative, truly her opposite. Gossiping, they make accusations against Giorgio, but Juliet apparently takes no notice of what they say. Before they go off, the mother seriously warns Juliet to take more care of herself.

When her husband comes home, Juliet wants to tell him about her dream adventure, but Giorgio falls asleep and calls out the name of Gabriella, his lover. Juliet is worried and, the next morning, asks for an explanation, but without results.

Val invites her to a meeting with Bishma, the man-woman. In the big hotel where the meeting is being held, Juliet thinks she sees a wedding feast, and then again when she is ushered into the room for a private audience with the guru: once more she sees Iris transformed into Fanny, the immoral ballerina who eloped with her grandfather years ago. In the car, Juliet tells her friends about that flight and of how, in her imagination, she saw her grandfather fly off in the old circus airplane followed by the family.

At home in the evening, Juliet encounters José, a Spanish friend of Giorgio's who is preparing the 'oblivion' drink that Bishma had foreseen. While Juliet listens to the conversation, attracted by the poetic nature of their guest, Giorgio points the telescope towards Susy's house, whose orgiastic parties have provoked innumerable protests. In bed, Juliet tries once again to speak to her husband and, late that night, discovers him on the telephone to his lover.

More and more worried, she takes Adele's advice, and goes to the Lince detective agency. While at the home of her sculptress friend, she remembers a scene from her childhood. Convinced that God was hiding behind the trap-door on the ceiling of the nuns' toy theater, she made a pact with her friend Laura that whoever saw Him first had to tell the other what he was like. During a play, Juliet, playing the role of

The director frames Sandra Milo in **Giulietta of the Spirits**

a little girl, is tied to a grate as a martyr, and is being elevated to heaven. She is just about to reach the trap-door when her grandfather interrupts the show and brings her back down in the name of reason, ranting against all forms of mystification and mysticism.

On the pretext of bringing her cat back, Juliet manages to make friends with Susy, who amiably gives her a tour of the villa, and introduces Juliet to her strange, ambiguous guests. A bicycle ride through the pine wood seals the women's friendship. But Juliet runs away when Susy invites her to be lifted in a basket to a tree house, where two boys are waiting to 'entertain' them.

Meanwhile, the detective's report on Giorgio is ready, and when she is shown the film of his betrayal, timid Juliet's reaction is to go to the party being held at her new friend's house. There, Juliet feels ill at ease and a little afraid of the guests, particularly Susy's Middle Eastern lover

and his very handsome son who, after a voyeuristic visit to surprise the couples making love, waits for Juliet in order to spend the night with her. Attracted by the boy's sensuality, Juliet is about to give in when, looking up, she sees in the mirror over the bed the martyr saint admonishing her, and she rushes off home.

Juliet gives a garden party for her and Giorgio's many friends, including an American psychotherapist. But the hostess is reluctant to go down to her guests, because she is in the throes of a new and more disturbing vision: the house is invaded by spirits. And she sees other ghosts when she goes down to the garden (the nuns, the martyrs, Iris and others). Giorgio goes off and the psychotherapist takes Juliet aside to make her own opinion known: unconsciously, she wants a definitive break with her faithless husband.

Juliet finally finds the strength to confront her rival, and goes to

Two opposing female characters square up to each other: the striking and slightly lascivious Susy (Sandra Milo) and the calm, passive wife, Juliet (Giulietta Masina)

Gabriella's house, ready to make a big scene. After a long wait, a telephone call makes her realize that Giorgio is now lost to her. At home, Giorgio is packing his bags and mutters excuses while Juliet stands in front of the television set where the close-up face of a clown looks at her in commiseration.

Now Juliet is alone. Spirits and real people invade every corner of the house and, in the bedroom, in front of a wardrobe door where God may be hiding, her mother appears, prohibiting Juliet from opening it. But this time, Juliet refuses to obey, saying that she is now no longer afraid. At these magic words, her beautiful mother immediately ages. Opening the wardrobe door, Juliet sees herself as the little martyr in the childhood show, just as her grandfather and Fanny arrive on the scene. The defeated spirits return whence they came, and Juliet sets off towards the pine wood, while a friendly voice murmurs that perhaps it can be of use to her.

The subject of matrimony is the pretext for *Juliet of the Spirits*, a story composed of various other stories, probably including that of the Fellinis. Juliet "exemplifies one kind of Italian woman who, due to her upbringing and what she has been told of the state of matrimony, believes that marriage automatically brings happiness. Each time she discovers it is not true, she does not understand or know how to face the situation."

In *La Strada,* Gelsomina nullifies herself in Zampanò, even though she is far superior to him. But Juliet, faced with a similar insensitivity in Giorgio – the vacuous second lead in the life of a couple in crisis – will learn through hard knocks not to defend him all the time; and, in time, she will escape from under that repressive education which has turned her into an insipid woman, an unhappy prisoner. In short, a rich, modern Gelsomina, she allows herself to be abandoned, only to begin living a real life again.

"In my movies I have often felt the need to represent the degeneration, the caricature of a marital relationship. It is problematic, the most problematic of all. It is profoundly individual. You cannot regulate it with collective norms imposed from the outside by the power of taboos. It ought to be forbidden to sit back in a marriage. Many of us stretch out passively on the laws of nature deformed by current usage and let ourselves be sucked out and swallowed by matrimony, neglecting its highest aim, the only one: the attempt to form a true union." Giorgio and his wife only achieve the appearance of a true union, a little like Guido and Luisa in *Eight and a Half.* The reference is not an accidental one, because in *Juliet of the Spirits* one gets the impression that Fellini wanted to complete the portrait of a marital relationship that had only been sketched out in the preceding movie, where Guido-Fellini was too distracted by his own crisis of inspiration to pay any real attention to Luisa's anguish.

Within the story of the protagonist, the simple autobiographical reflection of the fulfillment of a true

marital union is loaded with psychoanalytical meanings, touching upon communication, "a man's difficulty in speaking of woman", but of the contrary as well. As if, once having overcome the existential crisis to a large degree, Fellini felt the impelling need to expose the question of the couple's alienation, even while knowing that he had not the necessary clarity or honesty to do so. Here he aims, in words, at the intention of "giving woman back her true independence, her unarguable and inalienable dignity."

It is a first goal, a prophetic vision of the new feminine condition at a time when one scarcely heard the word feminism pronounced, and coming furthermore from the creator of *La Dolce Vita*, the man who exalted Anita Ekberg. This vision, however, was not shared by Giulietta Masina who, perhaps for the first time, opposed her husband with a will of iron on several counts. First of all, on esthetic grounds, because she wanted to look more attractive in the movie, but mostly because of the content. "Giulietta and I were in disagreement: each of us interpreted the future of the character in a different way. Because of my respect for her ability to delineate character, I asked for her advice. But from the moment her husband leaves her, our ideas were completely different. I stubbornly defended my position. But, with the passing of time, I came to understand that she was right. [...] In her opinion, Juliet was not on the point of finding herself, but of losing herself." This was because, as usual, Fellini the clairvoyant was too far ahead of the times. During that time, an abandoned woman with her upbringing would have actually been a woman destroyed.

Incontestable, however, is the heroine's flight into her very private world of memories. Under the influence of Bernhard and Jung – 'the older brother' – Fellini puts the dreams front stage, together with a whole series of symbols connected with them. Naturally, the director cannot help but begin with the world of childhood: like children, Juliet has "a hazy, emotional, dreamy relationship with reality. Everything is fantastic [...] a gigantic spectacle, gratuitous and marvelous, a kind of boundless, breathing amoeba where everything lives, subject and object, confused in a single unstoppable flow, visionary yet unaware, fascinating yet terrifying, from which the watershed, the boundary of consciousness, has not yet emerged." For Fellini, if those infantile visions had continued into maturity, they would probably swallow up one's entire capacity to think and act. "The important thing would be to rediscover, on the conscious level, that visionary faculty. Just because it is one of the possibilities of human nature and there is no reason to deprive oneself of it."

In the light of this information, one can get a better focus on Juliet's character, which is that of a woman who has to learn to walk alone, even while experiencing situations that put her in a disadvantaged position with regard to any sort

Sandra Milo, who in Juliet of the Spirits *also plays the part of the frivolous Fanny, enriches the gallery of spirits which haunt Juliet*

The mysterious, striking clairvoyant (Valeska Gert) will assist our heroine in overcoming the distress caused by her own imagination

of provocation, ready to bow her head right up to the threshold of middle age, when she is conceded that which was denied to Gelsomina and Cabiria: assistance from that particular power of her visions, not a repressed nebula, but assimilated into her personality as a balancing element. Having a simple nature, Juliet is prey to phenomena which, in a more structured personality, would have little influence, or at least be kept under control. Instead, she allows herself to be contaminated, to be influenced by that magical world inhabited by subhuman beings, petulant spirits, which she perhaps faces with less anxiety than she does the humans around her: hypocrites like Giorgio, the detectives, her sisters or women friends, swindlers like the lawyer, the sculptress, Bishma and his court, and the most repressive

and regressive of all, her very beautiful mother, the model of a woman and, at the same time, of a movie star (played by the superbly elegant and charming Caterina Boratto).

The magical landscape that opens up before this 'Alice in Spirit Land', with its intense colors (Fellini's first color movie), is an intimate part of herself, which is why Juliet forms an immediate familiarity with sinful Susy, who is so apparently different from her, and slips pleasantly into the ambience of her court of miracles, the very antithesis of the beautiful people who frequent her own villa at Fregene.

The spirit world that enshrouds the foundations of the subconcious deeply affect Juliet's life, even if they seem, at first, to escape from ordinary sensory perception. Far too much of a contrast to real life, but gradually more absorbing, little by little Juliet accepts them as representing 'another' reality that is gradually less frightening. At bottom, Susy's villa, the witch's house of fairy tales, belongs to all climes and epochs. "Our dreams and nightmares are the same ones that people had three thousand years ago. The same basic fears that enjoy living in our homes were experienced by them in their caves." With regard to the myriad characters and visions of her inner conflict, Juliet's courageous act consists of breaking that circle of fear and reliving the infantile role of the holy martyr to which her life has conformed by enduring her husband's lies, the superiority of her sisters, the repressions – including the esthetic one – of her mother.

Furthermore, Juliet settles accounts with the men in her subconscious who are – unlike the single one in her life – many: tempters, Middle Eastern satraps, bawling headmasters, barbarians, monsters. Her very human grandfather gets off scot-free, even though he abandoned her for the dancer Fanny. The reality of Juliet's soul finally emerges with the vision of the play, that is to say, when she manages to make contact with her childhood (the door behind which is God): an ingenuous dream to re-create, by recognizing it, her new personal equilibrium and a coming-

to-terms with the complex reality of her conscious existence, a long journey which gives her the strength to face life.

To return to a famous old quotation, one could really affirm, if it were still required, the ambivalent character of Fellini's personality: if the director was both Gelsomina and Zampanò, this time he really is Juliet in the deepest sense of the words: *"Giulietta c'est moi"*.

As we have said, *Juliet of the Spirits* is also his first feature movie in color. Color as an expressive element in a movie where the protagonists are dreams, and inner life constituted no small challenge considering that "the story, its structure, its feeling, are determined and come to life exclusively through the colors, and it is therefore only the colors that can relate it, interpret it, express it." And they are the colors of memory and of visions "concept, feeling, as in truly great painting… Those who dream may see a red meadow, a green horse, a yellow sky, and these are not absurdities. They are images saturated with the feelings that inspired them." From now on, Fellini will give them his utmost attention and *Casanova* will be the text of his personal theory about colors.

In *Juliet of the Spirits*, Fellini takes a vaguely impressionistic

At the party at Susy's villa, Juliet turns down the chance of becoming the lover of the young, attractive newcomer (Fred Williams)

direction: the eye, a selective organ, brings out the things that strike him most in relationship to the emotional and cultural burden of the spectator, but who must come to terms with the lens that records "what the light, so variable in its movement, suggests to him from moment to moment", trying to accommodate everything within a "result that interprets, by means of faithfully expressing them, his idea, feeling and meaning, his recollection of color without its whole being spoiled, betrayed by the imponderables of lighting, shooting and printing." To visualize thoughts, create the magic of dreams where everything monstrous takes on plastic beauty, was a problem that could have made the expressionism of old black and white despair. But no, because Fellini, very modern, grants color the recognition of its power, the capacity to enrich his 'living pictures' and give them a new expressive dimension. In other words, he paints the images with the colors he carries within himself.

The movie subsequent to *Juliet of the Spirits* was to be *Il Viaggio di G. Mastorna*. Fellini recounts: "My first idea came during a plane journey in 1964, as we were landing. It was winter in New York, and I had a sudden vision of us crashing. Fortunately for the cinema, that vision did not come true, but it transformed itself into the reflection of another vision, that is to say, the theme of *Mastorna,* which Fellini proposed in 1965 to De Laurentiis. The following year, the director fell ill, perhaps because "I was afraid of doing that movie, or did not feel I was up to it. The sets had been built, the people hired, the money had been spent, but I did not feel like going ahead with it. I was suffering from acute neurasthenia aggravated not only by the need I felt to outdo everything I had done up until then, but also by the usual debilitating arguments with the producers. I even thought the movie was killing me because it did not want to be made. However that may be, I found myself in a hospital room at the beginning of 1967, convinced that I was terminally ill."

Happily recovered from the illness (the argument with De Laurentiis not entirely resolved), Fellini has a new producer, Alberto Grimaldi, a new scriptwriter, Bernardino Zapponi, and a new office in the auspicious Via della Fortuna in Rome. All these are positive promontory signals for a proposal by Raymond Eger to make a movie of Edgar Allan Poe's *The Tell-Tale Heart* as one episode of three for a movie entitled "Three master directors for the master of the shiver". Fellini does not give a definitive reply. He waits for more signals, but in reality he is giving the project a lot of thought, sucking on it like a sweet to draw the last drop of taste out of it and then let it sink into his world of visions.

Poe is not an author easy to translate into images, his dense style being constructed on a 'philosophy of composition' with precise and deceiving rhythms. For Zapponi "to violate that intimacy is an impious as well as

Polidor, faithful Fellini clown, playing the part of a blind elderly actor who is awarded a prize at the opening ceremony of an improbable catholic Western (Toby Dammit, *third episode of* The Spirits of the Dead)

difficult proposal. There is something shameless about dissipating those mists, extracting the episodes, the characters, giving them their independence. In the light of the sun, those characters turn to dust, the reflectors of the cinema put the shadows to flight."

Terence Stamp portrays Toby, a character partially based on the hero of Edgar Allan Poe's story **Never Bet the Devil Your Head**

Even a dreamy and mercurial director like Fellini, well disposed to extra-sensory magic and fascinated by the mysterious, could find himself in trouble faced with the disturbing atmosphere of Poe, unless he managed to produce the same neuroses, even, perhaps, without actually working with the text itself. In fact, unconvinced by the choice imposed by the French producers, Fellini tries to find an alternative story, and commissions the 'historical' secretary, Liliana Betti, to make brief summaries for him. Fellini would like to use the story *L'Appuntamento*, but it is too hard to handle (he will take up the idea again for the movie *Venezia*), and he turns to *L'Angelo Bizzarro*. Finally, his imagination is captured by the clean, surreal demon of *Never Bet the Devil Your Head*. Not that he is entirely convinced by that "old limping man with the appearance of a venerable gentleman, as clean as his immaculate collar with a black apron and hair parted like a maiden's." But giving the devil the innocent appearance of a maiden, according to the mad law of contrasts, overturns the situation: "Is the devil ugly and evil? Let us make him attractive and innocent. He shall be a young boy. Better yet, a young girl" – in short, a familiar tempter, like the baby Cupid of Dr. Antonio or the tiny voice that offers help at the end of *Juliet of the Spirits*.

Probably due partly to the photo of the writer that Fellini keeps in his wallet, he galvanizes himself and accepts the commission. The advance payment and the chance of putting *Mastorna* to one side seem to have given him enough enthusiasm to begin. Except that, after signing the contract, the project, as usual, loses motivation due to a hint of indisposition and an associated rejection crisis. He wants to do a different story, proposes Zapponi's *L'Autista* (but the rights for it have already been sold) or a different Poe, *The Premature Burial*, to be located in the Castelli Romani. This idea is rejected by the producers, so that there is nothing left for him to do but hedge his bets on the 'devil' movie.

All he has prepared is "that ending, created with all the coldness of the great clowns", but there are the remaining 25 minutes of the movie to be thought out, the most interesting of the three episodes to be released in 1968 with the title *The Spirits of the Dead* (the other two entrusted, by a process of elimination, to Roger Vadim's *Metzengerstein* and Louis Malle's *William Wilson*).

And so begin long nights of cruising in the car with the scriptwriter, primarily in the Castelli area, full of mysterious ruins that are an antithesis to the pleasure trips outside town and the meals in numberless *trattorias* that display effigies of chefs offering inviting plates of *fettucini* (figures which, in the movie, will suddenly leap out of the darkness as anguished, disregarded signs of danger for the hero). With the problem of the location resolved, there remains the site where the hero is to die (it will be the broken bridge at Ariccia), but above all the selection of the leading actor.

Peter O'Toole would appear to be the perfect choice for the Shakespearian actor in his decline who comes to Italy to film the first 'Catholic Western'. After the first enthusiastic contact, however, O'Toole has second thoughts, probably recognising himself too well in the irascible and drunken Toby Dammit. Afraid of losing the public's favor, he declines, thus becoming perhaps the only famous actor ever to reject a part with Fellini.

After considering Richard Burton and Marlon Brando, the choice finally falls on Terence Stamp, rebaptized as Terenzio 'Francobollo' [literally 'postage stamp' in Italian], an actor sufficiently distraught and hallucinated to accept the challenge of an impossible wager. 'Terence Stamp,' Fellini writes, "arrived in Rome and, at first sight, I liked him for his boyish modesty. He was subjected to a long trial of make-up with Pierino Tosi, in an attempt to make him look as much as possible like Edgar Allan Poe, with imploring, frightened eyebrows. Then Pierino invented for him that

black velvet jacket with violet trimmings and a violet foulard. The result is a romantic, anguished hero, altogether similar to the timeless 'Edgardo' – as Fellini familiarly referred to the writer – for whom he nevertheless had such great admiration and respect as to impost upon himself a kind of detachment with regard to another artist's creative work whose primogeniture he recognizes, as he also did in the *Satyricon* and, more subtly, in *Casanova*.

Toby Dammit, an unemployed English actor and an alcoholic, is signed up to shoot an Italian Western financed by Catholic parties. He arrives in Rome and, while stuck in a nightmarish traffic jam, he is approached by a gypsy who wants to read his hand through the car window. But, at the sight of his palm, she flees in alarm. Toby sees a little blonde girl, who invites him to play with her by throwing him a ball. During a television interview, the actor replies haughtily to the reporters' stupid questions, stating that he believes in the devil who is a little girl.

During a social evening at an eccentric night club, a *Lupa d'oro* award is presented to a blind old comedian. When Toby's turn comes, he recites the passage from Macbeth, "Life is a tale told by an idiot/ Full of sound and fury/ Signifying nothing" and, disgusted by the human fauna applauding him, he drives off in a rage in the flaming red Ferrari the producers have given him.

Dammit, the cursed actor who stands out in contrast to the gothic Roman atmosphere of the cinematographists' party, goes after his own personal ghosts before reciting some Shakespearean verse

This despairing man's tragic destiny frightens the gypsy who reads his palm

His own father, Spagna (Salvo Randone), senses Toby Dammit's inner intensity, and feels foreboding about his desperate fate when he meets him at the airport

Driving aimlessly, he arrives at the Castelli Romani where, in the darkness, the car headlights illuminate the advertising cut-outs outside the restaurants, a flock of sheep, night workers and several closed streets, like the hallucinatory course of his disrupted mind. He finally finds himself at a collapsed bridge, where the little girl reappears and invites him to play again. Toby accepts and launches the car at full speed in order to leap the gap in the bridge. He succeeds, but his head is cut off by a cable stretched in mid-air. The ball bounces over to where the head is lying: the devil-child has won the bet.

In 1969, when all Italian society is being rocked by youthful dissent, Fellini shoots *A Director's Notebook* and the *Satyricon*, works which, at first glance, appear to be entirely removed from the new demands for change. The former, made for television, represents a pause for meditation, a director's interval of indubitable interest, not so much because it offers revelations of surprises to come or mere explanations of what has been, but because it is a vision, with commentary on projects, ideas, fragments which the director, always reticent about these things, has in his sights on the set of his imagination.

The part dedicated to *Il Viaggio di G. Mastorna* is almost as touching as the text published in 1964. A Utopian movie, a ghost frame, a journey and a character constantly pondered, periodically taken up anew, feared, hated and never made, but it is nice to think that *all* his work constitutes the dream journey of Fellini-Mastorna. In time, it was transformed into an icon of cult movies, for which reason a revisiting of his little troupe constitutes a fine monument to the dream of a dream, to *Fellini's Unfinished*.

And speaking of dreams, it is well to remember that along the route from neo-realism to the fantastic, which is to say from *La Dolce Vita* to *Eight and a Half,* there is to be found the *Book of Dreams,* which Fellini began to compile along the lines indicated by Ernest Bernhard, writing down drawings and comments about his inexhaustible nightly dream activity. He methodically devoted time to these notes for about twenty years, filling large notebooks bound in leather or Varese paper, writing with China ink or felt-tipped pens. They are preserved at the Fondazione Federico Fellini in Rimini, presided over by his sister Maddalena, and have never been published except for a few dreams in the magazine 'Dolce Vita', No.3, 1987 and No.12, 1988, in the monthly 'Il Grifo', Nos.1-9, 1991, and particularly those printed in the catalogue *Federico Fellini* edited by Lietta Tornabuoni for the exhibition/conference held in 1995. These are seventeen dreams in color with titles, dates, hand-written notes and a brief commentary: 'Il Cardinale', April 15, 1961 (about Fellini's encounter with Montini, Archbishop of Milan, later Pope Paul VI, as 'reparation' to the director for the negative position taken by the prelate towards the unity that the Jesuits and Father Angelo Arpa of the Centro San Fedele in Milan

gave to *La Dolce Vita*); *All'Indietro*, June 23, 1974 ('Myself at the wheel of a black car that sped dizzily in reverse along a path spiralling around a mountain'); 'Punti Interrogativi', August 22, 1974 (Fellini paints red question marks that run under the ironic look of Oreste Del Buono); 'Colla Acustica' and 'Su i Binari', October 30, 1974 (two descriptions: seated on some railway tracks with a woman in a large yellow hat, Fellini talks on the telephone, but the words are incomprehensible; and then a second scene, which was described, with some variations, in the television advertisement that Fellini shot for the Banca di Roma with Paolo Villaggio and Anna Falchi); 'Lucianona', January 1, 1975 (one of the typical women of Fellini's imagination – a hypnagogic image); '*Happy, Unhappy*', January 21, 1975 (the director's interpretation: 'A dream about a word game can be an invitation to recognize that, if you do not know English, a foreign language, just as the language of the unconscious is unknown to you, how can you dare to reach conclusions about the meanings of things and to make definitions and diagnoses that are based on premises deeply sunk in ignorance?'; 'Gigantic New-born Babe', April 1, 1975 (a hypnagogic image, a nude woman, 'P', seated on a cloud in a blue sky, Fellini blows, the cloud floats in space and the woman takes her big breasts in her hands while it rains); 'Folle Velocità', November 25 and 26, 1975 (an elevator that soars up towards room No. 672 of a hotel occupied by others, and a projection of the fears relating to *Eight and a Half*); 'Mastorna', September 9, 1978 (a photograph of the face of 'the elusive personage that has now been my obsession for years, stalking me and then abandoning me'); 'Le Belve', June 22, 1980 (a representation of the figure of the 'painter of wild beasts' who does portraits of lionesses that smile with human lips, in reference to women and the preparations for *City of Women*); 'Giuseppe Verdi', 'Giovanni Agnelli', 'La Mia Fine', 'Sempre Più Buio', 'Sandrocchia', 'Guerriera', are all dreams deliberately left without a date and an original text, but with the director's comment that they refer, in this order, to: shots of the backs of four women, all with very heavy asses, that make an airplane fly crookedly until the musician appears; after a party at the house of the Lawyer (popular nickname for Giovanni Agnelli, *translator*), a woman with a lovely round rear end gets out of the bed in which there are Fellini and Agnelli...; a hypnagogic vision of Fellini who, encircled by flames, is machine-gunned by the Germans; a crocodile grabs him by the waist to drag him 'endlessly into the depths of the river which gets darker and darker...'; the pet name Sandrocchia is for Sandra Milo as she appears dressed in *Juliet of the Spirits*, and there is also a black and white monkey who nibbles at the director's left hand; Fellini, blocked and turned to stone, standing before a grotto where a powerful woman is sitting on the ground, perhaps an Aztec, and above the arch of the grotto is written

'Everything you can do has already been decided long ago!', while a merry little boy is crouched down, laughing and saying: 'Yes! Yes! But making poo is something you can still always do!!! Ha! Ha! Ha!'

The cinematographic fantasy of the Great Dreamer, therefore, owes much to these nocturnal creations that he transferred to the heavy sheets of paper of the *Book of Dreams*, a sum of sequences, of visualized dream rushes, the precipitation of the effervescent Fellini solution of reality-dream-sleep-memory. This generally abstract activity, colored and fleeting, had absorbed him ever since childhood: "When I was about six or seven, I was convinced that there were two lives, one with open eyes and one with eyes closed. In the evening, I could hardly wait to go to bed. I had named the four corners of the bed after Rimini's four movie theaters: Fulgor, Savoia, Opera Nazionale Balilla, Sultano. The show began as soon as I closed my eyes. First, a velvety darkness, deep and transparent, a darkness that flowed into a second darkness. Then flashes began to break across the darkness like over the sea at evening when a storm threatens and the watery horizon is bombarded with lightening. Then I found myself deeper within it, the flashing happened behind me, and all around me as well. There appeared colored spirals, constellations, bright points, scintillating spheres, sometimes circled by rings like the planet Saturn. The dark sky was constellated by blinding forms and colors that began slowly to rotate around me at the center. The spectacle enchanted me. While rotating, little by little the splendor of the galaxy of light became attenuated and faded, like a merry-go-round that runs down. Everything became paler. This meant that, in that corner, the show was over, and I changed to a different corner of the bed. Once again the vortex of light started up, became filled with lights, was extinguished. I changed corners once more. These shows repeated themselves every night. For years. They were not real dreams – I saw the lights, heard the noises of the house…"

Even if Fellini, the great faker Fellini, had never dreamt all these things, the simple fact of having invented them for the written page would make him an extraordinary, eclectic narrator, an 'absent' artist, a little '*à la* Nino Rota'. So one can understand how *Il Viaggio di G. [Giuseppe] Mastorna* can open up the images of *Fellini: a Director's Notebook*, a notebook that, even while preoccupied with the movie that never was, is already sending out feelers towards the future incursion into the ancient Rome of the *Satyricon*.

Mastorna, a surname that Dino Buzzati casually took from the Milan telephone book, established itself in Fellini's poetic world as a synonym for obsession, perhaps of a most particular obsession connected with the figure of his friend

Bernhard, upon whose death in the summer of 1965 he writes this singular journey, a journey that neither begins nor ends. Like a dream somewhere between memory and oblivion, it truly has no point of origin, but does not want to die for at least twenty years, as long as, at Dinocittà, in the spaces occupied by Dino De Laurentiis productions, there are still the structures, the building façades and the great framework of the airplane with which Mastorna, landing in the piazza, was to have begun a story of death, a subject that was still far from the magic circle of the man and the cineast.

For the *Notebook* troupe, the same thing that happened on the set of *Eight and a Half* occurs once again, where, faced with the structure having to be dismantled, the force of the characters brought to life had determined the ending. In its own way, this ending was falser than false, because it was not written into the script, but invented on the set, that is to say on a duplicate of the spaceship meta-set.

Fellini, the cameraman, the sound man and the secretary roam among the surviving carcasses of the *Mastorna* sets, to which the director attributes a greater attraction than he did at the time of the project. Some young foreign hippies are living among those old structures, where they have even celebrated an 'alternative' marriage ceremony. The site and the objects there inspire one of them to write a poem, which sees Mastorna as a non-place, a ghost town, a storehouse of 'sleeping' materials: *I live in a place called Mastorna, which a madman's dream placed upon the grass, a useless place where no-one lives, where no-one loves, works, hates, dies. There is an airplane nailed down that cannot fly, and the shops have wooden doors that never open. Mastorna, sad and lovely town, with a beauty I love above all others because it is called Dementia, city of dust and rags, like all other things. I want to die in Mastorna, be buried in that paper church where no priests enter.*

Framed in the airplane's window, we see the silhouette of Mastorna/Mastroianni, on whose image the rushes focus. Here too, as in *Eight and a Half*, there is a character inscribed within an actor who, in turn, is filtered by the director, with the difference that Guido was saved from the girl at the spring, whereas now no character survives: Fellini's wind blows up strong, almost viciously, sweeps the landing area violently, shakes the young people, raises the dust, enters the fuselage and makes it look like a long coffin, brings on snow and, within its swirling, also causes Mastorna to appear from the back with his violoncello. But Mastorna's world arouses "something like remorse [in Fellini], as if I felt millions of eyes fixed upon me in expectation." And fleeing, as usual, from uneasiness, he diverts the spectator's attention, turns a page in his notebook and projects himself into the sites and sensations of the *Satyricon* to come: the Colosseum at night, populated by transvestites, homosexuals, hustlers and transexuals, disturbed by the spotlights of the movie cameras, a long flashback on the silent pictures about ancient Rome (the first movie that Fellini remembers having seen at the Fulgor movie theater was *Maciste all'Inferno*, 1926, directed by Guido Brignone).

There follows the conjuring up of Genius the medium, who 'senses' the underground presence of those ancient, joyful 'cutthroats', and knows how to make contact with them. A trip on the subway in the company of the expert becomes a visual experience, because the names of the stations are written in Latin, while a large group of ancient inhabitants look on and go along for the trip to a place where they find the practitioners of the world's oldest profession and, along with the images of the prostitutes, some 'wolves' howl and attract truck drivers from our own time.

The mixing up of past and present continues with an 'annotation' of Marcello Mastroianni's Roman villa, for which Fellini puts on a mini show dedicated to "dear, excellent Marcello: the faithful, devoted friend, the wise [other half of a] true, beautiful friendship based on a healthy reciprocal trust. It is a pleasure working with Marcello: discrete, helpful, intelligent, he enters his parts on tiptoe, without ever asking for anything, without even having read the script. [...] He allows himself to be made up, dressed, combed without objections and asking only the most indispensable questions; with him everything is soft, serene, relaxed, natural – so natural that he is even able to fall asleep at times during his scenes, possibly even during close up shots."

The actor is so prepared to do anything that is asked that he will show himself to American tourists from a terrace like a true Latin Lover. Old Snaporaz, who wants to make a movie about an aged Tarzan, or about Mandrake – *Mandrake de Frosinon* (a popular Mandrake from the country province where Mastroianni himself comes from, born in Fontana Liri in 1924) – is the extraordinary interpreter who yet is not able to satisfy his director in *Mastorna*, that monstrously complicated character, because he is not permitted to appropriate the part, as he himself will comment in the film testament *Mi ricordo, si mi ricordo* directed by Anna Maria Tatò.

Then the *Mastorna* idea comes back, impossible to put into focus in spite of the numerous attempts to define its invisible essence, to make it rational before going on to the artifice of the images. The rushes are nervous, agitated, full of tensions and people, and do not work because, as the director comments: "Marcello felt my uneasiness, he was disoriented by my uncertainty. We tried it with a moustache, without a moustache, with a wig, without one, contact lenses, but there was no Mastorna, he continued to implacably remain hidden." In spite of his fears, Fellini takes revenge on his elusive stone guest, who lives only in the hide-out of his anxiety. He takes note of this and goes on to another idea for the *Satyricon*, but not before Mastroianni makes one final attempt at helping his creator ("If you convince yourself that I *am* Mastorna, I *become* Mastorna.").

The final part of *A Director's Notebook* is entirely dedicated to the choosing of the 'faces' for the movie on ancient Rome. This, of course, brings up the subject of one of the cardinal apsects of his cinema, which owes a great deal of its plausibility, narrative atmosphere and evocative power to physiognomy.

The casting is a delicate, fundamental process, which comes immediately after the writing of the script. It is a sacred act, auguring well, in which the director places all his expectations and desires,

almost a small, independent birth, a movie within the movie in gestation: "I open an office, begin to receive people and let hundreds of faces file past me. It is a kind of propitiary rite for the creation of the atmosphere. For me, it is the most joyful phase: the one in which the movie is open to all possibilities, with everything still unsettled. It can become something quite different from what it was proposing to become. The point is to find the faces which will give it life. And, in the meantime, it remains in a kind of limbo, while my office becomes a police station waiting room, with my assistants calling London, New York, investigating, trying to find people on the basis of the vaguest traces. The photo archives are continuously searched, thumbed through. One discovers that, among the candidates for a role, one has fled to Latin America, another has had a sex change, yet another has turned from an ephemeral adolescent into a hairy, sweaty military recruit. I would like to see every face on the planet. I am never contented, and if I should be contented, I still want to compare the face that satisfies me with others, with all possible faces. It is a neurosis. [...] When I am in my office, the door opens and in comes an old man, a whore, someone who wants to sell their watch, a countess, a fat man. I see a hundred faces in order to cast two parts in the movie: but I take note of their clothes, their dialect, moustaches, tics, attitudes. [...] I have never chosen an actor on the basis of his acting skill, his professional ability, just as I have never discarded a non-actor because of his inexperience. Expressive faces are what I am after, with character etched on them, faces that say everything about themselves as soon as they appear on the screen. Furthermore, I tend to emphasize, with makeup and costume, everything that illustrates the person's psychology. I have no system for choosing. My choice depends upon the face in front of me, and on how much I can divine behind the faces of people who are generally strangers I am seeing for the first time. [...] Everyone has a face that suits them, he can have no other: and every face is the right one: life does not make mistakes."

The description of this ritual fills the final 'pages' of *A Director's Notebook*, first with the sequences shot at the Mattatoio di Testaccio (the old Rome stockyards, trans.), and then in the studios of Cinecittà (as will also be seen in *Intervista*), when a heterogeneous procession from a court of miracles begins to file past: faces, self-caricatures, improbable musicians, street vendors, pensioners, foreigners... In short, a chain of men and women, Roman and non-Roman of every size and shape, every age and condition, including those who are not actually looking for a part, but just hoping for a hand-out in cash, or trying to sell a villa or a painting by an unknown artist 'better than Raphael', up to the giant who, running the whole length of the corridor, stops in front of the movie camera and, with a kind of curtsy, greets the director, whose notes are scattered everywhere. In fact, Fellini is thinking of ancient Rome and the words of Genius at the tomb of Cecilia Metella: "It is not easy for us to grasp, to have a psychology that goes back to times before the Christian myth. I told you this about the butchers: eat, drink and enjoy. There was no sense of the suffering in life. They were butchers, but likeable", portrayed in a very beautiful, estranging manner in *Fellini's Satyricon*.

His encounter with Petronius goes back to high school Latin classes, extemporaneously recalled: "The professor was comical when he demanded enthusiasm from sixteen-year-old rogues for the recitation in his tiny voice of the last remaining verse of a poet: *Bevo appoggiato alla lunga lancia*, and I then became the promoter of uncontainable mirth." That long-ago memory turned into a 'constant and dark temptation' during the golden age of the Funny Face Shop, when he was commissioned to do a cover illustration for a new edition of the *Satyricon* of Petronius. The publisher will discard Fellini's sketch in favor of the one by his partner De Seta. But the book, in turn, prods him into the idea of writing a kind of musical about it with his friend of that time, Aldo Fabrizi, in the part of Trimalchio.

Having gone on to work in cinema, already during the creation of *I Vitelloni*, Fellini makes a kind of 'stop-gap' movie of the *Satyricon* (1969), one of those projects periodically presented to producers in order to make them finance the movie one really intends to make. His final re-reading of Petronius, during his convalescence after the great illness, triggers a kind of urgency in him to make it, almost a desire to start all over again. At the age of fifty, he has broken the ties with many of his habitual collaborators and has once again put off *Mastorna*, dissolving his contract with De Laurentiis. He has a good working rapport with his scriptwriter Zapponi, as well as with the young producer Grimaldi, who does not find the episode in *The Spirits of the Dead* enough to make him qualify as Fellini's producer.

When Grimaldi accepts the idea with enthusiasm, Fellini and Zapponi begine work on the script. The fragmentary condition of the *Satyricon* fascinates him, but, in one way, its disjointedness is not very suitable to the concatenations of film sequences. At the same time, this structure opens up new possibilities: those unexpected gaps make room for the imagination, hence for his favorite game of true and false, of the reality of the printed word and the artifices of the imagination; in that "unfamiliar landscape, shrouded in thick mists that occasionally part to allow a glimpse inside", Fellini faces his new challenge.

As far as the depiction of the ancient world is concerned, he perceptively chooses the right path by deciding to "nullify the line of demarcation between dream and fantasy, to invent everything and then objectify this fantastic operation, detach oneself from it in order to explore it as something at one and the same time intact and unrecognizable." At bottom, he shares many affinities with Petronius. Both of them sense, or better, have a premonition of the imbalances of their time and are capable of portraying them wrapped in a nebulous instability, in that feeling of uncertainty that precedes changes soon to come. The latter – while they mark the existential crisis of all transitional periods with a melancholy vein that leaves room for ambiguities which are never gratuitous – are faithful mirrors of the scenario of an epoch that is about to end in a state of economic well-being and the abandonment of positive values.

For Fellini, the movie must suggest "the boundaries, the reality of a world gone by, the life of creatures whose customs are incomprehensible, the rites and the daily life of a continent that has sunk into the galaxy of time." He calls his approach "an exercise of sorcery in ectoplasm" and, by moving the action from Magna Grecia to an unknown and extra-terrestrial Rome, leaps over the usual cinematic iconography – torment and joy of mythological movies – with its glossy marble, its broad, magniloquent gestures, its fierce beasts and reclining couches. In short, he thinks, writes and creates an inner Rome (like the one in *La Dolce Vita*), a fantasy Rome suspended between inaccessible antiquity and science fiction, a strange "adulterated mixture of the Pompeian and the psychedelic", a peplum of the mind. In this way, Fellini accomplishes his habitual expressionistic somersault: the more familiar we are with those ancient ruins, the less we know of that civilisation and, hence, must reinvent it.

That does not mean that Fellini neglects to carry out historical, artistic, linguistic and architectural research. He visits ruins and museums, gathers material and, above all, creatively filters all his impressions, keeping hold only of the feelings those texts or archaeological finds instill within him, rightly convinced as he is that the meaning of a work of art dies along with its epoch, and hence understanding the past and changing it into images is just about impossible, because that epoch can never be conveyed to modern man.

The same kind of problem exists on the linguistic level, and presents a few problems. What language should one put into the mouths of the men of that time? To underscore the incompatibility of the two worlds, their incommunicability, Fellini wants to try a form of invented Latin dialectic, then changes to a more comprehensible baroque Roman dialect and finally, only because of the producers' requirements, surrenders to Italian.

Undeniably, novelty makes his mouth water, and the further he gets into the reconstruction of another world, the more his taste emerges for challenge, courage, the desire to excite discussion, to wander picaresquely in the world of the dreams reflected in that somewhat murky and fearful Martian society. In his opinion, a point of contact between ancient Rome and the world of his time are the 1968 youth movements, the desire for liberty proclaimed aloud that inspire the main characters, Encolpius and Ascyltus, dissenters uninhibited to the point of immorality, refractory towards all rules.

Paradoxically, the preview at Madison Square Garden in New York after a rock concert was definitely a magical sign for Fellini. It was an event that confirmed his convictions, as he recalls: "It was a stupendous spectacle, that fabulous army of hippies that had arrived on incredible motorbikes and in brightly colored cars with blazing lights, a volcanic public with whom the *Satyricon* seemed to find its natural place. It no longer even seemed to be mine in the sudden revelation of so secret a bond, of such subtle, uninterrupted ties between that ancient Rome and that fantastic audience of the future."

Confronting Petronius with his own personal sensibility, Fellini seems to get younger, even though he has to renounce satire, an easy way to interpret the *Satyricon,* and a sure-fire way of making it a success. Having chosen to document a dream, he also abandons the sly winks and identification with the character, returning to the detachment displayed in *Juliet of the Spirits,* almost as if taking that world into a mediumistic zone, this time more mediumistic than ever before, required a special attitude of amazement. Because the pagan world cannot be figuratively retrieved, the director will shoot the dream of the painter of the final fresco, an icon taken from the subway episode in *Fellini's Roma.*

Faced with so complex a task, all of Fellini's baroque aspects come to the fore in the *Satyricon* – a negative connotation for many people, but an important component of his genius. It is the ideal way to express the precarious feelings of an epoch, the cognitive anxiety condensed in experimentalism which, in turn, creating a break with the limits of form and space, brings on complex geometries whose points multiply into a dynamic background. These points are Petronius's fragments 'replayed' in the director's figurative imagination who, within the missing sections – the dark zones between one episode and the next – creates 'his' *Satyricon* in *Fellini's Satyricon* (a title chosen to distinguish it from that of Gianluigi Polidori, a movie of scarce quality and success, shot in competition).

When choosing which dream fragments to reconstruct on awakening, Fellini avoids the extreme situations and avails himself of Luca Canali's advice (the Latinist who now, some thirty years later, is writing a new translation of Petronius, considering it to be unquestionably modern, thus confirming that Fellini's prevision had hit the mark). Stating in several interviews that he is creating historical fiction, the director intends to create historical fiction out of that remote past without excessive respect for the original text, immersing the fragments in an unhealthy atmosphere, the same atmosphere, with different facets, as he had created in *Fellini's Roma* and would create in *Casanova.* In so doing, he opened a phase of his cinema that could certainly not be

*Petronius according to Fellini.
In the centre, Fortunata (Magali Noël),
wife of Trimalchio (Mario Romagnoli)
during the feast at the home
of the rich ex-slave*

called sunny, and which would continue, more or less, until *The Voice of the Moon*. Thus, over the next twenty years, he portrays the mysterious, gloomy atmosphere of his totem-work *Il Viaggio di G. Mastorna*.

The hardest work lay in the preparations: Fellini worked incessantly for seven months in preparing it, and another seven in shooting it. His producer, Grimaldi, in partnership with United Artists for the guaranteed minimum, gives him free rein to choose his actors with non-modern faces, monstrous, matronly, a series of "masks which do not immediately display their characters, faces occupied with other thoughts, types that seem to have breathed a different air."

In fact, the parts of Encolpius and Ascyltus are given to two almost unknown actors, Martin Potter and Hiram Keller. Max Born is the ephebus Giton, while he chooses Mario Romagnoli, a Roman restaurant owner, as Trimalchio, after having tried to sign Boris Karloff, whose health would not allow him to accept, and having ignored Aldo Fabrizi, who badly wanted the part, and was resentful about it ever after. Salvo Randone plays Eumolpus, and Vernacchio, an invented character, is the comedian Fanfulla, while Lica was only later given to Alain Cuny. Constantly surrounding everything are new faces that are sometimes changed within a single scene in order to make the atmosphere more anguishing and upsetting.

Encolpio (Martin Potter) prepares to fight in a scene from **Fellini's Satyricon**

Encolpius is in a state of despair, because the ephebus Giton has been abducted. He meets his friend Ascyltus, who confesses to having lost Giton in a dice game with the actor Vernacchio. Encolpius searches for Giton in the slums, where Vernacchio is presenting a lewd farce in a run-down theater. During the play, a criminal's hand is cut off, but miraculously grows back with the intervention of an actor called Cesare. Meanwhile, Giton jumps down onto the stage from above in the part of Eros, and Encolpius reclaims possession of him. During a fight at the theater, which a judge who is present at the show tries to calm down, the two boys flee and pass through the slum area, which is overflowing with vice and human monsters, so the pair takes refuge in the Insula Felicles. They spend the night together and, when Ascyltus finds them, Giton, after a discussion, decides he prefers to go with him. A sudden earthquake destroys the Insula and Encolpius finds himself alone and despairing once again.

The old poet Eumolpus gives Encolpius a long tirade against riches, which brought about the death of art, then invites him along to the home of Trimalchio, a freed slave who has become rich and thinks he is a poet.

At the villa, there are many guests, grouped according to their importance. After their ablutions, the pair stretch out on divans. A sumptuous banquet is served. Then Eumolpus recites some of his poetry, but the guests prefer the verses of Trimalchio. Eumolpus calls Trimalchio the 'new Horace'. Flattered, Trimalchio recites another poem, but this time Eumolpus puts aside the flattery and accuses him of having copied Lucretius. He is beaten bloody for his pains. Trimalchio's wife dances and then abandons herself to the embraces of a woman friend.

The large company is led on a tour to Trimalchio's tomb, where a

fake funeral rite is celebrated. Genius tells the story of the matron of Ephesus, a widow who consoles herself with a guardsman on duty guarding the corpse of a hung man. When the body is stolen, the soldier is in despair, but the woman suggests hanging her husband's body on the rope so as not to lose her new lover. Meanwhile, Encolpius and Eumolpus find each other again and, before falling asleep, the poet predicts his imminent death.

On a beach, Encolpius sees Ascyltus and Giton again, who have been captured. Encolpius, too, is seized, and all three are taken to Lica's ship, a proconsul out to find new amusements for the emperor. After having challenged Encolpius, Lica falls in love with him and, dressed up as a bride, celebrates his wedding night with the boy.

The sailors catch an enormous fish. Caesar's ship is attacked, as is Lica's; the emperor dies and the proconsul is decapitated. A new emperor marches on Rome.

Two nobles, faithful to Caesar, decide to kill themselves, after having liberated the slaves and having placed their children in safety. Encolpius and Ascyltus reach their villa and discover the corpses, but, heedless, they spend the night with a black slave woman who has not fled the villa. At dawn they flee, while the corpses of the suicides burn, set on fire by the new masters.

During their wanderings, the boys encounter a small cortège conducting a nymphomaniac to the hermaphroditic oracle. Ascyltus pays the woman for her favors, but does not succeed in curing her.

A crowd of supplicants kneels before the albino hermaphrodite. Many have brought gifts, which are handled by two elderly assistants. Ascyltus and Encolpius, together with a predator, abduct the oracle, who dies along the way, needing to be kept continually moist and unable to bear the sunlight.

Thrown into the center of an arena, Encolpius must enter the labyrinth and encounter the Minotaur in order to win Ariadne. The boy is defeated, begs the monster for mercy, who, laughing, pulls off his mask and reveals human features: the festival of the God Laughter has begun. Encolpius is obliged to satisfy Ariadne in public and is unable to do so. The arrival of Ascyltus announces Eumolpus.

The old poet has become rich, and takes his young friend to the garden of delights in order to revitalize his virility. Before leaving, he gives him an appointment aboard a ship that is going to weigh anchor off Africa.

The brothel owner tells the story of the witch Enotea, who had captured a would-be sorcerer. As revenge, the sorcerer made fire disappear from the earth, and told men to look for it between the legs of Enotea, who is obliged to light all the torches in the village. Encolpius is not cured, and Ascyltus takes him to her. The witch, old, fat and ugly, manages to accomplish the miracle.

The two friends are back on the road, but Ascyltus dies in a fight. Eumolpus dies too, making his heirs those who agree to eat his body. While many are preparing for the macabre banquet, Encolpius who is opposed… it becomes a piece of a Pompeian fresco only decipherable in some parts.

As we have said, so complex a story requires an unprecedented effort, which negates once and for all the unmerited fame Fellini has always had of being an improviser. In fact, it would have been an impossibility to improvise 89 newly constructed sets and a multitude of extras. This was also a challenge for Fellini's collaborators: Piero Tosi for the sets, and Danilo Donati for the costumes, "the great expert of art incarnate in a variety show property man" (who,

On the slippery slopes of the hill, the gladiators are ready for combat

Fellini explains a crowd scene to his "ancient Romans"

at the very time he was working on this, received an Oscar for his costumes for Franco Zeffirelli's *Romeo and Juliet*).

Because the figurative rather than architectonic aspects are fundamental to *Fellini's Satyricon*, the sets are made of light, as in dreams. The demand for the figurative element's continuous, inventive capacity – dark colors and tones – means that the few open, clear spaces (the villa of the suicides, the flight with the hermaphrodite, the sea episodes, but little else), require "a constant, crepuscular, unchanging light, or rather, the vertiginous, anguishing darkness of the night."

Within the disorder of that ancient civilization, called to mind by the murky atmosphere, the mixture of races, the absence of the usual rubbish of 'Roman' cinema, Fellini feels himself to be "like a chameleon that must always be harmonizing with the colors around it", and, at a certain point, this search for harmonization begins to nauseate him, also because, as he goes along, he is progressively editing the movie. With his fussy perfectionism, he makes that dream world come true, particularly in the falsification of the false, which is to say in the invented episodes, the truly Fellini/Petronius ones, perfectly balanced within the

Fellini's irrepressible inventive genius creates a cosy, yet strangely futuristic femininity

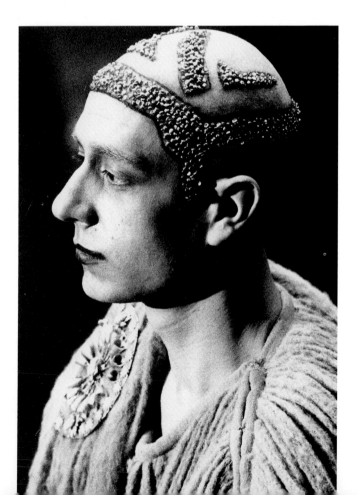

story as a whole. Avoiding every least trace of vulgarity, which furthermore is also missing in the original text (while still having a distinct commercial impact), the truculent effects of Trimalchio's orgy are cut in an attempt to rehabilitate these feasts, because movies have accustomed us to "seeing the usual fat men dripping with sweat who bite into lamb legs and dangle bunches of grapes into their throats, the usual greasy mouths kissing lasciviously and only detaching long enough from each other to gulp down wine." The freed slave Trimalchio, in fact, "is no fat man with a carefree, festive air, but an elderly, thin, tall, pigeon-breasted man, with the mean face of an ex-slave", while the ambience of the banquets, somewhere between wildness and melancholy perturbation, call up images of peasant wedding feasts in Romagna.

The ancient world, Fellini suggests, possibly never existed, possibly posterity only dreamed that it did, and the details of this dream have therefore remained isolated, inflated and rendered horridly beautiful, that is to say, sublime: its surroundings are dark, the sun pale, the circumscribed spaces tendentiously framed at a distance. The clothes themselves are opaquely colored, as if covered with the dust of those pagan times. Everything seems to be played out within the duality of counterpositioning. Just as Encolpius and Ascyltus are the two faces of the same coin, so are Trimalchio and Eumolpo: one the rich, trivial, aspiring poet who organizes his own bogus funeral; the other poor, cultivated, finally becoming rich and organizing his own real funeral, a macabre and poetic ritual because his body is the body of poetry.

Alongside the invented episodes, Fellini enlarges the characters of Eumolpo and Lica of Taranto (the invented episodes are those about Vernacchio, the suicides of the nobles, the emperor's assassination, the hermaphrodite, the nymphomaniac, Ariadne and the Minotaur). Lica, in particular, the last character to be developed through extensive changes to the original script, is turned from Petronius's rich merchant into an imperial envoy, neurotic, cruel and effeminate, who desperately loves beauty, almost as if his glass eye, besides making him harder and more disdainful, wants to snatch away everything of beauty and youth that appears before his eye. Lica concludes the parade of characters who are closer to us in their alienation the more fantastically far away they are, the protagonists of an intensely dreamed fresco.

Two excellent examples of the detailed iconographical and oneiric search undertaken by Fellini and his collaborators in order to create the faces and expressions of characters from an unknown world

When the Summing up Results in Poetry

The Clowns • Roma • Amarcord

Right from the time of his emergence, Fellini never ceased making reference to the motley world of the circus until finally, in 1970, he devoted an entire movie to it with *The Clowns,* made for Italian television. This came between the successful American project *Fellini: a Director's Notebook* and some others which fell through: Ex*perimental Hour* (an interview for NBC, another project by Peter Goldfard) and a series of contemporary 'portraits' which would have included Pappa, Rimini, Mao, a Tibetan convent and a U.S. factory. These works would have meant travelling, abandoning Rome and, above all, would not have taken into account that America was truly another world for the lazy singer of the Romagnolo countryside: "They have invited me to go and stay for twelve to fifteen weeks in order to get some ideas from this visit. My American friends, kind and generous, want to be my hosts, put their homes at my disposition, give me their time, their shows, their writers and coast-to-coast trips. And they tell me that I can visit the big cities and the provinces, and tell me to see everything I want to, because all my desires will be met. Once again, there would be meetings with artists, people of culture, all those who indicate that they would be happy to meet me, from Mailer to Woody Allen, from Capote to that fascinating, gentle specter that is Andy Warhol. They would certainly show me their homes, the places and people that they consider to be the most 'Fellinian', and who would make me feel totally embarrassed." A stimulating offer, but inferior to his artistic awareness of the differences: "I would not know how to make a movie in America, because even if their country fascinates me, seduces me and appears to be an immense set very congenial to my view of things, I would never know how to portray it on film. New York! It is stupendous, an immense spaceship set loose in the cosmos, without roots, depth, but suspended over an infinite crystal plate. Nineveh, Venice, Damascus, Mars, Benares, all the cities of the world fused together in a brilliant set, futuristic and decadent. New York is sweet, violent, very beautiful, terrifying: but how could I portray all that?"

Torn between his fascination with this great place so different from his fantasies, and the uncertainties, the sense of being lost that assails him as soon as he leaves Italy, Fellini, with the ever convenient excuse of working on the *Viaggio di G. Mastorna,* grabs at a clause in the contract to wriggle out of the American commitment. He proposes something quite different to RAI (Italian National Radio and Television): "Let's make *The Clowns,* the ambassadors of my vocation." And without using Teatro 5, his invented circus, he organizes the movie, together with Bernardino Zapponi, like a draft for a research paper, an essay '*à la* Fellini' about the circus and, in particular, about the lunar figures of the clowns.

In his imagination, the ideal circus-clown-Gelsomina-cinema sequence enabled him to avoid abandoning the circus ambience and its aura which, together with the wind of dreams, had pretty well characterized the universe of his childhood. It was enough for him to apply the peculiarities of the circus world to the movie camera and the thing was done, the trick had worked once again: the clowns become actors, the ring becomes the set, the people a troupe, while the performances, the shows, become the episodes, the plots, the stories, the cinematic representations. This goes on for an entire career, until the death of *that* circus and *that* cinema ordain the death of the clown, taking with it the fictional departure (the funeral at the end of *The Clowns* and of *Ginger and Fred*), prior to the arrival of the movies of lucid pessimism, of old age and death, even for the director of the Fellini Circus-Cinema.

All this is found in *The Clowns* (1970) and, as is well known, this juxtaposition of clown and death is not at all out of keeping with the ambience, inasmuch as the dramatic atmosphere, the irony, the fantastic realism of Fellini's cinema is immersed in melancholy and a sense of anguish equal to his declared intention of finally freeing himself from that love, of 'liquidating' the circus.

So then, for Fellini, whom by now we have seen to be a liar in small details but not in fundamental things – where, on the contrary, he deals in high artistic mystification – the cinema is nothing other than a metaphor of the circus. "The clowns, aberrant, grotesque, large-shoed, ragged, in their total irrationality, in their violence, in their abnormal whimsicality, seemed to me like the drunken, delirious ambassadors of an ineluctable vocation, the premonition, the prophecy, the annunciation of Federico. And the cinema, I mean the making of movies, living with a troupe that is shooting a movie, is this not like the life of the circus? Extravagant artists, muscular workers, technicians, extroverted specialists, women so beautiful as to make you faint, tailors, hairdressers, people who come from every part of the world, but nevertheless understand each other in a babel of languages, and the invasion of that ribald army from the streets and squares in a chaos of shouts and calls, anger, fights and the sudden silence that can sometimes be obtained by a loud howl. And underlying this apparent disorder, a schedule that has never been abandoned, a drumbeat miraculously respected, and then the pleasure of being together, working together, moving and travelling like an enormous family, realizing the ideal of a harmonious living together, of a Utopian society… all of this is what happens prodigiously during the shooting of a movie – is it not a circus life?"

With the two halves fused together, the clown becomes the image of Federico as a child, filtered through his sprite-women, mixed with the figures of clairvoyants, mediums and sorcerers, right up to the 'lunatics' of his final movie.

This hybrid, resulting from the two forms of mass entertainment found in Fellini's works, takes a leap in quality with the amount of the vital, the stirring and the compassionate magically contained within it. But perhaps one should say 'how much there *was*', because in *The Clowns*, the sense of something finished and past is most intense.

Awakened one night by the noise of the circus folk setting up their tent, Fellini the child cannot resist the fascination of the deserted ring, and goes out only to encounter the biggest surprise of his life. That evening, there is a show with the fire-eater, the strong woman, the dwarfs, the knife thrower and other performances including the tigers, the fakir buried alive for forty days, the mermaid eating little fish, the Siamese twins under glass and, finally, the clowns.

The sad memory of the evening introduces, in Fellini's voice, a small anthology of provincial characters: Giovannone, a slightly idiotic vagabond who watches the farm-hands work; the dwarf nun absorbed in her mission of salvation, who constantly commutes between madhouse and convent; and once again the faces of the denizens of the wine house, one of whose wife goes to fetch him with a wheelbarrow because he cannot make it home on his own; the invalid of the Great War and Signora Ines who knows all of Mussolini's speeches by heart. Finally, the railway conductors constantly fighting among themselves, and the station-master, Cotechino, who calls the Fascist police chief to protect him from the derision and the raspberries of the kids on the train; and Giudizio who, whenever he goes into crazy mode, puts on his uniform, takes up his rifle and, thinking a war is on, mimicks a military attack.

The scene changes to Fellini's office as the director dictates to Maja, his muddled secretary, a text about the world of the circus, a world gone by whose almost invisible traces he has decided to follow with his small troupe (Roy, the English cameraman, the sound man Alvaro and his mother, seamstress, and hairdresser, and Gasparino, the set's director). The first visit is to one of the most important Italian circuses, that of Liana, Rinaldo and Nando Orfei, where Fellini witnesses some moments at the end of the show with the clowns and the elephants – a prelude to the appearance of the 'panther', Anita Ekberg, before the communal dinner, with its recollections of those melancholy masks and their stories.

Next comes a trip to Paris to interview some glorious old clowns. The head of this whole tribe is Guillaume, the true creator of the drunken clown, extremely talented at covering his nose with his lower lip. He discharges himself from hospital in order to watch Foutite and Chocolat's performance, two colleagues whom he had never seen, and he dies at the circus.

In Paris, which has elevated the circus to an art form with the Cirque d'Hiver, Il Nouveau Cirque and the Medrano, the troupe goes in search of the best and most famous clowns, together with the circus historian Tristan Rémy. A few of them are still alive: Alex, Nino, Ludo – the only dwarf white clown – and Maïss. In a bistro, these old artistes discuss who had been the best clowns of the past. They talk about the famous Antonet, recalling his transformation of the white clown (the one with the sugar-loaf hat), and remember, in a wealth of detail, the fabulous costumes of their careers. It is an apt occasion for performing a sketch and to parade their gorgeous stage costumes.

The search goes on, with a few short visits to other personages: the ex-animal tamer Buglioni, previous circus directors like Hugue, and several clowns who, by now elderly, live in retirement homes, or modest houses in the center of town, or in the Parisian *banlieue*. These old people recall the good old days, anecdotes, a few show numbers and their great nostalgia for the ring, or for their home towns. They bring out photographs, posters from the golden age, and talk about the human affairs hidden behind those heavily made up faces.

During an evening with Pierre Etaix – film director, actor and husband of Annie Fratellini – as the time comes to show a rare movie about the famous Fratellini, the projector acts up, the film breaks, catches fire and gets stuck. To honor the magnificent art of Paul, Albert and François, Fellini reinvents the little shows they put on free of charge in hospitals, asylums and the trenches.

Then it is Père Loriot's turn, 68 years of career, 28 of them spent in the circus. He worked with the most famous clowns, among them Porto, Rhum and Bario, a Livornese whom the troupe goes to visit, where they shoot pictures of the rooms where he spends his days assailed by nostalgia for the circus and for Italy.

Trying to track down traces of Rhum, the clown who Rémy calls the greatest of them all, the director watches a film made by French television, which is too short to document the greatness of this artist. It is the moment of the clowns, most of them Italian, who perform the funeral of Fischietto. In a crescendo of gags, somersaults, absurd mimicry and verbal numbers, the clowns say their goodbyes to their departed companion.

At a certain moment, the hearse and horses arrive, a snapshot is taken, the workers put together the casket, the orchestra director and players appear, while the white clown, his stage companion, draws a terrible portrait. The widow is in despair. Fischietto is placed in the hearse, and the cortège begins to circle faster and faster around the ring. An enormous bottle of champagne is uncorked and, amidst music and confusion, the circling of the ring becomes more and more frenetic. The old clowns slow down and stop and, while shots are heard from all sides, and rockets go off, the clown firemen arrive amidst smoke and flames: the funeral celebration reaches its height, ending with dancing, music and the final cruel, romantic jokes of the clowns.

Amongst themselves, while the lights are being turned off, old Fumagalli talks about Fru Fru, his partner in the dead man performance: the two call each other by playing the trumpet, and leave the circus ring together.

"I have an embarrassing confession to make: I know nothing about the circus. I feel like the last person in the world who can talk about it with any clear notions of its history, facts, news. [...] On the other hand, I ask myself why shouldn't I? Even if I know nothing, I know everything about the circus, about its storerooms, its lights, its smells and even something about its most secret life. I know, I have always known. Ever since the first time I immediately felt a traumatizing, total connection to that clamor, that deafening music, those disquieting apparitions, those death threats." In this admission of presence and absence, we see the whole relationship of affection and fear, of sympathy and compassion, nourished with ups and downs for an entire artistic life. Conflicting feelings, doubtless, but highly synthesized in both the image of the clown and, above all, in what Fellini calls 'the party's over', the tormenting melancholy of the circus.

The cinema, too, is a party that is over, it is death at work, a manifestation of the collective creative chaos which makes one laugh and cry. It reinvents the comedy of life, just as the circus does which, possibly under a much patched tent on the outside – "a balloon, a spaceship that was not there the night before and suddenly is present" – presents a show with which one can identify, as one can identify with the clown, whether of the circus or street variety.

With his formidable bravura in choosing faces, circus faces that fill up reality, Fellini has thus traced a clean line of continuity between the historical tradition, its evolution, its slow death throes and the gallery of clowns – eccentric, melancholy and fearsome – with which his films are strewn. Continuity, because in one way or another the Fellini Circus guarantees the existence and perpetuation of the figure of the clown and, naturally, of the *Fellini clown* in the vast number of meanings that spans from Gelsomina to Ivo Salvini, from the White Sheik to Casanova, from Cabiria to Fred, passing through dozens of close-ups of people, extras, bodies, apparitions, shapes, ghosts, comedians, dancers, mimes, character actors, interpreters and actors, real and

unknown, entering and exiting from his fantastic frames. Agony, because unquestionably this buffoon no longer exacts a reaction in the social mirth of the last few decades.

Even if *The Clowns* is a television movie, and therefore feels the effects of an orientation somewhere between chronicle and a program edited in closed narrative blocks, it insists upon the search for people and their worlds, an expression of the antinomy that strikes at the form of a show when it is overtaken by another more modern one. The historian Rémy, the old pensioned clowns, their heirs and their families – all of these insist on the idea of the death of the traditional clown, of his inadequacy with respect to today's reality – but will it not be exactly the other way around, of the incapacity of the present to involve and understand the circus of the past, and the manifest impossibility of making people laugh as they once did?

With his affectionate investigation, Fellini indemnifies this world, altered by being forgotten, inserting amongst the interviews little scenes in which he resists not the temptation of thinking, conceiving and directing the shadows of the old-time clowns on the same level as the many performances and the concluding funeral ceremony. But if Fischietto's funeral is the funeral of the clown, there is no need to fear: Fellini does not kill off the clowns and their magical atmosphere, but, in 1970, he bears witness to a phenomenon that could be accepted by television. In the end, how could Fellini renounce the transgressing soul of the clown and thus lose his own, and how could he do without the irrational and pathetic comic quality of the white clown who fights with his side-kick, the Augustan one? In brief, he could not continue to make movies if he killed a part of his own ego, since "the clown is the incarnation of the fantastic creature that expresses the irrational part of man, the instinctive element, that part of the revolutionary and dissenter from the higher order which we all carry within ourselves. He is a caricature of man in his animal and childish aspects, of the mocked and the mocker. The clown is a mirror in which man sees his image made grotesque, deformed and comical. It is his very shadow. It will always exist. It is as if we asked ourselves "Is the shadow dead? Can the shadow die?"

"As soon as you construct a thought for yourself, laugh about it", or "If you construct a thought for yourself – white clown; laugh over it – Augustan clown." In his considerations of the figure of the clown he paraphrased from Lao Tzu, Fellini at one and the same time displays a snapshot of the *shadow*, the reflection of the body which one cannot deprive him of, except in particular conditions, along with an excellent introduction to the image of Rome, the city to which he is deeply attached by having given as

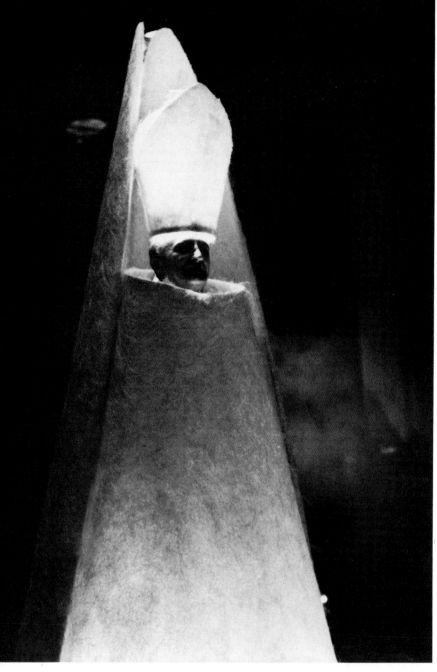

The imagination of Federico Fellini and Danilo Donati, accompanied by the evocative music of Nino Rota, is unleashed in the unique ecclesiastic fashion show in Roma

much as he took from its inspirational humus, its existential, historical and 'political' atmosphere. Thus, it was inevitable, if not a duty for him, to dedicate a movie to 'his' very special city. A movie which is not a movie, in the same way that *his* Rome is not seen as a city, but with the ambiguous figures of *his* imaginary and changing projection. It is a shadow, an idea of a city which exactly fits the principle of "As soon as you manufacture your thought about Rome, you must laugh about it" – certainly not to

deride it, but in order not to take it too seriously, thinking that you can easily delineate its boundaries and describe them. The creator of *La Dolce Vita* at the very beginning of the Seventies sees it and portrays what he sees with the following sequence of cadences:

In search of the first images of Rome, Fellini displays a large, ancient stone on the road to town (Rimini), and the notions learned at school: the crossing of the Rubicon, the armless statue of Julius Caesar, his death at the theater, the headmaster's lessons about the geese of the Capitoline, the monuments and churches of the capital being projected for the children of the boarding school, among which, by mistake, the image of the lovely bottom of a seated girl.

To complete the identity marks of *Fellini's Roma*, one must add the pope's Sunday benediction on the radio, the silent film screening, and the Luce newsreel that portrays a gymnastic celebration of Fascism. But the Roman way of being in those days is also the simple evocation of a name, Messalina, which is enough to conjure up the image of the pharamacist's wife thirsting for sex…

The picture of Rome seen by someone far away is consummated by the comments of the people in the café, and the train stopping on its way to Urbe in Rimini's small station under the gaze of a small boy dressed in a sailor's suit (Fellini).

The same gaze observes its own arrival by train in Rome in 1939. The Termini station is jam-packed with people vociferating in big-city confusion. The twenty-year-old who plays the part of Fellini goes to the boarding house for artistes in Via Albalonga, run by a big, big lady. There, he takes a room and gets to know its special guests (a seasoned actor, a prostitute, someone who resembles Mussolini, a Japanese, etc.).

It is summer and, in the evening, one eats outdoors at the *trattoria* below the house amidst small family events, wisecracks, pleasant slang, singers and beggars. One makes the most of the abundant food and the typical Roman dishes, until night empties the streets, brings out the squads to repair the tram lines, the shepherds lead their sheep across town, the prostitutes stand like wild beasts among the remains of the past.

After the encounter with Rome at the end of the Thirties, Fellini and his small troupe attack the city from the Great Ring Road. Traffic is chaotic and noisy on a flooded road, narrow and full of holes, with accidents, student protests, sirens, trucks of every variety, carts, motorcycles, Neapolitan soccer fans, prostitutes, hitch-hikers, small factories, industrial buildings, historical sites and ruins in a crescendo that ends with a gigantic traffic jam at the Colosseum, and thousands of flashing lights.

A third approach from above, with the camera mounted on a crane, shows the panorama on a beautiful sunny morning. A bus full of American tourists, the inescapable Roman 'latin lover', a group of students talking with the director, while several people comment on how the city is going to hell. The handing out of lunch boxes puts an end to this scene, but not before the director, convinced that everyone must only do what he finds congenial, introduces the long episode to follow, the Teatrino della Barafonda during the war.

During the variety show, there are performances by mediocre artists, risk-taking amateurs, mimics, singers and dancers, all confronting the implacable, terrible audience of common people, so involved that it does not miss the slightest opportunity for mocking, criticizing, shouting provocations and playing heavy-handed tricks on other members of the audience and the artistes who, in turn, pay them back in the same coin. When the news of the war arrives and the alarm sounds, the tawdry occasion breaks up as everyone rushes off to the air-raid shelter.

Another part of Fellini's description of Rome is concerned with the construction of the subway across the city. The visit to the underground construction site takes place in the company of the head engineer, who explains the enormous difficulties due to both the eight layers of terrain and to the many archeological finds which are unearthed, and thus block progress or force a change in route.

At the end of the gallery, the technicians have come to a halt, because the transmitter has signalled the presence of an empty space, a cavern, perhaps a catacomb. With an automatic drill, a small passage is accurately opened, which reveals an ancient Roman house with frescoed rooms and a statue, all in a perfect state of preservation. But the air that penetrates through the opening causes the frescos to dissolve before the dismayed eyes of those watching.

The liberty that contemporary young people have gained, and openly display, takes Fellini back to the times of the brothels, described in a variety of manners according to the different types of people and ambience. A series of scenes portrays the various phases: the arrival, the waiting in a group, the display of girls, the choice, and going up to the room (a practice that not even the young Fellini deprives himself of).

The ecclesiastical fashion show held in the palace of the Princess Domitilla is another of the thousand aspects of Rome, the papal and aristocratic Rome. A world that has survived time, but that harbors a

cardinal, a high representative of the clergy, diplomats and nobles with their heirs, waiting to see a demonstration of religious habits, in an accumulation of images and scenographic solutions, culminating with the figure of the pope bathed in light.

The tour in search of the real Rome moves to the 'Festa of Noantri in Trastevere, perhaps the most 'Roman' quarter of all. The camera roams among *trattorias*, tables in the street, pizzerias, taverns and stands full of *porchetta* (whole pigs roasted on the spit), of candy and

Above: *In the modern day episode about the construction of the underground railway, the journey through the underground tunnels leads to the discovery of ancient frescoes, which are completely turned to dust by the air they let in*

Left: *Life in the brothel, a narrative location devised for the imaginary man of the Fascist years, creates the scene for a series of characters who are often local heroes within a microcosmic tragicomedy*

watermelon, shouting Romans and many tourists strolling around the narrow streets, the characteristic carriages, a boxing match, and wandering musicians. It catches salacious comments, snatches of often incomprehensible dialogue, while the youths of Piazza Santa Maria in Trastevere are chased off by the police. In this lively confusion, Fellini, off camera, interviews Marcello Mastroianni, the American writer Gore Vidal, Alberto Sordi, and Anna Magnani. Each of them relates his relationship with Rome from his own personal point of view.

At the end of the *Festa*, a hefty group of motorcyclists depart from Ponte Garibaldi for a tour of Imperial, Seventeenth Century Rome, illuminated by the reflected light of the summer evening and by the evocative artificial lights. Filing in front of the baroque churches and some of the most beautiful and famous spots – the Castel Sant'Angelo, the Piazza di Spagna and Trinità dei Monti, the Piazza del Popolo and its gate, the Muro Torto, the Quirinale square and palace, the Teatro di Marcello, the temple of Vesta and the Colosseum – the rumbling motors leave the ancient walls behind them and head out via Cristoforo Colombo for the new EUR quarter.

"The intellectuals and artists who always live in a state of friction between two different dimensions – reality and fantasy – find here [in Rome] the impulse needed to free their mental activity with the comfort of an umbilical cord that keeps them attached to solid ground. Because Rome is a mother, and she is the ideal mother, because she is indifferent. She is a mother with too many children, and so is unable to give you her whole attention. She asks nothing of you and expects nothing from you. She welcomes you when you come, and lets you go when you depart, like Kafka's court. In this there is very ancient wisdom: African, almost prehistorical. We know that Rome is a city loaded with history, but her evocative power lies in something prehistorical, something primordial which is clearly demonstrated in some of her boundless, desolate aspects, in certain ruins that seem like fossils, bony, like mammoth skeletons." These few lines contain all of Rome's attractions for Fellini, an intuition of the real influence that also affected other cineasts – from Pasolini to Greenaway, from Aldo Fabrizi to Verdone, from Luigi Zampa to Ettore Scola and Nanni Moretti – and autobiographically breathed in, metabolized and returned by Fellini's sponge in the form of poetic images.

Whether it is a question of the ill-mannered, greedy, generously plebeian Rome, or the middling Rome of clerks, the *petit bourgeois* and the sated mediocrities, or of imperial, papal, fascist, aristocratic Rome (not to mention the artistic, cinematographic, governmental and political, lay, religious, bureaucratic, commercial, alternative, slum Rome, or the Rome outside the city and even outside the province) – to whatever Rome you may refer, in short, the special thing about Fellini is that he has depicted almost all of them – either directly or obliquely, with characters or with a face, with real places or constructed sets, with a quotation, a single name, the summoning of more or less historical

figures, in the use of dialect, in a hundred other narrative and visual ways, his Eternal City is the true representation of the Shadow of the Great Mother in whose opulent womb all find hospitality.

In many aspects, Rome is the irreconcilable opposite of New York, the Big Apple, the crucible that makes everything possible as long as it reflects the future of the "magnificent destiny and progress" of the New World. In Fellini's Rome, the embryo of the Old World, *the first*, there is no need to do, everything has already been said, done, seen; all that is left is to observe with the inner eye or the eye of the camera, to be a witness and travelling companion of a piece of the past, of history, of time. But one must be a lucid and disinterested witness, motivated by love, but disenchanted and ironic, otherwise that shadow will be dispelled in the exploited stereotype of a chaotic, lazy Rome, suffocated by traffic and environmental, as well as human, degradation, aspects which Fellini always felt as foreign to him.

Fellini's Roma (1972) is Fellini's point of arrival, the place where he lives and works, where the presence of the city is figuratively strong and decisive for the narrative, as the context for the Cinecittà sets within the folds of his imagination. In a word, his cinematic subconscious is Roman, and composed of progressive stratifications like the seven layers of earth below it.

Already in *The White Sheik,* the arrival by train portrayed the Rome of the Holy Year, disenchanted and distracted by the vicissitudes of Ivan and his bride. In *I Vitelloni,* Fausto and Sandrina go to Rome on their honeymoon, Alberto's city, on whose outskirts the circus of *La Strada* is camped. The whole of *Il Bidone* would be meaningless outside the Roman context, in the same way as the 'slum hut' reality of Cabiria would be between the *Passeggiata Archeologica* and Via Veneto. Not to mention *La Dolce Vita*, the prototype throughout the world of Fellini's Rome, and all subsequent movies up until *Amarcord*, a moment of transition and preparation for the mature, concluding phase. This homage to a particular Rome, and Marcello's journey through its splendors and shame, is metaphorically an act of love in order to possess its ambiguous fascination, a charm which has been extended beyond the center of town to the modern EUR residential quarter, where the moralist Mazzuolo lives, or the psychoanalytical Fregene of *Juliet of the Spirits*, not to mention the nocturnal and Gothic Castelli Romani of *Toby Dammit,* and the imaginary city of *Fellini's Satyricon*. In Fellini's accounting, *Fellini's Roma* closes the books on the debt to Rome, just as *The Clowns* liquidated the circus and *Amarcord* will liquidate the provinces. So then, the last liberating show for seeing the Roman circus, according to Fellini, is in these episodes, which are to be thumbed page by page like a precious illustrated art catalog.

The first page opens the memory of Rome coming from the misty north. A distant Rome, remote, perhaps just a name like any other. It is the milestone outside Rimini, the statue of Julius Caesar, the outing to the Rubicon. The signs of approach continue with the didactic-religious projection, an amused pretext for an introduction to the contradiction enclosed in the walls of the holy city, an authentic Fellinian twist where the historical/sacred images are interrupted by a girl's bottom, a competitor to be feared by the 'cupolas' of the Christian basilicas. And then, the theater – the death of Caesar – and the radio (the benediction *urbi et orbi*), which is to say the pre-cinema techniques and language, are those that contribute to increasing the distinctive signs of Roman-*ness* reflected in silent movies.

Thus, when Fellini recalled his Roman roots, and when, like Moraldo, he feels he must leave, he takes the train that, as a child, he had so often seen stop at the little station with three people and two hens aboard and, when he gets off in Rome, the first of his life's journeys is ended: that from the provinces to the capital of Italy, of Christianity and of cinema. It is a journey transformed by the prerequisite of all the preceding and subsequent mental journeys, a sequence of variations on a reality observed through the deforming lens of the imagination.

His arrival in Rome is an invented projection, a 'debarking', if not 'science fiction' like *Fellini's Satyricon*, at least a caricature, now exaggerated and now distorted by the exigencies of making movies, occasionally marked by moments and linguistic expressions that must have struck the young man from Romagna, who freely recalls them in statements and interviews: the greetings exchanged by two friends at the Termini station, the overcrowded tram with the back door left open because of the excessive number of passengers, the snapshot recollection of a fat man washing at a public fountain as if he were at home, the comment on the price of meat and other pet expressions in Roman dialect.

From the start, Fellini frames building facades in a few fleeting upward shots, only to return immediately to the street that leads to the arch of Santa Bibiana, from where they reach Via Tiburtina and the San Lorenzo quarter with the Verano cemetery. A choice of life or death, like the street where the outdoor meal was held, almost on the tram tracks, a microcosm of the common people, the 'big Roman heart' with its customs, its faces, funny and grotesque, ancient and vulgar, the fat faces and bodies, a little worn out, from which Fellini knows he can draw out a very tasty Roman sauce – at least as tasty as the flavors and smells of the numerous dishes that come and go on camera: "Cannolicchi

Beneath the gaze of Princess Domitilla's Roman ancestors (invented by painter and friend, Geleng), ecclesiastic mysticism and simbolism glorify the macabre, grotesque ritual of the unusual fashion show

with cheese and pepper, penne all'arrabbiata, macaroni… rigatoni with anchovies, schiaffoni al norcino, fettuccine with chicken giblets, bucatini alla carbonara, coratella, facioli co' 'e cotiche, ch'a sarciccia, tripe, snails, la pajata…" an alimentary orgy, a coarse, elemental exaggeration of the good life ("as you eat, so you shit", or the assimilation of the food-sex-death chain) that the young Fellini gets to know, along with the indolent and only seemingly gross character of the Roman. A paradox that closes with the fine scene of the proud prostitute-wolf among the ruins, a symbolic image of synedochic eloquence for the strident contrast which, in Rome, takes on the fracture – or the continuity – between past and present.

The big outdoor dinner is the favorite collective ritual for advancing the choral action within the group, while detailing here and there a few close-ups or minor characters in Fellini's mosaic bestiary, for the purpose of creating 'confusion'. It is the *mise en espace* of the many artistic rehearsals preceding Fellini's cinema, the many drawings created while pondering the movies still to be made. If one were not to consider the preparatory phase, the visual traces and the surrealistic automatic writing of the sketches and drawings in which Fellini's bizarre creative imagination discharges itself, his movies would simply not contain that cause and that chaos which is indispensable to reconstructing the sense. It would be like a dead body without veins, blood or members. "This almost

subconscious, involuntary doodling, making caricature notes, interminably drawing puppets that stare at me from every corner of the page, this automatic sketching of obsessively hyper-sexual female anatomy, the decrepit faces of cardinals, candle flames, and again breasts and backsides and an infinity of other hieroglyphics, constellated with telephone numbers, addresses, delirious verses, tax figures, appointments – in short, this spreading and inexhaustible graphic rubbish heap which would delight any psychiatrist, may be a kind of track, a thread, at the end of which I find myself on the set, lights blazing, for the first day of filming."

Fellini's sketches are independent, pre-filming expressions, which also serve to communicate with his collaborators in the preparation of everything necessary for making the movie. They represent characters, moral likenesses, and are expressions of his avid curiosity, of his not wanting to lose anything of what passes before his eyes and through his mind. Images of cultured people in all their crude reality, their habits, their ways of speech and, in the specific details which become the seasoning of the movie: "If it is true that, in Rome, there are very few neurotics, it is also true, as the psychoanalyst maintains, that neuroses are providential in that they are a way to make deep discoveries about ourselves. It is like diving into the sea to find the hidden treasure of fairy tales; they oblige the child to become an adult. Rome does not do this. With its big belly like a placenta, and its maternal aspect, it avoids neuroses, but it also halts development, true maturing. There are no neurotics here, but neither are there any adults. It is a city of unambitious, skeptical, rude children. They are also a little psychically deformed, because it is unnatural to block development. This is also one reason why, in Rome, there is such a strong attachment to the family. I have seen no other city in the world where one speaks so much about relatives. 'Let me introduce my brother-in-law. This is Lallo, my cousin's son.' It is a vicious circle: one lives among a circumscribed number of people, immediately recognizable for sharing a common biological element. They live like nestlings, in a brood [...] There is even comfort in the very common phrase: 'Who the hell are you? You're nobody!' Because it is not only disdainful, but also liberating. [...] Receiving insults like no other city, Rome does not react. The Roman says: 'Rome sure isn't my responsibility.' This invalidation of reality, which is the Roman when he says, 'So what the hell do you care?' comes perhaps from the fact that he has something to fear, either from the pope, the gendarmes or the nobility. He encloses himself within a gastro-sexual circle. His interests are extremely limited. [...] Certain Romans say 'I am going to visit papa, or I am going to visit uncle', and then one discovers they mean they are going to the cemetery. [...] This takes the anxiety out of death, the neurotic anxiety: it is enough to remember that Romans call death 'la commare secca' ['the dry buddy', trans.]. Buddy – so then, almost a relative itself. And then certain other fine expressions: '*andato agli arberi pizzuti, sta a fa tera pe' ceci*' (more or less 'pushing up daisies')."

And if anyone should think that this snapshot of the Roman taken by Fellini is labored or, at least, referable only to the first post-war years or the Fifties, all he needs to do is to go and trace the last phase of the careers of Roman personages from the Italian comedy to verify the full reality of a symbolic description somewhere between tails, the religious habit and the sleeveless undershirt which, deep down, does not change, or only changes very slowly.

And if it is true that Fellini's Roman cannot be of help to him on an individual level because he is "an ignoramus who does not want to be bothered, and is the most exact product of the Church"; and if there is also truth in his "heavy image: quite gloomy, dull and suggestive of a leaden, pessimistic view of things, downward looking, sleepy, disapproving, uncurious, or rather not believing that curiosity is of any use", Fellini's love for the city of the Romans is still undeniable, which, once it reaches you with its "ancient enchantment, all the negative judgements you may have made of it disappear, and all you know is that it is a great fortune to live there." Feeding on its defects and decadence, it becomes a necessity for Fellini to portray

through a movie how things are going to be in a year's time for the loved and hated Rimini of *Amarcord*.

Fellini had four other parts in mind for *Fellini's Roma*: the *circolare notturna* (the night tram that circles Rome), the Roma-Lazio soccer game where the two local teams play each other, Roman women, and lastly the *ponentino* evening wind and clouds. Cut from the script, these elements make their way into the movie in a different way. The *circolare*, a two-car tram that once called at many metropolitan quarters, is turned into the chaotic ring road. An orgy of steel plating and noise, of auto vehicles, people and objects squeezed into a space that could reasonably only hold cars and trucks.

In his excited and exaggerated vision of traffic, there is, on the one hand, a prophetic intuition of the round cage which that peripheral race-track circle was to become and, on the other hand, the presence of a rich variety of fauna, from those boxed inside their cars (similar to the 'mannequins' of *Eight and a Half*), to a horse, to the calves spread out on the ground after an accident, to the chained dog that barks while another, presumably a thoroughbred, slips away in its luxury car. And then there is the man pulling his cart, the prostitutes with their bonfires beyond the guard-rail, the hitch-hikers, and all the other unidentifiable figures on the outer edge of the confusion. Finally, there is a shot of the crowd motif, the *Fellinian crowd*, made up of small assemblages that fill the frame, often saturating it in such a way as to exponentially increase the effect. For example, the ones of the Termini train station, the main floor of the vaudeville theater, the people at night in Trastevere.

The confusion of the ring road approaches the image of what we could call the *Fellinian Finale*, a great decadent fissure rather than a total disaster, as the words of Gore Vidal confirm when interviewed at the 'Festa of Noantri': "You ask me why an American writer lives in Rome? First of all, because I like the Romans, who don't give a damn whether you are rich or poor. They are neutral, like the cats. Rome is the city of illusions. It is no accident that the Church is here, the government and the movies, all things that produce illusions, as you do (to Fellini), as I do... The more the world approaches its end from overpopulation, too many cars, poisons... and what quieter place from which to wait for the end from pollution, from overpopulation. It is the ideal point from which to observe, whether everything ends or not."

At the time of *La Dolce Vita*, Marcello was content to hide *inside* Rome. Now everyone, the common people, intellectuals, and the bourgeoisie, can stand at the window and *look*, also through the grand illusion which is cinema, at the rubble of a dying civilization, wait without anxiety to see… one never knows. The other people interviewed are almost like guest stars representing a golden frame for the picture of a Rome which, the longer one observes it, the more it seems to flee, slip out of one's grasp like Mastorna's city. At the same time, hiding behind its robust entrance door is Anna Magnani, "symbol… of the city. A Rome seen as a wolf and a vestal virgin, aristocrat and bag lady, gloomy, comical…", who does not trust Fellini and sets the movie off towards its epilogue.

The ecclesiastical fashion show is a true *tour de force*, a synthesis between the analogous scene of the white clowns (in *The Clowns*), and the illuminated pit of the television studio (in *Ginger and Fred*). This is a moment of great cinema in which Fellini optimally expresses the ironic/visionary aspect of the sets (with the masterful collaboration of Danilo Donati and Gino Landi), supported by Nino Rota's original music. The Church and the Roman aristocrats – "a cemetery full of cadavers who don't know they are dead" – are gathered together for the fashion show. The show is clear and vital in displaying the styles in a rhythmic crescendo, vaguely macabre and sublime, up until the papal empyrean: from the creation called 'Petite soeur de la tentation du Purgatoire', to the red 'Au Paradis toujours plus vite' for prelates on roller-skates. But it is also dark, old, dead and mummified in the dust of centuries, represented by the audience, a pathetic, infantile funeral choir that accompanies that magnificent agony, very slow and sumptuous, lugubriously eternal, to which Rome seems destined by the circularity of time and the history of progress.

The irreversible destiny of some pre-modern symbols will characterize Fellini's project for a movie about Venice, the city *par excellence* of the much-invoked 'End'. This movie was never made, but was at least partially sublimated in the world of *Fellini's Casanova*. However, there do exist some quite beautiful pages written by the director on a subject rich in ideas, where "the city seems to present fascinating figurative and pictorial seductions that are most congenial to a certain way I have of looking at cinema, or better, cinematographic narration. This would be a series of pieces that, as in a mosaic, separate and disintegrate the narrative, the situations, the characters, in a molecular decomposition that is continually menaced by even further fragmentation, but which, in its entirety, offers a mirage of unity, of vision, of a panorama and, in this case, of a city which can appear even more to shimmer and shake because mirrored in water and palpitating with lights and reflections." Perhaps *Fellini's Roma* is really to Fellini's Venice what *Amarcord* is to the city of Mastorna.

That the director always likes the less showy aspects is exemplified in the flaking away of the frescos in the ancient Roman house. That wind which usually stuns Fellini's

men/children, brings on dreams and fantasies, flash-backs or surprising flash-forwards, now unconsciously liberated, soughing, destroys those who brutally 'awaken' the sign of the past with the horror of the movie camera. The frescos of the Roman house, opened after who knows how long, are other shadows that vanish before the impotent eye of an acritical progress, just as the brothels vanished. Always in a condition of semi-destruction, these are the sites where female faces and symbology are concentrated. Thus, they do not intend to represent the world of commercial sex, as much as a cinematic imagining of the Body of Rome, a variation in the idea of the prostitute. Just as Sylvia was Woman and Cabiria a prostitute/clown, the prostitutes of *Fellini's Roma* are Rome, vulgar and protective, 'maternal' and aggressive. They incarnate the other mother, the tolerant one who does not put obligations on you, does not create duties, does not sit in judgement. She is not jealous or possessive. She welcomes you when you arrive and lets you leave whenever you like. The brothel and the prostitute "have been a surrogate which, in the straight jacket of our education, helped to smuggle in at least a part of what had been forbidden to us."

The Barafonda Theater, a world apart, reflected in the world of its own of show business, another microcosm of Rome in a reinvention of the historical site of vaudeville, the Ambra-Jovinelli theater. Fellini is fascinated by the audience rather than with the show itself. That is where the real actors are, a place loud with cruel remarks made in Roman dialect, that the director depicts with the swift strokes of a master. Moments, situations, characters and jokes that reach the stage from the audience in the auditorium, and return again to the hall. A cocktail of cynicism and gutsiness in the fight between the 'mob' and clumsy, amateur artistes, which reflects events that have been occurring for centuries in the streets and squares of the real world, comments on them in low linguistic forms, in the improvised gags, in the parodies and belly-laughs, rather than with the brain. A treacherous and grotesque exhibition of improvisations, therefore, a show of extroverted spectators, of decidedly ball-breaking hecklers which, while it places the vaudeville show somewhere "between the Circus Maximus and the brothel", reverts to the two crude qualities of *cynicism* and *viscerality,* and would be able to rewind the movie to its opening shots. There, among the aphorisms of the cutting language of the people which had already accompanied the young Fellini's initiation as he was about to become a paying guest in the Palletta family, the young author hears a scene played out on the stair landing which, in itself, subsumes the Roman character, fugitive and wise, mocking and lazy, good-natured and irreverent. An intermezzo suitable for making the curtain fall, without regrets, on the bitter, caricature-like fresco of *Fellini's Roma*, a mosaic that sparkles with pessimism and gratitude, mental indolence and sweaty carnality, in the anti-rhetorical portrait between being and appearing in the inner life of a city. A movie that tells its story simply, and without which that masterpiece of ironic observation, *Amarcord*, could never have existed.

The changing of the seasons sets the rhythm for the life of the small suburban town on the Romagna coast during the Thirties. The beginning of spring, like the 'fogarazza', the winter bonfire, is an occasion for a festival for the various characters that, one by one, introduce themselves into the story. In order of appearance, they are: Giudizio, a trouble-maker who is always hanging around, and prepares the faggots and old wood for burning; the barber/musician,

the beautiful Gradisca, and Titta's family, the messenger boy in the events to follow. The owner of the Fulgor Cinema (a double for Clark Gable) is present, Biscein the pedlar, and the people in the piazza who greet the end of the cold with a brass band and fireworks. Even Count Lovignano celebrates the same propitiatory rite with his small family in the courtyard of his villa. During the final events of the evening, Cantarel the blind accordion player, Volpina the nymphomaniac, the Venetian veteran and Lallo, brother of Miranda, who is Titta's mother, all arrive on the scene. A motorcyclist riding over the embers ends the festivities.

The lawyer, devoted to local history, gives information about the town, its people and its province, in spite of having to deal with a mysterious, witty heckler who interrupts his learned discourse.

Titta's class, together with the principle, Zeus, and all the teachers, are gathered for the school photograph. Then, one at a time and according

Fellini with the eccentric Biscein (Gennaro Ombra), the incredible story-teller in Amarcord

"It's the year of the snow". The village youths bombard an amused Gradisca (Magali Noël)

to their subjects, the teachers come up to the lectern and demonstrate all their defects during the explanations and the questioning.

Titta's family life is introduced by Volpina, who goes to Aurelio's workplace, the head of the family and chief engineer of a small construction company. Everyone is at home for dinner, including uncle Lallo, Gina the maid, and the lively grandfather, Aurelio's father. Amidst shouting, the soup, chicken and cabbage are consumed, interrupted by a quarrel between father and mother because Titta pissed on the hat of the distinguished Mr. Blondi from the movie theater balcony.

During the evening walk, the kids do not miss the chance of a bit of fun by molesting Gradisca, while the other characters are immersed in the routine of provincial life. The lawyer continues his discourse on architecture, the Fascists march up and down the main street, as do the principle and the teachers. The end of the evening is marked by the arrival of the new 'fifteen' – the change of shift at the local brothel – the closing of the movie theater and the turning off of the lights.

Just to give vent to his erotic thoughts, Titta confesses to the priest Don Balosa: the tobacco woman with her overflowing breasts, the mathematics teacher, the bottoms of the farm girls on their bicycles, the chance meeting with Volpina, the clumsy pass made at Gradisca in the deserted movie theater. The distracted priest absolves all the boys who,

at the end of the episode, masturbate together in the car parked in the garage.

The festivities for the foundation of Rome, on April 21, are held in euphoric adherence by the Fascists, including races, ceremonies and gymnastic exercises. Ciccio even imagines that the Duce is personally presiding over his marriage to Aldina, his haughty comrade who prefers someone else. Aurelio, who is an anarchist sympathizer, remains at home because Miranda will not let him out. But, when a gramophone in the bell tower begins to play the 'International', he is seized by the Fascists for interrogation. He will return home at two in the morning full of castor oil, which has its rapid and inevitable effect.

The elegant world of the Grand Hotel announces the arrival of summer, the sun and amorous adventures. It starts by recalling the affair of Gradisca and the prince, which changed the girl's real name, Ninola, after the girl freely offered her favors. There follows the odalisque scene, and Biscein shooting off his mouth with a lie about having had each one of the thirty highly-guarded wives of the emir. In the evening, on the terrace, uncle Lallo and his good-for-nothing friends pick up some foreign women for love and sex adventures that will fill their winter tales.

A hot summer day favors an outing by Titta's family to their country home. They take along Aurelio's brother Teo, who lives in a mental hospital. According to the doctors, he is basically quite well, but, in the carriage, he displays the stones he keeps in his pocket, and then, after asking them for a stop to relive himself, he wets his pants. After lunch at the farm house, Teo profits from the others' distraction to climb a tree and shout that he wants a woman. Then he throws stones at anyone who tries to approach him. In desperation, Aurelio organizes a fake departure and other ruses to make him come out of the tree, but only when a dwarf nun from the hospital arrives is Teo convinced to come down and return to the institution.

The Rex, a large ocean liner on its way from America, is going to pass by in the night, and all kinds of boats take to the water during the late afternoon, taking the whole town to see its sudden, swift passing.

The great autumn mists make everything unrecognizable, packed in wadding and unsettling. The grandfather and the youngest grandchild get the worst of it. But Titta and his friends cut up on the terrace of the Grand Hotel, closed for the winter, dancing around in order to shake off their melancholy. Then there is the 'Thousand Mile' automobile race. Titta and Ciccio imagine that they are famous racing drivers, and that they have won the heart of the mini-skirted Gradisca, for the former, and have snubbed the haughty Aldina, for the latter.

The adventure with the tobacco woman at closing time results in uselessly strenuous attempts by Titta to demonstrate his strength, who ends up in bed with a fever for his efforts.

A heavy snowfall arrives – the year of the 'big snow' – to the delight of the boys, but Aurelio's displeasure, and changes the appearance of the town's streets and squares. The mysterious motorcyclist, however, continues to appear out of the blue with a loud rumble. The young, and not-so-young, throw snowballs at each other and at Gradisca.

Miranda is taken ill, and receives a visit from her husband and eldest son, who does not realize how seriously ill she is. At the funeral, Lallo faints when Aurelio criticizes him and is about to take revenge for having kept him all these years. Now, with the house silent and empty, Titta goes to the sea, and as he stands on the wharf, the spring breezes appear once again.

It is the season of beginnings, and also a good time for the wedding of Gradisca to the police officer, Matteo. At the wedding banquet, amidst rhymed toasts, mimicked excuses by the kids, and the inevitable photograph, a very brief downpour soaks the blind accordion player, Cantarel, who is accompanying the dancing on the meadow. As the melancholy music plays, goodbyes are said, and the married couple leave. A few people remain to finish off the party. There is a fade out in black, the sound of the wind and the surf, and the title of the movie appears… Amarcord.

After La Strada, The Nights of Cabiria, and Eight and a Half, Amarcord (1973) also won the Academy Award the following year as the best foreign film, immediately gaining unanimous international critical acclaim, as well as public favor. In fact, it has all the ingredients to please both the professional press, the intelligentsia and ordinary movie-goers of all ages. For his part, the critic can perceive in it the director's third and definitive liberation. After the circus and Rome, Fellini finally puts the provinces behind him with Amarcord, those of his origins, and the other, broader provinces of the movies of the early Thirties, in which his movie is intuitively set. Intuitively,

Aurelio (Armando Brancia), Titta's anarchic father, is questioned by the Fascists, because someone played "Internazionale" in the square on the anniversary of the Foundation of Rome

because those years are not entirely reconcilable and, if we did not know Fellini's habit of intentionally covering his tracks, there would be some question marks, which are fortunately resolved in Tullio Kezich's thorough biography ("It could be 1933, the year of the VII Mille Miglia and the maiden voyage of the transatlantic steamer, The Rex, cited in the movie. But it could also be 1935, when, with the war in Ethiopia, one began to sing 'Facetta nera'; or 1937, when Shall We Dance? came out with Ginger Rogers and Fred Astaire, of which we see a poster.")

In one of these years, or perhaps more plausibly in the chronological anthology subsumed in those five years, the same process occurs as in Eight and a Half, when real and cinema personalities freely came to the (double) director's mind, who could do nothing but welcome them all in the confused universe of his fantasy. The characters of Amarcord create a similar invasion for the artist to deal with. And, if one remembers that here too 'I am another', and that one of the titles considered for the movie – along with Hammarcord, Vive l'Italia, Romagna, and Il Borgo – was L'Uomo Invaso ('The Invaded Man'), one understands the intentional direction and the symbolic presence of the personalities and masks of this suburban town.

Entirely constructed at Cinecittà (including the scene of

Gymnastic display by the local schoolchildren: on the right, Titta (Bruno Zanin), and on the left, his classmate, the unfortunate Ciccio (Ferdinando De Felice)

the passing transatlantic Rex), the Rimini of *Amarcord* is similar to the Rimini of Ostia reinvented for *I Vitelloni*: truer than the real thing, and thus cinematographically and superlatively false, realistic and convincing, an aggregate of obsessions that had always pursued the director, filtered through the scurrilous, ironic loudmouths of *Fellini's Roma*, and sifted through the real characters and clowns of the circus essay. Through this process, Fellini finally manages to clear away the "decrepit and ever contagious little theater of Rimini", whose marionettes, despite their different roles, all work together to compose a "rosary of dusty samples", a village fair in which the style and the group story respect the rules of choral works, except, naturally, for the subjective invention of memory, precisely *a m'arcord*.

Like an animal tamer who both loves and fears his animals, the director uses sugar and the whip, feeling and grimacing in sending his camera wandering through the streets, the psychology and behavior of a typicalness bound to local history – "the mocking character of such

populations, which have Roman and Celtic blood in their veins, and a character that is exuberant, generous, loyal and tenacious…" – and, because of this strong identity (also negative), recognizable within other realities outside of Romagna.

In fact, the movie brushes up against several primary units of society, from the small to the large. *The family*: Titta (inspired by his friend Titta Benzi); Aurelio, master clown; Miranda the housewife; the lively little grandfather, with his unforgettable erotic gesturing; 'little lord' Lallo, good-for-nothing Fascist. *The school*: represented in the delicious vignettes involving the teachers of the Fourth Latin School, in hierarchical order from gloomy principle Zeus to the religious studies teacher, and parish priest Don Balosa, who alternates the scholastic catechism with rapid sexophobic confessions. These, and many others, typologically inserted with all the caricatured tics deriving from their profession: the physics professor protected by photos of the king, the pope and Mussolini, who explains the laws governing the pendulum by the use of a rock; the history professor who questions Titta about Tiberius and Agrippina, but is only interested in keeping the ash of his cigarette from dropping; the sullen Alfieri, who is tested by the Italian teacher in a stormy atmosphere; the philosophy professor who moves excitedly around the classroom trying to reconcile the ideals of the State with those of the Church; the mathematics teacher and the Greek teacher, who are dreadfully afraid of the students' pranks. And finally, the most delightful character of all, the little art teacher, who explains Giotto speaking rhythmically of "per-spec-tive".

Within these tableaux, there are fluctuating sensations of memory, an affectionate look taken at a time when life was serene and unproblematic, but, at the same time, the worrisome awareness of the ideological/political, authoritarian, obtuse, old and fundamentally anti-educational elements behind it all. With regard to ignorance and adolescence in particular – fertile ground for what the movie has to say – Fellini insists on the historical responsibility of "personal" Fascism, thus making of *Amarcord* a movie that is attentive to the social and political realities, as well as an explicit warning about the significance to be attributed to this. "Politics – I mean to say, a political view of life where the problems of living are stated and confronted only in collective terms – seems to me to be a limitation. Everything which risks obliterating, hiding or altering the individual and his very personal story, turning it into abstract, schematic reality, confounding itself among 'categories', 'classes' and 'masses', instinctively repels me, I must confess. […] If, on the other hand, by politics one meant the possibility of living together, to function in a society of individuals who have respect for themselves and who know that their personal liberty ends where the freedom of others begins, well then, my movies seem to me to be political, because they do speak of these things, perhaps by denouncing their absence, by portraying a world in which they do not exist. I believe that all of my movies try to unmask prejudice, rhetoric, schematicism, the aberrant forms of a certain type of education and the world which produced it. What else can one do?"

One can, as Fellini does very well, portray Fascism using the truth of simple language within a single episode, that of the Christmas festivities in Rome, with the rhetoric and the 'Roman' destiny of Fascist Italy reduced to a few salient moments: the late arrival at the train station, the hierarchy on the flight of steps, authorities, teachers, various VIPs and, finally, the gramophone and the castor oil. Moments which, all on their own – "Of all the seas, the Adriatic has always been the most Fascist" – pungently depict a "psychological, emotional way of being Fasicst, a sort of block, an arrested development in the adolescent phase." When then the author states that "I seem to discern the eternal premises of Fascism precisely in being provincial", one cannot help having before one's eyes the suburban Fascists, the good-for-nothing friends of Lallo, and Lallo himself, youths who are already old, and whose jokes, swims, hair nets and snow balls are a substitution for the awareness that comes with growth, causing them to remain as eternal children, seeing that "Fascism and adolescence continue in some degree to be permanent historical stages of our lives."

More eloquently than a documentary, the connections in *Amarcord* between ignorance, adolescence, the provincial and Fascism are developed into something like a radical cure for that kind of thing. Thus *Amarcord* is another of the countless therapy movies against something, a satirical wringing out of Fellini's sponge in order to liberate mental space and leave the door open for the equally critical *Casanova* and, in particular, *Orchestra Rehearsal*, the stage where those castrating historical bonds are absent and are recklessly replaced by the unreasonable, deafening confusion of contemporary chaos.

In this family scene, Titta, who has been up to all sorts of tricks, tries to hide from Aurelio's anger

The tobacconist (Maria Antonietta Beluzzi), a typical large Fellinian woman, subjects our young hero to a suffocating sexual initiation, while the Supreme Poet watches with puzzled sterness

To free himself of these burdensome traditions, a director like Fellini, constitutionally unsuited to following the schemes of the old political movies, must necessarily avail himself of irony and the structure of the funny story, because he is too attentive to details, irrelevant, intimated, submissive and unusual facts. Therefore, descending, as it were, the hierarchical social order of *Amarcord*, after Fascism, the church, the school, there are the family, the coffee bar, the movie theater, the class photograph, the piazza, the community, including the closing meal at the Paradiso *trattoria*.

In these moments, like the blind man's accordion, the movie elongates itself into broad frescos – the bonfire, the passage of the Rex, the Grand Hotel in autumn, the 'year of the big snow' (which was, after all, in 1929), the count's peacock, the wedding banquet – only to narrow down again by focusing on (self)portraits, scenes and incomparable personalities. From Titta himself, uncertainly moving between carefree and emotional states, to Uncle Teo with his cry of "I want a woman!", to Ninola 'Gradisca' and the prince, to the grandfather with his mortal fear of the silent mist ("I feel like I'm no place: if that's the way death is, its a bad job. Shove it !"). And the grandfather again: "My pa's pa used to say that, to stay healthy, you have to piss a lot,

like dogs do", and you had to believe him, because at 106 his sex life was still going strong.

The sketches of Titta and his parents are also exemplary. Aurelio, the father, with that circus clown's head of his, slaps himself hard across the face when angry, while Miranda (Pupella Maggio) seems to be very sensitively playing out her role again as housewife Concetta in Eduardo De Filippo's play *Christmas at the Cupiello's*. And, furthermore: the south Italian lawyer who takes his bicycle along on the boat, the priest who sniffs at his fingers during confession, Ciccio and the other kids, the tobacco woman – emblem, quotation and premise for the gallery of *City of Women* in gestation – and all the other actors, present, past and future of the Amarcord Circus, the little adolescent hot-air balloon that came from a sleepy provincial town.

Several sequences were excluded from this closed world of Fellini's youth and nostalgia, including the one of the man, Colonia, cleaning out the cesspools and searching for the countess's diamond ring (eliminated because it would be incomprehensible in the United States where, Fellini thought, this kind of scavenger would be unheard of); the tornado that was meant to come between the Uncle Teo sequence and the passing of the Rex, but not shot for financial reasons; and finally the Chinese tie seller (a scene that ended

A lively scene involving uncle Teo (Ciccio Ingrassia), the family madman. He will only climb down from the tree, where he has taken refuge and is loudly asking for a woman, when the dwarf nun peremptorily commands him to do so

Titta in the concluding scene of Amarcord

The walk down the main street is an opportunity to bother alluring Gradisca, while the poster of Gary Cooper reminds one of the drawings which Fellini did as a boy for a picture house in Rimini

up, Kezich recalls, together with the cesspool one, in the television special *Fellini nel Cestino* ('Fellini's Waste Basket').

In a reduced world where, however, Fellini's oblique resentment is unable to leave out the pleasant group feeling, the life of comradely relations, where others are like oneself, one can more easily feel at home in the same places: at the coffee bar where they tell the same old stories, at the Fulgor movie theater where everyone waits for the snow to come, where Titta pursues love, Gradisca dreams of a husband like Gary Cooper in *Beau Geste* (a movie that the faker Fellini has fun passing off as the non-existent *La Valle dell'Amore*). And in the piazza, too, where there is a place for everyone, from the mysterious horseman to Biscein's tall stories; in the 'exotic' Grand Hotel between the elegance of the 'vecchia signora' and the closed, deserted atrium; in the nocturnal wait for the transatlantic steamer, with the idea of the always possible, but never actual, adventure, like the painted sea of the false liner; and finally, in the two collective moments of the ending, Miranda's funeral and Gradisca's wedding.

In the rites of death and of life, analogous to what he did

at the end of *Eight and a Half,* Fellini once again presents the whole cast in order to close this anthology of faces and characters that his imagination – and particularly the poetic imagination of Tonino Guerra, the Riminese of the suburbs – have bestowed upon cinema comedy.

The melancholy motif of the story fades out splendidly, a little at a time, in the light of the equally melancholy finale, in the fleeting merriment of a party that has ended and only just begun. The tone is almost subdued, suggested by the wide-angle shots of the toasting, of the photograph and the continuation of the movie after Biscein's goodbye, the unconscious desire to avoid the words 'the end', which Fellini never attached to his pictures. The movements of the camera, corresponding to those of the director in the town set, and the atmosphere created by the music, untiringly depict impressions and memories solicited by the never absent wind which, at the opening, brings the springtime and, at the end, together with the sound of the sea, suggests once more the maternal character – enveloping, fecund, unstable and deep – of the basic elements of the cinema of memory, of his Great World Theater.

The Wind Blows Where It Will

Fellini's Casanova ● Orchestra Rehearsal ● City of Women ● And the Ship Sails On

"It is easier for a person to change his deep convictions than to change his clichés," Fellini remarked with regard to *Casanova* (1976), the movie that possibly caused him the most suffering and turned him into the protagonist of "one of the most dreadful clashes in the history of cinema" (Bernardino Zapponi). The dual-name *Fellini's Casanova* could be considered the classical producer's *coup*, a really big deal, because the director's name appeared alongside that of the most legendary seducer, which, almost by chance, Fellini had proposed to Dino De Laurentiis. The idea, as had happened with *Mastorna,* came to nothing for many reasons, among them the director's refusal to cast an American actor (Robert Redford or Dustin Hoffman) in the title role.

The project was taken up by Andrea Rizzoli for Cineriz, who eventually dropped it for being too expensive to produce, as well as for its weak cover funding on the foreign market. Finally, in 1975, Alberto Grimaldi entered the scene, on the strict condition that, in order to keep down the costs, it had to be filmed in London studios and in the English language. Director and producer finally reached a compromise: it will be shot in English, but at Cinecittà, and the lead is to be Donald Sutherland, closer in appearance to the physical type Fellini had drawn in many sketches. Three years passed from the first negotiations until the movie was finished.

Casanova is another 'stop-gap movie', like the *Satyricon* and the hypothetical projects for a *Decameron* or *Orlando Furioso* – "a protective system of intentions, excuses, desires and convictions whose sole purpose is to allow me to make the movie that I need to make at that moment in time." One of those movies in which the producer must, as often happens with Fellini, do nothing but believe in the project and accept everything the director wants. Grimaldi is not accepting enough, and the work is plagued by friction, mostly due to an increase in costs, which was not actually very great.

Fellini takes up Casanova's *Memoirs* only after having signed the contract and, from this moment, the trouble begins: "I waded into the endless paper ocean of the *Memoirs*, into that arid catalogue of a quantity of facts amassed with the statistical rigor of a file clerk, finicky, meticulous, cramped, not even much of a liar, and annoyance, alienation, disgust, boredom, were the only variants in my state of mind, depressed, disconsolate. It was this rejection, this nausea, which suggested the approach to the movie."

The project proceeds punctiliously, the director feels less and less emotion on reading the Venetian's ponderous diary, and the same goes for the Eighteenth Century, "the most empty, exhausted, drained of centuries. What was European society on the eve of the French Revolution if not a cemetery?" It is this very funereal atmosphere that is taken as a paradigm, to accentuate the eternal juxtaposition of love and death, or better, love and non-life, a constant in the melancholy progress of a man who is a prisoner of his origins. In effect, the historical Casanova, overbearing male, great seducer, immoderate in all his ways, holds as little interest for the director as does Casanova the writer. Fellini shares out the boring task of reading the diaries with Bernardino Zapponi and Tonino Guerra, filling his pages with acid comments, noting all of antipathy for the character, an antipathy that will lead the director to portray him as an unfeeling marionette, a strange vampire who "never dies because he was never born, an aquarium fish", in short, an eighteenth century *Nosferatu* whose life is "a frenetic, mechanical dance without any purpose, something out of an electric wax museum."

Using his beloved law of opposites, the director begins to overturn even the hero's physical traits: for the tall, robust and vital Giacomo Casanova, he substitutes *Fellini's Casanova*, a smooth gigolo and unctuous sexual athlete, constantly and futilely searching for public recognition of his qualities as economist, philosopher, alchemist and what you will: a search constantly frustrated by the demand for that one and only thing: his sexual services, which conclude every scene. Substantially, a Casanova who is the victim of an ineluctable destiny, made by his own hands, a solitary

anti-hero, a romantic misunderstood by the immoral humanity with which he comes into contact, from the lowest to the highest ranks. A neurotic Casanova who finds his *raison d'être* not so much in sex as in reveries, in fantasizing, not a woman's body, but a single great intellectual opportunity.

Be that as it may, from the memories of an old embittered man, the director distils what, in his opinion, is the very essence of the man, who possibly never was the victim of a mother complex, as suggested by the false clue thrown up during the meeting with his mother in Dresden – an expedient for making him more human, after the antipathies and reservations aroused on every occasion. One can accept or reject this psychoanalytic interpretation, but there is no doubt that Fellini, with his capacities as a 'medium', has sucked out the best to be found in his subject, targeting his sensibilities as an old good-for-nothing, as a smoke vendor, or as an Italian man conditioned by the woman-mother-lover figure, having little credibility with his cumbersome fame and yet modern, a man greatly curious about the world, born in the wrong century.

Fellini's Casanova opens with titles that scroll across the waters of the Grand Canal in Venice. Near the Rialto, carnival season is being celebrated with the flight of the ceremonial angel, today known as the Colombina, as the masks respond in chorus to the oration for the city in the verses of the Venetian poet Andrea Zanzotto. The Doge cuts the ribbon, and the angel falls from above into the canal, as an enormous figurehead takes shape on the water through the noise of the *festa* and firecrackers. As the populace recites *La mona ciavona*, a cable breaks, causing the head to sink: this is a sign of disaster, but not for Giacomo Casanova who, masked, receives a note with regard to an amorous *rendevouz*.

It is an encounter with Maddalena, the mistress of the French ambassador, a voyeur who watches the union, delicate and ritualistic, to the beat of the mechanical bird that the great Venetian lover always has with him. Taking advantage of the invisible observer's satisfaction, Casanova – not only an able and intense lover, but a scholar of philosophy, mathematics and economics – does not hesitate to ask, in vain, for a letter of introduction for France, a country he loves like a second homeland.

On his way home, in the very midst of a storm over the lagoon, Casanova is arrested by order of the Messer Grande and the inquisitors. Unjustly found guilty of practising black magic, of possessing books placed on the index and of despising religion, he is condemned to prison in I Piombi, Venice's lugubrious, insalubrious prison.

In his horrid, narrow cell, Casanova remembers his earlier life of freedom, the erotic encounter with the woman who loved being whipped from behind, and of the episode with the anemic embroiderer, Annamaria, whom the intuitive Casanova had saved from debilitating blood-lettings and had 'cured' after a night of love.

The nocturnal escape from I Piombi, which Casanova himself calls "a masterpiece of intellgience, of exact calculation, intuition and courage, all of which qualities were rewarded with good luck," leads the Venetian to Paris, and the esoteric salon of the Marquise d'Urf, surrounded by magicians, occultists, clairvoyants and mediums – among them Cagliostro – whose one and only purpose, apart from magical or philosophical disquisitions on the conception of the

Madonna, is to realize the Great Work: to die and be reborn as a man who will live forever. This will be possible after carnal union with an initiate of her own pyramidal sign, such as Casanova, who, with the help of Marcolina, his temporary bed companion, succeeds in making love to the withered countess.

Two years later at Forli, he meets Henriette, a French girl travelling with a Hungarian officer who, being obliged to continue north, entrusts her to him. Giacomo falls madly in love, and goes with her to the fête organized by the hunchback Count Du Bois, an arts patron and homosexual. There, after discussions about the female soul, the guests hear a short metaphorical opera on love, entitled *La Mantide Religiosa ('The Praying Mantis')*, composed and sung by their host himself and his lover, Gianbruno.

The sudden clandestine departure of Henriette, indissolubly bound to a great, mysterious European personage who has total power over her, throws Casanova into the blackest depression, and he considers becoming a monk or even killing himself. This despair will be equalled only by a despair he feels many years later in London, due to two

women, "the infamous Charpillon and her daughter, who is completely worthy of her." These two, after infecting him with syphilis and robbing him, abandon him with his few bags to the adverse destiny of wretched, generous spirits. Determined this time as well to kill himself, he puts on his best clothes and wades into the river. But upon espying a very tall lady in the company of two dwarfs on the opposite shore, his lively curiosity is attracted and he desists from his intention.

In his search for the giantess, he arrives at a circus where, amidst shows, rides, masks, human jokes and tattoos, he also witnesses the presentation of the 'Great Mouna', a kind of throat, whale's belly, symbolic cavern in whose depths everything originates and can be found. A friend unexpectedly comes to the rescue, and informs him that there is also a giant woman at the circus, young and from the mountains of Veneto, very tall, very strong, but also fair and gentle. Sold to the circus by her wicked husband, the woman now puts on a show at fairs and circuses, beating the most robust men at arm wrestling. Two Neapolitan dwarfs take care of her and, under Casanova's discrete gaze, they bathe her lovingly and are moved when

In mist-covered London, Giacomo Casanova (Donald Sutherland) is discarded by his last lovers (Diane Kourys and Carmen Scarpitta)

she sings a llittle dialect song, the dirge of her hometown. The following day, the circus has folded its tents and Casanova leaves London.

One of his unforgettable days was one spent in Rome, first in the presence of the smiling pope, whose hand he could finally kiss over and over again, and then, in the evening, at the party of the English ambassador to the Holy See. In the ancient palace of Prince Del Brando, some rather lusty, primitive games are played, such as a wine contest. Casanova's fame as a tireless lover leads the host to organize a contest between Casanova's more 'intellectual' approach, and the brute instincts of the prince's coachman, to see who can publicly make love the most times in one hour. The couples are formed. Casanova chooses the Roman model, while a noble lady puts herself at the disposition of the servant. After some respiratory exercises and drinking eighteen eggs mixed with spiced Spanish wine, Giacomo wins the contest and is carried around in triumph.

The travelling Giacomo experiences his next sexual encounter between Berne and Dresden. In the latter city, as guest of the entomologist Moebius, he is taken ill, perhaps because of witnessing the insects being pinned down alive by the scholar's two young daughters. Feeling better, thanks to their loving care, he falls in love with Isabelle, and makes an appointment with her in Dresden so that they may live together for the rest of their lives. The girl never shows up at the Inn of the Moors, but Casanova still has a night of unbridled sex with the singer Astrodi, an old lover from Venice, and the insatiable little German hunchback.

The following evening, at the end of the opera *Orpheus and Eurydice*, when the theater is deserted and the great candelabra extinguished, Casanova happens to meet his mother, who, now almost paralyzed, lives in the country. He carries her to her carriage on his back, and tries to find a way of remaining with her for a while, but the carriage goes off into the snowy night.

During the years that follow, he finds himself in Holland, Belgium, Spain and Norway, where he is taken seriously ill, but finally ends up at the brilliant court of Wuerttemberg. There, he tries to convince the duchess to intervene for him with her brother, but the fête is extremely noisy and full of unexpected surprises, the atmosphere tipsy and

Going into the belly of the whale (the Grande Mouna), one of the most significant circus sideshows, from the London episode of **Fellini's Casanova**

The tall lady, Angelina (Sandra Elaine Allen), assisted by her dwarf attendants as she bathes, sings a gentle Venetian dirge after her routine circus exhibition

military, and the music deafening, played by organists roosting on high stools, which make it impossible for him to be taken seriously, and the same is true for the projects he proposes. The court sings the melancholy, patriotic ditty "The Hunter of Wuerttemberg" and, seeing the mechanical doll Rosalba, his disappointment is transformed into the most lively interest for the magnificent automaton.

Unable to resist temptation, he goes down into the salon during the night where, to the playing of a music box, he embraces Rosalba and dances with her. The doll with a porcelain face moves jerkily, but Giacomo, excited, uses it to make love.

The memories of his last years relate to his life in Dux, and its long Bohemian winters. There, Casanova has been librarian to Count Waldenstein for a long time, a job which he holds very dear, because it allows him to sate his unextinguished thirst for knowledge. But his indignation is roused for two reasons: the necessity of having his meals in the kitchen with the servants, where he does not always find 'maccaroni', and the dishonest behavior of the major-domo, Faulkirchner, and his mistress. These two take their revenge on the old man by smearing his portrait, and the first page of his novel *Icosameron,* with excrement.

During a fête in honor of the young count, Casanova recites a passage from his beloved Ariosto, which is not appreciated by some, who furthermore thought he was long dead. Offended, he retires to his rooms and the consolation of his books. Thinking about Venice, where he now feels he will never be able to return, he remembers a dream…

It is night. On the gray and gelid waters of the moonlit Grand

Canal, a young Casanova goes to meet Rosalba, while several of his women run towards the Rialto Bridge. On the other side, very brightly lit, a golden carriage arrives, drawn by four horses. It stops, the door opens, and inside there is the pope, smiling and nodding to him. Half hidden at the pope's side is his mother, whom he saw for the last time in Dresden many years ago. Once again with the Rialto as a background, in the half light of the moon and the soughing of the wind, Giacomo Casanova dances once more with the genteel automaton to the sound of a music box… The red and puffy eyes of the old Venetian are dissolved in the last romantic embrace of the two waxen figures, who slowly rotate round themselves.

Of all Fellini's movies, *Casanova* is the one that is most inspired by painting. It is as if the director, in his supposed antipathy for the character, had turned all his inventive inspiration to creating vast pictures – the episodes of the rake's life taken from his memoirs – drawing upon the heritage of eighteenth century figurative art. During the early stages of preparation, he appears to be very busy, keeping himself amused by drawing, making little models, studying costumes and details to be constructed in the studios of Cinecittà…. Everything in *Casanova* is clearly fake, and yet true to life, a product of the mind and hands of the artisan of genius, who wraps his creations in an aura of melancholy.

And so, these claustrophobic sets are created, which

Angelina (on the right) challenges the strongest men in the tavern to a test of strength, and beats them all

Through the wide-open mouth of the whale, the Venetian libertine sees the "light of the origins"

remind one of the interiors of Pietro Longhi's paintings, the papier-maché Venice and the plastic lagoon, the exact opposite of Canaletto's radiance, the opening of space and light that, whilst exploring the lagoon city, had seemed to Fellini to be too 'sunny', even during the darkest hours, so that he rejected the idea of shooting the film in its natural setting. For the director, the colors and light had to complement the dark wedding of Eros and Thanatos, the sadness of love without feelings, underscored by the example of the bed/coffins that host Giacomo's virtuoso performances. As in *Fellini's Satyricon* then, crepuscular tones prevail, which open to the light only in the Henriette episode, true love, the only woman to whom Giacomo says 'forever'. Dark gray, brown, deep green, black and red, these are the colors of a century that was dirty, and is shown to be such in the bad smells of the inns and taverns, and the courts swarming with crude and vulgar personages. Casanova himself is often in underwear and corsets of an indefinable color, rather than white, and in sharp contrast to his highly colored, rich clothes: velvet waistcoats, lace collars, golden buttons and powdered wig.

At this point, it is worth remarking on the complicated business of casting Donald Sutherland as the lead and, above all, his edgy relationship with the director. A skilled, professional actor, Sutherland's looks and sensibilities were still far from Fellini's idea of Casanova. Imprisoned in a 'sea-horse' mask with a protruding chin, a humped nose, shaven head and eyebrows personally designed by the director, the actor underwent a daily crisis, until Fellini explained that he had to let himself go, give up the stereotype and put himself at the disposition of the dream Casanova.

In his long career as a lover, Giacomo never excluded any type of woman. A champion of love even without feeling, he chooses women who can complete him, without concern for their beauty, except in Henriette's case. Fellini therefore accentuates the crossed eyes of Maddalena at the paroxysm of pleasure, Annamaria's hysteria, and the daughter of Moebius the entomologist, who enjoys the erotic/intellectual game between Giacomo and her sister Isabelle. She is beautiful, but it is a funeral kind of beauty, as slick as that of Rosalba, the inexpressive and obedient mechanical doll. Angelina has the same characteristics, an enormous doll with a body as large as her brain is small, an inaccessible myth whom Giacomo does not even try to touch. The other women in the movie are horrid: from the old, libidinous Marquise d'Urf, to Marcolina, shapely but disfigured by a black eye. Then there are the hags like Charpillon or Astrodi, the prostitute and the princess of the sexual contest in the Roman episode.

If Casanova – half poet, half adventurer – really loved every woman, Fellini does not believe it and turns that love

Acrobatic sideshows and amazed expressions create a protocinematographic atmosphere, full of nebulous mystery, in the oneiric fresco depicting the restrictive, gloomy world of the eighteenth century created by Fellini

into dark misogyny, even taking care to provide a psychoanalytical justification: through his mother's fault, Giacomo cannot have a real woman. And he demonstrates that woman is a symbol of perdition by inserting the drawings of his friend Roland Topor into the magic lantern at the London circus.

Fellini's gallery is enriched by Hogarth's style in the London adventure, and the encounter with the great whale, one of the most symbolic and pictorial in the movie. In his monograph on Fellini, Mario Verdone remembers having met him at an exhibition of circus posters, standing in front of one entitled 'The Whale Theater with the Magic Lantern', that he was to use exactly as it was in his movie. In the long line of people waiting to enter the whale's stomach, there is also Giacomo who, in front of Topor's disquieting images, will fall back into his nightmare and, physically, fall among the human variety of monstrous circus charlatans who populate the tavern, and is redeemed by the presence of Angelina, a victim like himself, and therefore part of his inner world.

The Dresden scene is divided into two parts, with the common background of the Italian opera. It is the occasion for the chance meeting with his mother and Astrodi, mother and mistress, that is to say the two faces of woman, broken into pieces, which Casanova does not succeed in recomposing. And if Astrodi will further exalt his love-making capacity, his superficial side, his mother will make him once more compare himself with his phantoms, his condition as victim of the woman who gave him his first refusal. With the infinite tenderness of a child looking for affection and petting, Giacomo announces his successes (not sexual ones) at European courts, and receives only indifference in return. At this point, Fellini can no longer lie, and briefly reveals a wave of sympathy – and fraternity – with the unfortunate chap. In short, his exterior opposition dissolves in the images of that lake of solitude and intense humanity reflected in the glance of his personage, in a cul-de-sac.

From this moment on, ever gloomier colors and events accompany the Venetian on his road towards old age and death, which has been all too often announced. When sexual athletics no longer sustain him, he will become painfully aware that not even his fame as a scholar will be enough to earn him consideration. He is no longer credible, no longer believed, but only just tolerated. Old, irritable, isolated, dirty and untidy in his outmoded clothes, his mechanical bird out of order like himself, he will live, forgotten, in his study in Bohemia, keeping his last amorous thought for the doll Rosalba, the only one who cannot judge him.

At the gloomy court of Dux, Fellini's wind will begin to sough again – and forcefully – when the dream of the old Casanova is recounted. That same breath of wind will carry him back to his beloved Venice, to the frozen Grand Canal,

The first romantic encounter in Casanova takes place during the Venice Carnival, when Giacomo meets up with Sister Maddalena (Margareth Clementi) in order to satisfy the voyeuristic tendencies of the Ambassador of France

Images from the subconcious (the sketches are by Roland Topor) contained within the unique portrayal inside a cetacean's stomach, a figurative metaphor of the eternal, somewhat stereotyped, myth about sex

in the company of the automaton, before closing his eyes and returning to that mother who, from her carriage, finally sends him a benevolent gesture.

From the Venetian adventurer's large, prolix diary emerges a reckless combination of cavalier and genius, and Federico Fellini extracts a most beautiful, complex film, in which he contemplates himself non-narcissistically in the mirror. A mirror visually very rich, pictorial, dream-like, to express the autobiographical solitude of Casanova, and his own artist's melancholy in seeing his creative energy frustrated, almost foreseeing the events. Precisely what will happen in *Orchestra Rehearsal*.

The sonoric commentary to the great ring road episode of *Fellini's Roma* is dissonant and unpleasant, to the point of visual saturation in the emblematic Colosseum traffic jam. For the titles of *Orchestra Rehearsal* (1979), Fellini reverts to that sound-track once again, as an introduction to the movie.

And so, in this musical *prova* (rehearsal, trial, trans.), one finds once again the theme of accumulation, of baroque exaggeration, of clairvoyance, of *contemporary chaos* according to Federico Fellini. It is an apocalyptic/ironic picture of social life and politics, a prelude to those sketched in *Ginger and Fred* and *The Voice of the Moon*. Analogously to what occurs in Ingmar Bergman's movies – to which, sometimes in an instrumental manner, his movies have been compared – Fellini's *prova* intends to direct itself elsewhere. He is interested in nosing around, digging into the *before*, primarily among the folds, but also in the *after* (a little like in Bergman's theater piece *After the Rehearsal*) in order to analyze the effects produced in the individual and the collective, the conductor and the orchestra, by the pretext of a performance to be tested, rehearsed, modified.

In the same way that he had tried out elsewhere, Fellini assumes the fictitious and discrete role of the interviewer, interested in showing what lies *behind* or *ahead* (of a personage, event or context). He is interested in the *surroundings* as well as the *inside*, being aware that the internal dimension is implicit, acquired. This, too, is the reason why he repeatedly shows the movie camera, the *mode* in which cinema images are made, because he has always known and felt – and with him the spectator – that the fascinating thing is not the *what* but the *how*. With regard to what there is of the political in the fable behind *Amarcord*, it would be equally reductive to trace back the political 'message' in *Orchestra Rehearsal* to the collapse of general order in the system, to the annulling of some rules of behavior, to the confusion and uncertainty of an epoch (for Italy, 1978 means the year of Aldo Moro's kidnapping and assassination by the Red Brigades, and the first government the Italian Communist Party voted for).

Fellini is an artistic thermometer, apparently superficial, but deep in substance: deep because, with the objective eye of the camera, he analyzes the small daily gestures of the musician-personages, and their behavior due to being part of a cohesive group, or what is supposed to be such, bound together by music; superficial because, in refusing didacticism, he places the observer both within and without the business, through the acting out of a senseless, provoking musical rehearsal.

An old oratory that holds the tombs of no less than three popes and seven bishops has been turned into a concert hall. The old copyist, who is putting the parts on the music stands, is explaining things to the television crew that has come to interview the orchestra and conductor. He talks about the different stages of transformation of the place, its marvelous acoustics and his own imminent pension.

The concert-master arrives, a Piedmontese who wants to relate the history of the oratory. Then Mirella, the pianist, enters with two other musicians and, a few at a time, others arrive and begin taking their places in front of their music stands, arranging the chairs and tuning up their instruments.

There is a lot of the usual talk about everyday life, about sex, the characters you meet in heavy traffic, and, while the players are finishing their preparations, various things take place. Some are listening to the ball game on the radio and others, like the concert-master, check the humidity on the barometer before starting to quarrel with another neurotic violinist. A few are still eating sandwiches; one trombonist finds a balloon in his instrument, which inflates as he blows and explodes… in short, a series of jokes and scenarios.

The orchestra manager comes in, as does the Sardinian union delegate, and officially announces the presence of the television crew (which not everyone is happy about). Immediately after, two muffled knocks are heard from a distance, and Clara the harpist arrives.

A series of interviews begins with the musicians talking about their own instruments: the piano is the most difficult; a young, slightly eccentric, Tuscan lady shows off her flute and, like many of the others, compares her instrument to the human voice. There follow the trombone and the percussion instruments – almost isolated because the violin and flute treat them with detachment and condescension – the violoncello, the violin again, the bassoon, the clarinet, the trumpet. Behind every instrument there is obviously not only the musician, but the human being as well, whose job it is to describe the qualities, defects and betrayals which each one experiences in his professional, artistic and personal relationship with his instrument.

During the preliminary doodling of the musicians, the union delegate expresses his own ideas, and while the small organizational details are being settled, the German conductor arrives, the preliminaries are ended and the sonoric arrangements for the rehearsal begin.

The music is interrupted and repeated various times in order to correct rhythmic, timbric and dynamic errors. The rehearsal proceeds as best it can, while those who are not playing continue speaking, giggling and chatting, and some still listening to the radio…

The conductor is not at all happy with the situation – he complains and throws away the score, while the musicians regard him with annoyance, sarcasm or mockery – and wants to start again at a

Under the roof of an ancient auditorium desecrated by the musicians' protest slogans, we find the cineast, surrounded by a cloud of dust created by the scuffle in Orchestra Rehearsal

The German conductor (Baldwin Baas) vainly tries to get the members of the orchestra to play in harmony

different passage, introduced by the piano. It is necessary to begin again several times *da capo,* because the sound is not compact enough. The constant incitement of the conductor's harsh words, emphasized by his German accent, finally causes some of the musicians to remove their jackets and shirts, or fan themselves and take a handkerchief to mop up the sweat induced by the hard work.

When the conductor asks for the clarinet to play a passage by himself, the situation, already tense, becomes really problematic: the clarinet player refuses, saying that the contract and the union agreement do not call for such services. Offensive remarks are made by both sides, which are interrupted by a new noise, distant and disturbing.

The horn is not present at the rehearsal which, meanwhile, is suspended for a double pause of twenty minutes, unilaterally called.

During this break, some of the players go to the bar, while others remain in their places, and the interviewed musicians comment on the conductor, the joys and pains of the profession, the value of music and the instruments, the obsessions and tics, vices and other extra-musical topics.

While the oboe insists on his absolutely determining role in the orchestra, the old copyist takes the television crew to the conductor, concluding his remarks with a criticism of modern methods compared to the rigor and respect of the past.

Now it is the conductor's turn, concluding the series of interviews with a mixture of exultant memories about his beginnings and completely negative judgments about the state of music, the law and musicians.

As he is about to remount the podium, a blackout occurs, and the conductor wants to continue the rehearsal by candlelight. Looking into the hall, he discovers that a rebellion has broken out against him, and the supposedly dictatorial powers and arrogance that the musicians believe that he represents. His role, function and usefulness are contested, inkpots thrown against the portraits of the great composers of the past, and the walls covered with insulting, offensive graffiti of various kinds. Political music for all is called for, but the union delegates do not even try to intervene, and later fight among themselves.

Confusion and rebellion increase and, under the conductor's mute, impotent gaze, the musicians give way to vandalism, sex under the piano, quarrels and vindictive slogans, slapping. Meanwhile, plaster begins to fall from the ceiling and the drums beat the rhythms of the devastation in full sway.

Struck by a violinist, the harpist, who was the only one not to give an interview, now expounds her poetical views on the harp – a devoted friend and not merely an instrument to play for a living.

"Orchestra. Terror. Death to the conductor." "Orchestra. Terror. Anyone who plays is a traitor." These are the slogans that accompany the entrance of the 'new conductor', a giant metronome, disliked by many. Groups of dissenters form, verbal and physical violence take place, no holds barred, and then an elderly violinist, who until that

moment had been silent and looking lost and dazed, pulls out a pistol and begins shooting into the air…

Silence ensues, except for the muffled noises that are now closer at hand. On the wall opposite the podium, deep cracks appear, and a steel ball, a very heavy wrecking ball, creates an enormous hole in the wall.

Everyone is paralyzed, pale with terror, speechless amidst the dense dust, and sorrow for the dead harpist buried under the rubble.

The conductor brings the situation back under control, restoring faith in music, in the work of each individual and the love for each one's instrument. The podium is restored to its place, the musicians all return more or less to their places, the rehearsal begins anew, while the dust settles and the faces of the musicians are more recognizable.

The music of the strings move some of the players, others smile as if in peace, recovered and fused in music… But the conductor begins

The tidy arrangement of the music scores by the elderly copyist (Umberto Zuanelli), who has vivid memories of that musical venue, is now scattered in this Fellinian fantasy, which also marks the last collaboration between Master Rota and the director

The rehearsal begins, and the slightly anonymous, depressed faces of the members of the orchestra register boredom, ill feeling and frustration with the "real world"

For the benefit of the cameras, a strange, slightly disconsolate expression on the face of the sentimental copyist, a thoughtful witness to the rehearsal

to… act like an orchestra conductor, to criticize harshly, to mistreat the musicians with that Germanic Italian of his, hard and metallic. The picture fades and his stentorian voice gives way to the music and the end titles.

Contrary to the norm, Nino Rota wrote the music for *Orchestra Rehearsal* before the filming to be used in playback: *Gemelli allo Specchio, Piccolo Riso Melanconico, Piccolo Attesa* and *Grande Galop* – a quartet of anticipatory compositions, creating a crescendo alongside the events of the movie, and a '*prova*' of its nightmare. However, it is not simply an anticipation, as it is flanked by Fellini's pre-vision of the great uncertainties of the end of the decade.

If art serves to interpret the past and to scrutinize the unknowable future, and even though the director concluded the interview in Costanto Costantini's book by saying: "I foresaw nothing. What happened had to happen, it was in the nature of things. We are all subject to a kind of fatal predetermination", it is still true that the presence of Fellini's genius in the art and society of the Twentieth Century allows anyone who knows how to, and actually wants to do so, to rend the cultural veils, to instinctively sense and reveal the changes. Fellini opened up views of things which it was not incumbent upon him to enter and gaze upon: the rot, the corruption and the stupid intolerance; nor was it his place to find solutions. Fellini was a director and, with a movie, the most you can do is open an abyss in the concert halls – in the political headquarters? – with heavier sledgehammers than the enormous weight of obtuse collective behavior, foolish greediness and the imposition of the judgement and privileged position of the uncultured – those same uncultured whose basis is insensitivity and incapacity for moral order and the understanding of the beautiful.

This describes that little movie that was made while awaiting financing for *City of Women*. A little movie in length (lasting hardly seventy minutes), but great in the nobility of its non-partisan conception of politics. A picture dedicated to the search for simple and collective harmony, which is reached for a moment towards the end after the self-destructive catastrophe, when the conductor manages to scratch up a pinch of individual dignity and bring the agitated back to their senses. More shocked than satisfied for having unleashed their frustrations and their ignorant rage at the conductor and the podium (symbols of power without which art cannot exist), they return to their places and exert themselves to seek some justification and consolation, and approach the maestro to get his consensus, his responsibility and guidance. But it only lasts for a moment. As often happens in Fellini's work, here too an overly desperate or excessively 'happy ending' conclusion would be superficial, and easily intriguing or exploitative

Both the outside world and the world of music seem to be collapsing beneath the powerful, demolishing blows, until the temporary Fellinian reconstruction

The stress and strain of the rehearsal provokes unseemly behaviour, and slogans are chanted to the beat of the metronome to drown out the "ineffectual" and dictatorial orchestra director

(should we not say unrealistic?). The harmony is splintered again by generational and cultural immaturity. And the stereotype of the German 'commander' who uses his harsh, biting tongue, a messenger of disdain and poetry with that strident "da capo!", annuls the lovely moment of music's victory over the banal and fragile quotidian.

A wrestling match sustained for the whole of the film, from Nino Rota's music in the interruptions of the musicians, in their airs of self-sufficiency, in their disdain for musical quality and love of their instruments – a love which, on an individual level, does come through here and there during the interviews, amidst frustrations, mediocrity, wrong choices and senile delusions. Some of the orchestra musicians play as it they were going to the office, attempt to open contractual negotiations and even let themselves be convinced to put their welfare in the hands of defenders who guarantee such a degree of conflict that will shield them from their true nature as musicians. The refusal of the clarinet player to play for a third time not stipulated in the contract is perhaps one of the most evident examples: he was saved from the eternal mists of his home town on the Po thanks to his instrument, he is proud because the maestro told him: "Bravo, young man. Finally I get to hear a clarinet with a beautiful sound", and yet he refuses to play a passage solo, particularly after the conductor had contested a dramatic passage which he considered comical. Perhaps on a point like this, one could have established a different kind of contact, rather than bet on the introduction of a metronome to fictitiously settle all problems.

And so, Fellini's metaphor in *Orchestra Rehearsal* would no longer address only the feeling of a progressive collapse, announced by revealing signs that were ignored until it was too late even for short respites. "Maestro, but how did this happen? When?" some of the musicians, who do not know how to explain events to themselves, ask of the conductor. And their chief reacts to scurrilous vulgarity and the musical ignorance of the masses and the lack of ice in the champagne bucket by buying houses all around the world

Federico and Marcello, as the woman in the train (Bernice Stegers) has to kiss Snaporaz (Mastroianni) at the beginning of City of Women

A padlocked wedding dress is the feminists' provocation, as they hold their convention in the Miramare hotel where, following to the newcomer, chauvinist Snaporaz will turn up

and, as soon as he gets the baton back again, begins impassably anew from where he left off.

So then, Fellini's metaphorical *Orchestra Rehearsal* would no longer seem to need television to accentuate the chaos that, within a short time, the very language of television would become part of. The orchestra musicians take advantage of television to speak ill of the conductor and the union delegate (who takes bribes under the counter), and the latter provokes a rebellion that leaves things as they are. Little does it matter that he will have the death of the poor harpist on his conscience, who had the premonitory dream of a horse in her room (the enormous demolition ball in the oratory).

So then, Fellini's fable in *Orchestra Rehearsal* will have to show other emblems of epoch-making rubble and of their looming apocalyptic pessimism, and, for this, one will only need to await the forthcoming movies. The general climate of Fellini's cinema is worsening, the circus-oratory is getting uglier, with nastier, colder, more aloof faces. By pure luck, there still remain some modest moments of alienation and unessential realism: the invisible waving of the threads in the spider web when the trombones vibrate, the stolen gesture of comfort for the cellist's haemorrhoids, the former Greek professor in *Amarcord* and, most of all, the old copyist.

He speaks to the scores that play tricks on him and, with a leap, manages to get clear of the falling masonry. Even if Fellini's scenarios are turning ever darker in color, one will find it again in *City of Women,* in the guise of a memory magician, and in *And the Ship Sails On* as the singing teacher who makes music with water glasses, a *trait d'union* in the new and pessimistic discourse initiated by *Casanova,* the lover of women.

With a great metallic noise, a train enters a tunnel. Marcello Snaporaz has dozed off in a compartment and, upon wakening, finds a lady wearing a busby and boots seated in front of him by the window.

Struck by her charm, he meets her in the restroom where, after an intense kiss, he immediately tries to have sex with her, but is frustrated by a sudden halt in open countryside. The woman gets off and Snaporaz, because of his sexual excitement, follows her into the Fregene pine wood, and there, for the second time, the mysterious, headstrong woman leads him to believe that she consents, only to leave him with closed eyes leaning against a tree like a fool.

Seeing her enter the Hotel Miramare, the man decides to continue following her, and he discovers that there is a crowded feminist congress being held there. Looking for his woman, Snaporaz roams through the rooms full of girls, attends anti-masculine seminars, ironic shows about the exploitation of housewives, collective liberation rallies, and slides against usurpation by masculine power. He is observed with

Here Snaporaz walks through the gallery of sound and images which record the romantic encounters of Sante Katzone (Ettore Manni), a former schoolmate

great suspicion and hostility, made the butt of jokes, derided, threatened quite openly and forced to leave the rooms where the congress is being held.

Inexplicably, two girls help him find the elevator, and together they reach the gymnasium. Putting on roller-skates, he may manage to make a getaway, and after wobbling around a bit he rolls down the stairs and finds himself in the boiler room, where the robust boiler woman offers to take him to the train station on her motor scooter.

As they travel through the countryside, the girl stops at some greenhouses covered with plastic awnings. On the pretext of wanting to get seeds for the stationmaster, the girl leads him inside to make love with him. Snaporaz, who has no desire, is saved by the providential arrival of the boiler woman's elderly mother, who kicks the girl around for her uncontrollable lustfulness, which allows Snaporaz to make for the station, again in the company of a girl.

He gets into a car full of punk girls, dazed by music and drugs and, when night comes, finds himself near an airport landing strip, where the group watches planes land, and one of the girls wants to shoot at

them with a pistol. Snaporaz leaves the punks, whose number has now grown so that they require three cars, which chase him threateningly. He arrives at the home of Sante Katzone, an ex-schoolmate and symbol of masculine virility, who lives in a villa with three large dogs, and defends himself from the women with rifle fire. Sante asks Snaporaz to stay for the party, held in celebration of the ten thousand women he has had so far. While waiting for the guests to arrive, Marcello discovers some erotic objects that Katzone keeps around to enhance his consideration for the phallus and, in particular, admires the gallery/cemetery of his female conquests, accompanied by a loud commentary on the most successful performances.

Before the extremely exhausting ceremony of extinguishing all the little candles (Katzone deals with those placed on high with a jet of pee), Snaporaz runs into his wife Elena, who drunkenly reproves him for the crisis in their relationship and the passing of the years. In a trance, Katzone's last mistress stuffs coins and pearls into her pussy and, a little later, the policewomen break in: they have killed one of his beloved dogs and destroyed the laboratory where he was making his ideal woman. The party, also attended by the roller-skating girls, is suddenly interrupted.

Snaporaz and the two girls perform a kind of Fred Astaire dance routine, then he is accompanied by the housemaid and Katzone's old governess to his room. While a tempest rages outside, Elena, hotly excited, joins him in the big double bed, her face covered with skin cream. She wants to make love with him, but ends up falling blissfully asleep.

Hearing some voices, Snaporaz crawls under the bed and finds himself at the opening of a long, winding slide, which is suddenly illuminated with many lights, operated by three old men, three strange little wizards in tails.

Sliding down in his nightshirt and bathrobe, the illuminated circles act as mirrors of memory at every curve and stretch of the run, and cause Snaporaz to relive certain moments from the past: the provocative laundry woman; the fish seller with her wriggling eels; the German nurse at the spa; the two motorcyclists dressed in black leather; the female bather spied through a hole in the cabin wall, who seductively walks towards the sea; the starlette of the silent film, with the male audience that indulges in collective masturbation underneath the sheets. And finally, the brothel, where the grotesque madam is at the cash register, and the large-assed prostitute in the bedroom.

At the foot of the slide, the three wizards, feeling cold, are taken away by their patient wives, while Snaporaz, captured by a feminist rally, is put into a cage and sent to a shed run by homosexuals, where he will be prosecuted by the female population who, sometimes masked and sometimes not, charge him, as a man, with a whole load of crimes.

Inquisitive about noisy shouts coming from a nearby arena, Snaporaz learns that some male combatants are fighting for the ideal woman, under the watchful eyes of a feminine crowd. He wants to go and watch and, after passing through a long, narrow corridor, he finds himself in the blinding glare of floodlights in front of the tiers of the arena crowded with women, who throw flowers and firecrackers at him, whistling and jeering, while a young terrorist mockingly observes him from beneath his hood. Two girls dressed up as Laurel and Hardy point out an iron ladder to him, at the top of which is the deserted ring, and the old governess informs him that he has won the fight. The audience begins to disperse, and Snaporaz is helped into a balloon poised for take-off. The balloon is shaped like a curvaceous girl, with a luminous halo like the madonna's over her head.

Free at last under the stars, Snaporaz is happy, but the masked girl shoots at the balloon, which deflates and falls to earth. Snaporaz grasps at the cables, to which another woman is also clinging… He awakens from the dream. In front of him is his wife, and the woman in the busby enters the compartment, followed by the roller-skating girls. He watches the women for a while, picks up his dark glasses with one lens missing, and is about to doze off again, looking forward to a continuation of his dream. The train enters a gallery.

If the first impression leads one to consider *City of Women* (1980) to be a modern fairy tale, in which Snaporaz is a helpless Little Red Riding Hood lost in the feminist wood, or else to be one of those visual dreams to which Fellini has got us accustomed, in reality, if one thinks about it, this movie

is a wave. And, like a wave, it is in continuous motion (the travel theme, an inquisitive search, a true quest), rushing headlong only to break and recompose itself endlessly (the encounters and clashes with the feminists), growing and developing only to exhaust itself and grow again (the forms of desire), overtaking itself, dissolving into fragments and finding its crest again in other subsequent waves (the

In the central room of the museum/cemetery, our hero seems overwhelmed by the feminist images and voices, a prelude to his flood of memories

dynamics of memory, of an infantile and adolescent *amarcord*, a little curious and more vague in its anxiety). Like a tireless, never-ending wave, it posseses a slow-motion inner rhythm (the unnatural pace of the dream and the story), and an external rhythm that depends upon other things (the rhythmic language of cinema, the energy of social or vitalistic moments). And, of course, it is an incoherent, wave-vague movie, cold deep inside (in the gallery/cemetery of women/tombs) and hot on the surface of events (the train, the feminist congress, the Katzone episode, the slide).

Naturally, the wave does not exclude the dream, on the contrary it exalts it, presents more symbols to be elaborated, invented, imagined, explored. All of these are aspects around which, as we know, Fellini's pictures have always completely revolved. And yet, in *City of Women,* the outcome is, in some way, much more familiar than usual, encountered if not exhausted in the earlier works. In the female characters – completed in the social chronicles and history by the 'feminist' ones – as in the character of

Marcello/Snaporaz/Fellini, and his other half, Katzone, or the internal dramatic settings, metaphorical, congenial to the idea of swamps, of labyrinths, of aspirations to sinking and thus to its opposite, flight: in all of this, one can find the sense of the movie. If there is a stairway, or else a wave – and even in *City of Women* there are several – one can try to go up, stride over it, go down, fall, drown, sink into it. To laugh grotesquely under the scourge of dreams when one is low is a sublimation – completed by illusion – of elevation, of penetration (the tunnel and the woman on the train), of the revisitation of the male, of what there is between earth and heaven, man and woman, clown and the anxiety of passing time. The final slide completes the transformation of the incoherence of the wave: only immutable on the surface, it is actually Fellini's creative shuttlecock which insists on the dream dimension.

Attempts to understand the other half of oneself and the female universe having turned out to be sterile or obsolete, the 'old Snaporaz' – and, with him, the sixty-year-old director who, after the fable of *Orchestra Rehearsal,* is no

The shell bed enfolds Marcello and the two young soubrettes, Donatella (Donatella Damiani) and Sara (Rosaria Tafuri)

The trial of a (Fellinian) man is almost complete, and Snaporaz, imprisoned between his own paranoia and the Jungian impossibility of fully understanding a woman's world, awaits his destiny

longer on the same wavelength as the 'in crowd' (the young punks, music, feminism) – once more takes refuge in the maternal, reassuring circus of thought, of memory, of time past. Another *déjà vue* parade of women: a housemaid from Romagna (one imagines one can smell freshly washed laundry, together with the sweaty potato-peel odour so often recalled by Fellini); an excited, exciting fish seller; one of the nurses from the spa in *Eight and a Half;* and the blonde motorcycle riders. So then, we have once again the circus and popular shows, the soubrette in a bikini who is a kind of anticipation of *Ginger and Fred* and, to close, the balloon, for a moment a Woman/Madonna who might give him the illusion of having overcome the macho complex of Sante Katzone and of forgetting the movies.

But it is not possible. The dream wakes the dreamer at the moment of the fall – has the anxiety of Gido returned in the opening of *Eight and a Half?* – and the wave, with its rhythmic, magmatic, erotic flow (the boiler woman, the slide, the balloon), replaces the manifestations of the incongruous political context, moves it away and returns to the opening dream image – the lucid intoxication of the cinema. In the train compartment, Snaporaz sees the dream take on the recognisable connotations of reality: his wife instead of the mysterious woman (she wears her busby), his eyeglasses which had fallen and lost one lens in the dream adventure, the two soubrettes sitting in the vacant seats. The looks exchanged are almost of astute complicity for a dream – one which Snaporaz, happy and languid, prepares to rejoin *in reality* in the darkness of the tunnel, a black hole where one glimpses a little light (which anticipates the dawning light of the moving reflections in *The Voice of the Moon*).

Rather like the end of Hitchcock's *North by Northwest,* which makes the ascendance/penetration a metaphor for the end of the action and the marriage to be consummated, the circle of *City of Women* is the last of Fellini's innumerable excursus "into the body of woman". Kezich, the first to use the Hitchcock ending, has noted that the Italian director "does not succeed in being equally consolatory." This is not entirely true, since consolation would have given continuance to the flight of the subconscious and of eros over the blessed fields of Fellini's nocturnal imagination. The poet Andrea Zanzotto, Fellini's friend and amused collaborator on some precious occasions, recalls in the introductory pages to the text of the movie that "walking around in the city of women, everyone, even while noticing that they had been placed in the center of a spinning top moved by a delicate rod, finally feels, after the appearance of a balloon destined to disintegrate, that they have gone into a free fall that may be true liberty."

But if Fellini the dream magician were as consolatory as Hitchcock the thrill magician, it would be taken as complementary to his refusal to flirt with the public in a film where masculine psychoanalytic incursions into the mysterious sphere of the feminine come into play, and the variations of a statistical age that make one see things in a different, darker light. This is also due to events such as the sudden deaths of Nino Rota, of his friend and factotum Bevilacqua, and of Ettore Manni, the portrayer of Sante Katzone. And yet, in spite of all this, as always with Fellini, the dream of the imagination is what generates cinema. Furthermore, one should not forget that, for Fellini, Jung's words about the female image are totally valid: a man cannot know her because he projects onto her the dark and unknown side of himself (and so if that dark side is unknown, how can woman be known?). Just as there is no difference in the comparison between the cinema and woman, inasmuch as "in the alternation of light and dark, of images which appear and disappear, the cinema is itself woman. As in the maternal womb, one sits still and focused at the cinema, immersed in darkness, waiting for life to be given to you from the screen… One ought to visit the cinema in the innocent condition of a fetus… My movie is the after dinner jabbering of someone who is slightly drunk. It is a fairy tale about the women of today and yesterday, as told by a man who cannot know women because they are inside of him: like Little Red Riding Hood lost in the woods. It is a dream, and it speaks the symbolic language of dreams. It would please me if one could watch it without being blinded by the temptation to understand: there is nothing to understand."

And with this declaration, we can, for now, take leave of *City of Women,* because a gust of that strong wind that Snaporaz felt strike him while going down the slide, will gradually lift us to *The Voice of the Moon,* the film-testament of *listening* as opposed to *understanding*: "Woe to those who try to understand", the poet of images continues to implore. Contemporary mediocrity could, at this point, agree with him, but perhaps it still needs some other ineffable, deadly support to convince itself of this. And Fellini is a director who is very attentive and helpful to everyone, as patience is certainly one of his best qualities. He will wait. He will wait until his other films of the Eighties get through, the last decade of his very fervid productive life.

"Making a movie today is like taking off in a plane without knowing where, how and when you are going to land. Since the purpose, route and end of the trip are unknown, there is nothing left but to tell about the trip for its own sake." And this will be *And the Ship Sails On.* Between *City of Women* and the preparation of this movie, more than three very long, inactive years pass by, in which Fellini lives through and comments on what he had portrayed in

It would be the end of Snaporaz/Fellini if it were not for the enchantment of memories, represented by the ghostly slide, and Donatella's skates which conveniently allow him to escape

Orchestra Rehearsal – that is, collapses, modifications and a sort of inevitable lack of preparation, both personal and generational. The recognized master of international cinema has (the usual) difficulties in making a movie, finding the right producers and coming to terms with them. In the end, he begins to find himself in the condition of someone who had given a lot and is now left to one side – regally – a little in the shade, by himself. The one exception is receiving the Golden Lion for his career at the 1985 Venice Festival, a prize that its beneficiaries generally consider to be midway between a golden handshake and an artistic gravestone.

So then, during these three years, between the ironic, the poisonous and the melancholy, Fellini recalls himself as "standing at the street corner to watch how the world and the movies were changing. If you place yourself at the street corner, you meet everyone: the tramp, the thief, the prophet, the assassin, the mystic, the apocalyptic preacher, the bankrupt, the suicide. It is the only way of knowing how the world is changing, what direction things are taking. Thus, as I was standing at the street corner, I understood that movies were changing, that it was no longer what it used to be, had nothing to do with pictures as we used to make them, while all around I heard the drumbeats of the invaders, the Attilas, the Genghis Khans, the Star Wars, the

electronic directors, who shoot for the maximum while demanding the minimum. To satisfy a spectator molded by television, the movies must make as much noise as possible: once the firecracker explodes, it no longer exists, just like fireworks." And if bitterness for the missing workplaces – the studios of Cinecittà – synthesizes with "where churches stood, they now open brothels", one must certainly not think of those constructed from his images, but rather of the idea that the Great Demolition of the Imagination was working at full speed with tremendous damage.

This pessimism, while keeping him from falling into the trap of making a movie *against* the current, is a contradictory fluid which, capably and laboriously, Fellini transforms into a creative proposal. *And the Ship Sails On* (1983) expresses an evident nostalgia, since metaphorically the funeral that is being celebrated in the memory of the singer is also that of the (old) cinema, an art that is disappearing or already gone, a traditional author's way of turning images into a narrative, and not viceversa, an artistic philosophy of which Federico Fellini had been one of the great voices.

Black and white film images document, with the typical hum of silent movies, the preparations taking place along Wharf Ten at the port of Naples for the departure of the steamer Gloria N.

Scrutinized by workers and curiosity seekers, the cars of the wealthy passengers arrive. Some captions inform us that the month is July and the year 1914, and the journalist Orlando, let us call him the 'special correspondent', explains that it is a very important funeral ceremony.

The people who are about to board the ship are artistes, opera singers, sopranos, tenors, orchestra conductors, actors, impresarios, friends and devotees of the greatest singer of all times, Edmea Tetua, whose ashes were brought in a magnificent hearse and, under close guard, taken aboard the ship as the band plays and the film gradually changes into color. The ashes are to be thrown to the winds off the island of Erimo, the birthplace of the divine singer, for which the ship will head in obedience to her last wishes.

The color comes in as the sailor with the urn goes up the gangplank. Then everyone, including the engine room firemen, sings in salutation as the ship weighs anchor.

In the ship's large kitchens, they prepare meals that the busy waiters serve in the elegant dining room crowded with very staid people (shot in slow motion). There is the soprano Ildebranda Cuffari, rival and now heiress of La Tetua, with her family; the Italian tenor Sebastiano Lepori, with his Argentine wife/manager and his theatrical agent; the homosexual comedian, Ricotin, who is on board only for the publicity value; and the Englishman, Sir Reginald of Covent Garden, with his wife Violet, hyper-attentive to the glances of the men.

The journalist Orlando clumsily allows the introduction of the other passengers, including the superintendents of both Milan's La Scala and the Rome Opera, the latter accompanied by his secretary cum medium; the orchestra conductor and ex-child prodigy, Von Rupert, with his mother; the tenor Aureliano Fuciletto; the two superintendents of the Vienna Opera; the columnist Brenda Hilton; the basso profundo Ziloev; the mezzo soprano Valegnani, with the likeable Ines Ruffo Saltini; the Rubetti brothers, both singing teachers; the orchestra conductor David Fitzmayer; the famous dancer Svetlana.

*As **The Ship Sails On** its symbolic voyage, a love-sick rhinoceros requires constant sprinkling with water*

Passengers and crew of the Gloria N. form the lively, grotesque characters of the fantasy news report about the funeral rites of the famous operatic singer, Edmea Tetua

A seagull, its hunger awakened by espying Fuciletto's meal through the window, enters, creating confusion among the elegant guests before flying off and allowing the Grand Duke of Herzog to make his entrance for lunch at a separate table with his retinue – his sister Lherimia, the blind princess who sees the color of musical notes; the Prime Minister, defence minister and police chief.

Meanwhile, life on board consists of resting on deck, visiting the various parts of the ship, a very much applauded concert by the Rubettis, who make the glasses in the kitchen vibrate, the red sunsets (like the sea, so false as to appear real), the observation of the stars, the apparition of a young, spiritual maiden, and both personal and professional occasions in memory of the late Edmea. The evening concludes with the eager, excited, jealously erotic game between Sir Reginald and Violet, while the Count of Bassano, custodian of the memory of La Tetua, remains all alone and watches the projection of a movie about the divine singer, but is interrupted in his private – and perhaps not disinterested – adoration by the passing by of the Princess Lherimia.

The following day, the group tour of the boiler room turns into a singing competition for the benefit of the hot firemen who, down there among the boilers, greatly appreciate the short, intense performance, which naturally ends with a high note from Cuffari.

The second outstanding event of the day is the visit to the hold, where there is a stinking rhinoceros in a cage. The love-sick animal will not eat or move, which worries its Turkish caretaker not a little.

Orlando is in the gymnasium, briefly interviewing the Grand Duke. After some problems of procedure and translation, he succeeds in learning from the Grand Duke that, in the future of the world, there are

three "boom-boom-booms" suspended metaphorically on the edge of a mountain, or tragically in the mouth of a volcano.

During the long hours of navigation, they watch porpoises and take souvenir pictures of them. The young, fat Grand Duke is unable to resist the fascination of the camera, while the Prime Minister surreptitiously courts the princess, and Ziloev manages to hypnotize a hen using his voice. All of this is recorded by the ever-present, but discreet, movie camera, which has been at work since the start of the voyage, even taking shots of the funeral urn deposited in the captain's cabin.

Amidst singing practise and walks on deck, the rhinoceros problem is resolved. Its strong stink is eliminated with a shower.

Still tracing the memories of Edmea Tetua, it becomes clear that the legendary secret of her greatness did not only depend upon her lungs, diaphragm and vocal chords, but on an energy-catalyzing phenomenon that the soprano obtained following the spirals of an imaginary sea-snail's shell, which enabled her voice to rise effortlessly. In order to evoke her spirit, a seance is held in the library: a book falling on a picture of the Gioconda gives the answer to the question of what her favorite opera was. The medium materializes La Tetua wrapped in a white shawl. This evocation, in reality, is the fruit of the excessively romantic Count of Bassano dressed in the clothes of the august departed.

The following morning, the passengers discover that something new has occurred. During the night, a group of Serbs was taken on board because, as the captain explains, as a result of the assassination of the Austrian arch-duke visiting Sarajevo, Austria has declared war on Serbia, and the terrified population has attempted to escape by sea and reach Italy.

Amidst problems of cohabitation and the sense of humanity, between the hunger of the refugees and the exquisite dinner of the passengers – the unsufferable Violet will serve food to those people – and after the complaints of the Grand Duke's ministers, who fear for his safety, the situation is resolved by music and singing. Initiated by the gypsies, who begin to dance around the fire, the action, little by little, begins to involve the musicians also, in a collective and liberating choreography. In the meantime, Princess Lherimia calms the Prime Minister, who is secretly plotting against the Grand Duke, by telling him of a good dream she had, and by sealing their meeting with an intense lover's kiss.

At dawn, everyone is awakened by the menacing appearance of an Austro-Hungarian warship demanding the surrender of the Serbs. The news that the Grand Duke is on board momentarily resolves the problem, and allows the Italian ship to continue on its way.

Off the coast of Erimo, the solemn, elegant funeral ceremony takes place on deck. The wind disperses the ashes of the world's greatest singer, while a gramophone broadcasts her voice, greatly affecting all present.

Once the rites are over, the princess orders the police chief to arrest the Prime Minister for treason, while the warship crosses their bows and awaits the handing over of the Serbs.

The next episode and the ending are dedicated to the story told by Orlando who, exchanging his black ceremonial dress for a bathing suit, cap and life jacket, alternates the 'anything but east' reconstruction of events with the Chorus of the Lombards (and other things) sung by those passengers who have remained on deck. The Grand Duke and the Serbs board the lifeboats (together with the ethereal maiden in love with love, who has been smitten by the young refugee Mirko). The young Serb launches a home-made bomb at the side of the warship, which ends up in the cannon compartment, and provokes an historical catastrophe. It is not easy for the journalist to accurately report what happened: the bomb could have been a pretext for firing at the Gloria N. and thus provoke an international incident with its repercussions; the fact remains that the ship is bombarded and begins to take water, as the participants at the funeral save themselves in the lifeboats, singing in chorus with the firemen. The images of the short film about Edmea Tetua and the epilogue of the singing precede the explosion of the warship, which lists to one side.

In the strong wind that has blown up, the cameraman continues turning his crank for filming the closing scenes before the set at Cinecittà is revealed, with a great platform swaying on a false sea at the center of the sound stage. All around are large floodlights, movie cameras, technicians, photographers and members of the crew busy with the filming.

The images have reverted to a slightly sepia tinted black and white, showing Orlando at the oars of a lifeboat as he gives final instructions: many have managed to save themselves, and he has brought the rhinoceros on board which, he says, will supply excellent milk.

Zoom and close in, with the same hum as at the beginning, freeze the image of the little boat in the distance with the sparkling of the plastic sea until the final fade out.

At a certain point in the voyage of the Gloria N., the journalist Orlando puts away his professional guise for a moment and, as the ship sails on, perhaps in order to

Beautiful, romantic Dorotea (Sara Jane Varley) lingers on the bridge with the gregarious journalist Orlando (Freddie Jones), who is constantly on the look out for interesting gossip about the radiant celebrities on board

Dorotea's smile highlights her innocence, in sharp contrast to the feigned respectability of the other passengers

determine the route, seems to take on the role of Fellini himself. It is night, all the characters have been presented, the reasons for the voyage amply explained, the context as well defined as that of the silent film era brought to mind by the very elegant costumes of the artistes. Somehow, the impasse is the same one that tormented Guido in *Eight and a Half.* I have nothing to say, but I want to say it all the same, confessed the anguished director. Now, with *And the Ship Sails On,* Fellini puts similar words into the mouth of the guide Orlando: "These are some notes I have been jotting down… for a diary of mine. I write, I narrate. But just what is it that I want to narrate? A sea voyage, the voyage of life? That is not something one writes about, one simply does it and that's enough. Its banal, is it? It has already been said! And better… But everything has already been said! And done!" Even the style in which Fellini – who supposedly has nothing to say – continues to brilliantly portray that hypothetical nothing, is the same, even if more nostalgic.

The structure of the movie is, in fact, a ritual regret made possible by the lack of the authentic, the absence of something true and genuine (the great late singer) that manifests itself as a voyage/pretext of self-referential homage, in which the author intends to "look with a certain irony on the dangers of hyper-information." Impersonated by the journalist Orlando, a correspondent of the Ruggero Orlando type (a well-known television journalist typical in his gestures and style of communication), he turns up in Fellini's vision of show business in the early Eighties, a messenger of nostalgic feelings for what is past and which, like nostalgia, "reaches us in the form of information."

Ildebranda Cuffari (Barbara Jefford) is an old rival of the lovely Edmea, whose ashes will be scattered off the coast of Erimo Island

A few examples of the many different types of people on board Fellini's fantasy ship: Serb refugees and nymphomaniac noblewomen (Norma West)

Perhaps Fellini's ship is sailing somewhere, but the goal is neither that of the tunnel in *City of Women*, where nostalgia is still overcome by memory, nor the initiatory circuit illuminated by the lights and shadows of the Eighteenth Century in *Casanova*. The covered space where the personages, models, narrative solutions, perfume of an epoch and of cinema falsification is much more the hall of *Orchestra Rehearsal* which, bearing the past of defunct illustrious personages, is changed into an up-to-date place in accordance with the cinema's eye for the manias of the travellers.

The division of the roles into sailors, firemen, waiters, artistes, singers, actors, intellectuals, and then the prince and the Serbs, corresponds to the places of the various instruments in the orchestra, among which little groups are formed that confide and collaborate amongst themselves, different from and indifferent to the others when not outright hostile. And, if in the affairs of the rebellious musicians, irony is midway between caricature and degraded professional comportment, *And the Ship Sails On* produces some frescos of ambience: the beginning on the wharf, the passengers' pastimes, the high notes in the machine room, Schubert's *Moment Musicale* played on water glasses, the hypnotized hen, the unhealthy, feigned jealousy of the baronet, the pre-finale and the finale.

What in *Orchestra Rehearsal* was a constant motif, always disquietingly the same, is entrusted here to a 'nonchalant' discourse on music: "A solution that may even appear sacrilegious, blasphemous and will no doubt make lovers of opera howl. I had a new collaborator, maestro Gianfranco Plenizio, who followed me confidently, and sometimes guided me, in this dare-devil musical adventure which aroused my enthusiasm. Once again, I was priveleged to have the collaboration of the poet Andrea Zanzotto, who had fun – at least I hope so – substituting verses of his own for the words written by Piave or the other librettists of Verdi or Rossini." And this ironic little game, while setting the cadences for the phases of the film, relieves the growing gloominess of the preceding orchestra rehearsal. At the beginning we have "*Seguiamo sui flutti/di gioe e di lutti/la rotta più ardita/la nave che va…*" and, immediately afterwards, Čajkovskij *Nutcracker Suite*, a triumphal march for the entrance of the Grand Duke of Herzog, and finally the ersatz Italian melodrama of the passengers and sailors against the Austrians and in favor of the shipwrecked Serbs: "No, no, no. We will not surrender them…"

The heavy wrecking ball which caused the revolution to stop also reappears under the guise of the Austro-Hungarian warship, with which it shares the same metallic molecules and gray color, the menacing presence and the immobile perilousness which will bring about the same consequences. The former sets its seal on contemporary chaos, and the latter brings to account a polished world of uniforms, hats, lacework, strings of pearls and Nineteenth Century *bel canto*, photographed in July 1914 with the eruption of World War I. But when the war comes, the true reality, that is, Fellini has already finished the voyage, or rather he rushes to end it, closing the vastness of the expanse of water in the frame. He evidences once again the irony to which he had entrusted the construction of his great mirror of the false at the beginning of the voyage, a falsity projected in the smallest details with

The ineffable head waiter (Ugo Frangareggi) standing next to the effeminate, extremely odd comedian, Ricotin (Jonathan Cecil)

The refined Italian opera singer, Lepori (Fred Williams) communicates the theatricality of this world with a simple gesture

total dedication to the movie and its sublime cinema artifice. "How marvelous! It looks painted!", says a singer, looking at the false sunset in the false sea that is even more beautiful than the one in *Amarcord*.

And where, in the pre-finale of *Orchestra Rehearsal*, the ball swung heavily after the rhythmic and fallacious movement of the metronome, now the regular rolling that had visually accompanied the entire voyage is shown in its spectacular fictiousness. And never before as in this picture does Fellini's *where* become the movie itself, form and content of its journey/tale. The revealed set increases the fascination of the scenography, the furnishings, the rich costumes, and emphasizes that, in Studio 5 too, they can

produce effects not necessarily super-technological and special to recreate atmospheres more real than reality, and close the narrative circle by taking the lifelike aspect of the movies back to its original centrality. Fellini seems to be hiding behind the silent film beginning and ending, behind the crane, the strong floodlights, the dollies and the movie camera – in short, behind the cinema, a ship that, by now, is proceeding on its own without a real helm.

When Fellini moved within the non-places of his imagination, he was quite at home among the displacements, illusions, magical gusts of visionary realism, like a disorderly person within his own disorder. Now that he seeks guarantees from the producers, signs of public and private interest that no longer disassociate the director's image (difficult) from that of the personage (a world emblem), he is no longer at ease, and is content to remain inside the unstable shell of his creative obsession in order to continue *making* films as he likes to – as a craftsman, methodical, very orderly, detailed. "It is good enough to hammer in a nail, put a wall into a set, set a wig on an actress's head, check that some makeup is right. In a word, move around busily in the midst of a troupe of people who look at me with the respect due to age and also perhaps a little embarrassed and amused. Shoot, adjust a drape, a chair, a light, arrange an actress's shawl, try to make an actor understand how to raise an eyebrow. That's it – to live not only the characters but the objects too. Yes, this continuous flowing is a power that identifies with volumes, people, things, lights. It is mercurial, unseizeable. […] I hand over my body and my mind or talent to a kind of current. A current that solicits me, obliges me, forces me rapidly to embody many things, people, thoughts, attitudes. And it is in that moment, when I do not exist because I am in so many places and occupied with so many details, that I believe my strength lies."

Being part of that group of movie people for whom the parentheses between one movie and the next – real life – are only cruel interruptions, Fellini cannot help but react with the cynic's faith in the things he does. He is an artist who will not renounce a craftsman-like reinvention of the dream in 35mm, and who wants to continue liberating himself from the many encumbrances of the intellect and the unconscious – for example, the symbolism of the false rhinoceros. But he also knows that he cannot continue wearing himself out for long in the attempt to reconcile the idea with money, reason with passion, and so he is already thinking of getting past the (maternal) marine metaphors in order to follow the destiny of his next movie, the last grateful and devoted homage to his Giulietta, the faithful companion of the terrifying voyages on the treacherous seas of private life and the world of Italian movies and television.

The Silence of the Clown

Ginger and Fred • Intervista • The Voice of the Moon

Ginger and Fred (1985), impious portrait of television and bittersweet reflection on ageing, is a movie that combines the two souls of Fellini's kaleidoscopic world. Ginger is the female character who changes from the soubrette of *Variety Lights* into Cabiria by way of the clown woman – Giulietta/Gelsomina. Fred, played by Mastroianni, is Fellini's usual alter ego. This disarmed and disarming critique of television and its fearful rules could have no other interpreters than these two beloved actors towards whom Fellini feels a great debt: Giulietta Masina, whose tragi-comic clowning nourished his imagination for some thirty years, and Marcello, opposite side of the genetic coin, who could certainly not be excluded from this quaking, masculine *Amarcord* of the movies, and the stage of a past epoch.

Like the ship without a goal of the preceding film, whose passengers are shadows that sing and live out a (melo)drama because they know they belong to an epoch that has been superceded by the movies, Fred too is a relic, a symbol of the survival of his derelict art, like that of Ginger's, another bit of flotsam from the Fourties. Around them moves the cold empire of the television screen, with its indifferent soldiers, in an exotic and motley aquarium to bring an emblematic affair to life. Certainly not the one imagined by Dino De Laurentiis who, before deciding not to produce the movie, complained: "I have read the script. Why the hell waste time with this crap? Give me Mandrake! Don't you realize that you are Mandrake?" On the contrary, this is a blistering photograph of Italian commercial television.

To the music of 'The Continental', and a photo of Ginger and Fred in evening clothes amidst the Manhattan skyscrapers, the opening titles are shown, followed by the arrival of a train. Amelia Bonetti disembarks, an elegant little lady who, during the Forties, appeared on stage under the name of Ginger. The Christmas season is in full swing when she arrives at the Termini station in Rome. The station is crowded with people of all kinds, as always, and plastered with advertisements showing an enormous Lombardoni type *zamponi*, a Christmas sausage. Amelia has been invited to appear on the television show *Ed ecco a voi* where, after many, many years, she will dance again with Fred, real name Pippo Botticella, in an imitation of the famous couple Fred Astaire and Ginger Rogers. This number was their war horse in many a seedy vaudeville show during the Forties. A forbidding lady hostess accompanies the bus, whose passengers include two Lucio Dalla imitators, a Neapolitan transsexual and an old, senile admiral covered in medals.

They arrive at the Palace Hotel, a large establishment on the outskirts, located near a tremendously tall television tower sprouting parabolic antennas, repeaters and a conspicuous revolving something or other. No-one among the rude, distracted hotel employees pays any attention to Ginger, who nevertheless finds her room, where the television is on and is alternating pieces of a movie with advertisements. Almost sorry that she came, and in order to free herself of the attentions of a Clark Gable double, friend of an unsuccessful imitator of Proust, Ginger goes down to the restaurant with the transvestite. She dances a little by herself as she waits outside for Fred, who is late in arriving. She is interrupted and frightened by a group of rowdy motorcyclists, and then by a strange young man who asks her for a handout. When the bus finally arrives with a group of performing dwarfs, the 24 Los Liliput, Pippo is not on it. Back in her room, Ginger cannot get to sleep because the man in the next room snores. She will discover that the man is Fred, grown very old and run down who, in turn, does not recognize his ex-partner.

In the morning, the pair practice their dance routine with the piano. They are interrupted by the confusion and excitement of the television people, who are rounding up the 'bestiary' for an animal program featuring a cow with eighteen teats.

On the bus to the television studios, a slightly crazed mother and son play a recording of voices from the next world, and Fred becomes sad, thinking that the things of this world sometimes regard him in a strange way, as if saying goodbye…

When they arrive at their destination, they cannot get off the bus immediately, because the boss Catanzaro is arriving under police escort to recite a poem on television, and particularly because Fred sets off the metal detector alarm with the horseshoe he carries in his pocket.

There is still a little time before they have to go into make up and put on their costumes. Stopping at the big coffee bar, they get to see, both live and on the monitor, the other 'stars' invited to the special Christmas show: the engineer Armando Bitossi, who has beaten all records for his time spent sequestered with kidnappers, and for the size of his ransom; a girl from Romagna who abandoned her family because she fell in love with an extra-terrestrial; Fra Gerolamo di

*Giulietta Masina and Marcello Mastroianni in **Ginger** and **Fred**, a poignant symbol of a time which has now passed*

Trivento who levitates when he prays; a priest who has (not) renounced the habit for love; the plastic surgeon who will remove the bandages from his most recent patient on live television; the writer being urged to promote his latest book; the clan that has fun with Fred's extemporised sexual proverbs.

There are unknown journalists from small papers. The merry Barbara from Teleflash interviews the dance team, and Fred gives a short lesson in tap dancing, which was invented as a morse code by black plantation slaves.

On the way to their dressing room in the company of Toto, a friend and colleague from the good old days, Ginger and Fred encounter people in costumes, dancers, strong men, vampires, gypsies, monkey trainers, a political figure who is on hunger strike against hunting, real hoboes, the decorated hero, etc, etc. Finding a quiet spot, they put on their evening clothes and Ginger is possibly thinking of what Toto said about the depression her ex-partner suffered right after the separation, a crisis that had even seen him admitted into a mental hospital. The two partners exchange a few youthful memories, try out a couple of dance steps, and express ideas about the television system and the 'philosophy' that conditions an audience of sheep.

In the makeup room, among the crowd of those almost ready to go into the recording room, Ginger is overcome by a panic attack to the point of wanting to leave, but Lombardoni, president of the television network and, in his youth, a Fred Astaire imitator, leads her into a few dance steps and thus reassures her.

The guest stars are now in the long, dark corridor waiting to enter the studio. They wait, some enter sighing, there are long silences and the subdued advice of the bored television personnel. Ginger refuses to state her age in order to coax the sympathy of the audience, and Fred laments the lack of another glass of cognac against the cold (or his fear?). Finally, one enters 'on tip-toe, as in church', and among the

technicians, the suffused lights, nervousness, the extorted applause, exaggerated trumpet blasts and the highly illuminated curtains of the scenography, the conductor Aurelio makes his entrance (Franco Fabrizi, dubbed with the extraordinary vocal inflections of Alberto Lionello) who opens the program.

While waiting to go on, walking in the boxes marked on the floor, there is an alternating of advertising with the guests on stage and off: the ostensible ex-priest kisses his woman, Lombardoni sausages with corn meal mush combine with the man who studied black magic along the Amazon and makes women pregnant with a look; an enormous plate of macaroni with ragout and parmesan cheese unites with an olive oil to try on a girl's bottom; the two crazed people who hear messages from the dead are mixed up with the story of the transsexual, and the inventor of edible women's underpants gives a quick demonstration of the article.

The show continues with the flying monk, the fasting politician, those who hear voices, the Spanish number of the dancing dwarfs, right up until the turn of Ginger and Fred (a little agitated), and the decorated admiral is helped into their waiting place by the nurse and attendants.

Before our couple goes on, there is still the moment of the heroic housewife who had studied voice: she cries into the television camera, confessing to have taken money, cursed money, to go for a whole month without watching television, a dreadful experience that she would never repeat again. The advertisement for Lombardini roast pig is used as a curtain for presenting Ginger and Fred's number. Just as they are about to begin, there is a black out. The whole studio is in darkness and nobody must move. The two dancers sit down on the floor and then, frightened, decide to profit by the situation to make their escape. The lowing of the multi-teated cow is the signal. Fred is finally going to get out of his system the urge to make a spiteful gesture towards the television audience of sheep, but at the very moment he bends his arm the lights go back on. The couple dance as well as they can manage – tripping up a few times, breathless, some cramps, and Fred briefly falling down – accompanied by the immortal tunes of American musical comedy.

At the Termini station by night, Ginger is about to return to her daughter and grandchildren at Santa Margherita Ligure where, as a widow, she has been running a very small business. Fred, who sells encyclopedias, after having sold his little dance school and separating from his wife, has decided to stay in Rome for a few days as Toto's guest, perhaps under the impossible illusion of becoming a television host like the one for *Ecco a voi*.

Two girls and a young smiling black boy who is a dancer ask them for their autographs. Ginger 'loans' Fred, who is obviously in a bad way, the 800,000 liras that she got for her performance. They say goodbye with melancholy affection. Ginger gets on the train, the lights of the enormous sausage go out, Fred is already in the bar and, on the last television screen, the final image is the Lombardini advertisement.

All one needs are the few notes Fellini jotted down in 1985 for 'Corriere della Sera' to give a synthesis of television in the Eighties and supply a motivation for the making of *Ginger and Fred*: "Note: The abnormal, the monstrous, the delirious, the alienated, the exceptional things that television suggests as the most obvious, normal, familiar and usual daily fare; and, on the contrary, the banal, the insignificant, the informal, the collective, the undifferentiated presented with the solemnity, the blare of trumpets, floodlights, choreography and rhythms of a sacred ceremony." And added to this description of television, which gigantically enlarges and emphasizes

Neon lights and dancers contrast with the absurd television show "Ed ecco a voi", where true stories, twins and tales of former bravery follow one after the other

everything, there is the effect of annulling, flattening, drowning in syrup that every person, event and story ends up experiencing when placed inside the magic box.

A paradox, for by definition the magic box is something Fellini ought to like, who, as from a magician's top hat and the illusionists of his cinema, could extract from it some real surprises, true reality, true cinema. Instead, on the contrary, he cannot stand it, because it is the arrogant proposal of something impossible, an unbearable resonating chamber habituated to the ugly and the bad taste created by and for the box itself.

A memory box with all the conditions for being profoundly Fellini-like. Television preserves everything, can file away any image in the world at any hour of the day or night in an uninterrupted flow which, however, due precisely to the accumulation, no longer allows any one image to establish itself on the eye, the brain or the heart of a director like Fellini. Lord of images, but of imagined ones, not those of the void. And the television void is located at the center of its screen, collected in the hypnotizing funnel of repetition and the passive conditioning of the viewer – or better, of the consumer.

One might object that, in a certain sense, Fellini is spitting into the plate he is eating from when he criticizes television, seeing that he is making his movies with television money. Not only that, he criticizes the interruptions of movies by television commercials. If, in the former case, one should remember that, at first, the language of television had aroused his interest for its immediacy, in the latter he became a champion, along with many other Italian directors, of a crusade under the slogan: "One does not

Master of ceremonies, Aurelio (Franco Fabrizi), high priest of the paradoxical show, introduces a guest

In spite of the years and the difficulties he has endured, Pippo Botticella, Fred on stage (Mastroianni), has not lost any of his protesting spirit, and definitely does not share the ideas of his calm dance partner, Amelia Bonetti, alias Ginger (Masina)

interrupt a story, one does not postpone an emotion." In fact, there is no contradiction, because to shoot television commercials, as Fellini did, does not mean that these must be used to interrupt movies; otherwise, he says, the commercials could also be inserted into masses, processions, and so on. To shoot commercials (aside from the money involved) meant for Fellini trying to tell a story in a few seconds, a fine challenge for a cineast, an interesting test of one's professional ability – as were his commercials for Campari, Barilla and the Banca di Roma. In both the last and the first, trains played a determining role. Furthermore, the commercial for the aperitif brings to the director's mind memories of his very first trip to Rome, when he saw images of landscapes rolling past the window as on a movie screen, which he transformed into a purely dream dimension for the bank's advertisement.

In *Ginger and Fred* then, television is presented as a container of nothing, a self-reflecting mirror in which people, bodies and faces begin to take on the structure of the products they advertize: they become things made of synthetic materials, rubber, nothing human, and they turn into aliens, even those who, attracted by the money or the eye of the television camera that bestows visibility on them (identity, that is to say), go and exhibit themselves and their

Whilst waiting to go on, the elderly couple, now pitifully made up, have some very real doubts

Private television advertising about Lombardoni salami hammers home its message with frequent, vulgar shots of giant products

vulgarity or else, conversely, the simplicity of normal people from the provinces or the city, or intellectual swaggering. But the gelid atmosphere of television language or of the camera have mercilessly consumed them, chewed and digested them through its cathode tube and its production and commercial apparatus. Florenzo, the assistant director of *Ed ecco a voi,* would never have been found on a Fellini set, where there was room for all except someone as careless as he, who looked at the actors' photos in the dark. He too looks no-one in the eye, but wastes time following the screen test of an improbable Queen Elizabeth double from Apulia, nor does he hesitate to interrupt Ginger lamenting that she and Fred are not married: "It works better that way. The audience likes love stories: companions in art and in life."

deep humanity. It is enough to look at the types who file past in the movie to get an idea, to have a prophetic Fellini type of vision, which in the middle of the last decade foretold the matrix of the degeneration of these last years, entirely insensitive to the message which is also contained in *Intervista* and *The Voice of the Moon*, and to the decisive, unheeded appeal for a return to Humanism.

For instance, the girl who fetches Ginger from the train station could easily be of the type who met Fellini at the Termini station in 1939, as represented in *Fellini's Roma*. She has the same origins, the same 'I don't give a damn' attitude and stupid indolence: she meets the 'old people', carrying a placard bearing the name of the television program, refuses to look you in the eye, chews gum, knows nothing, and her first words are "an hour late". Then she sits next to the uncaring driver on the bus and hands over the guest stars to the equally indifferent personnel at the hotel, who are absorbed in watching a soccer match on television.

Therefore, an immediate connection is established between the types inhabiting the Barafonda Theater, and the typical Fellini madhouse, somewhere between a brothel and a circus, with the only difference being that the television context portrays the breakdown that has made these same faces go to rot, these bodies, these farcical masks. Let it be clear that they are still the same ones already seen in *Fellini: a Director's Notebook* and *The Clowns*, for example, or in the *Satyricon,* expressing the same natural

One of the last memorable pictures of Giulietta Masina in one of Fellini's movies. She is once again wearing the cape which she has kept since La Strada

The characters of the two protagonists are revealed even when it is dark in the studio: Ginger is as suspicious and fearful as Fred is mocking and impertinent, ready to jeer at everything in classic Fellinian manner

Their sad farewell at Termini station is evidence of the realization that they will never get back together again

For his part, the other assistant director handles the various doubles of Lucio Dalla, Brigitte Bardot, Marlene Dietrich, Reagan, Kojak/Telly Savalas, Woody Allen, Celentano, as if they were chess pieces, packages with faces. The only thing that counts for him is creating enjoyment for an audience of "25 million viewers" sitting in front of their televison sets. During the visit of the president Lombardoni to the makeup room, the two assistants vie for his attention. Florenzo gets the number of teats on the Borgosole cow wrong, and includes Fred among the authentic hoboes of the real-life episode "On the Margins of the Metropolis". The other one goes after him, and corrects him in order to make a good impression, insistently talking about the great amount of work required to prepare the program, which worked out perfectly, particularly due to the presence of the hunger striker.

Then, when the two of them lead the army of guests down the corridor, and Ginger refuses to reveal her age, the second assistant has already taken over. First he hushes everyone up and then, suppressing a yawn owing to the boredom of the routine, he tells her: "It's for your own good, very much so, because the audience gets sentimental, emotional, and applauds when it sees a woman of your age tap dancing. Believe me, its for your own good." Then he ushers the herd of guests into the studio in religious silence.

But no-one knows the tastes of the audience, or can touch all the right chords as well as the master of ceremonies, the model of a television show host, including those terrifying quiz shows. Aurelio, in his sky-blue jacket, subsumes all characteristics, negative and sordidly arrogant, and, as a true star, will stop at nothing in order to sacrifice a victim to the audience, managing to change his tone – often with total nonchalance – and to be completely convincing. He is insincere, screaming and cursing everyone in the wings, only to display a smile as captivating as it is false in front of the television camera. Fellini entrusts the part to the ex-

Tired but never beaten, Mastroianni, dressed in the "patched" clothes of Pippo/Fred, says farewell to a show business world with which he is unfamiliar

'vitellone', Franco Fabrizi, a youthful elderly man with the face you love to slap, a bit of the dirty guy, a bit of the amoral sneak, the type suited to showing the void of the two faces of the show/container, but above all to put into relief what binds them: advertising.

The exact purpose of this is to underscore the diabolically ambiguous, ruthless and idiotic nature of what Ginger calls "their system" – the selling of merchandise and individuals. A grinding machine for the feelings and private lives of people (attracted by the money and the flattery of appearing in public) and their artistic lives (when 'those there' include within their number that wreck of old admiral Aulenti, and all of it flavored with Lombardoni products).

Apropos of the way Fellini's movies portray falsities, it was said that the director expressed a *cruauté*, an expressive piece of nastiness of the metacinematographic type, which is to say, something for the sake of creating the movie. But during the mid Eighties, his maliciousness underwent a change, his falsity became nastier, demonstrating his great wrath against a television that did not respect the work of cinema directors. Then Fellini's indignation with the god of advertising is turned into the obtuse cruelty of the master of ceremonies, like that of television itself and programs such as *Ed ecco a voi*: unaware, harmful, overbearing, exaggerated and a tremendous mirror of that ignorant void created by summing up true, eccentric, human stories, that obliterates sincere fictions and makes an entirely false non-stop show out of them. A gigantic idol with feet of clay, thinks Fellini, and as that jinxed dissenter Pippo Botticella, called Fred, would say. But a powerful giant in which reality and life go to rot within the life and reality of that great television stomach, which has nothing to do with the *'grande mouna'* of *Casanova*. In the latter, there was the obscure origin of all things, while here there is only the superficial spectacle of money and pain.

Ginger and Fred is far from being able to put paid to the business. A movie is not enough to get something heavy off your chest. It's a tough cookie – the television eye is not the cineast Fellini's (false) television camera filming its pseudo-investigations, which are still cinema, which is to say picture stories that begin, develop and end – exactly the opposite of what happens in eternal, unstoppable television, where even the doubles and the grotesque characters lose their magic to become empty shells, a consumers' showcase. Something much stronger is needed to get rid of the rhinoceros with antennas than to do away with the romantic myth of the musical and the old-style charm of the evergreen Fred Astaire and Ginger Rogers. More film is needed for Federico Fellini's second morality play against the vulgar incursions on Hertz waves of a society that is rapidly being widely vulgarised. The end of *Intervista* is required.

Mario Verdone, in his Fellini monograph, introduces *Intervista* (1987), calling it "*a special* for television, more improvised than meditated." And yet the meta-cinematographic, dovetailing structure of this movie turns it into a reflection, not so much of itself – as it is already a real working diary like *A Director's Notebook* – as of the movies in general, of Cinecittà and the director's work. A reflection of the language and the apparatus of film making, because, the way cinephiles like it, cinema through the mirror exhibits, in narrative form, its production techniques. A reflection of Cinecittà as a historic site of the Italian image factory, to which Fellini added lustre, and from which he was given affection, technical/professional competence, and which also served as an *excuse* and a *redoubt* in which to take shelter, as in the safety of the maternal womb, and to falsify his artistic horizons. And finally, it is a reflection of his entire output, because in seeing *Intervista* one cannot avoid returning at least to *Eight and a Half, Amarcord, The Clowns, Fellini's Roma, A Director's Notebook,* assuming that one does not want to include *Il Viaggio di G. Mastorna.*

Once more the reticent, mysterious Fellini, secretive about his projects even with his collaborators, does not hesitate to put himself narcisistically and modestly before and behind a camera to endorse an intimate kind of movie about the love for, and the art of, movies. A little nostalgic, summarizing, melancholy, and sometimes amusing, he

Above: *Pippo and Amelia doing a Fred Astaire and Ginger Rogers number: a sedate, elegant, nostalgic moment before the rude interruption of the usual Lombardoni advertising*

Right: *Aurelio's pandering insincerity fails to spoil the brief enjoyment of having met up again, and of their successful performance*

Pietro Notarianni, production director of Intervista *and other films by Fellini, pictured here with the director, who has persuaded him to play the part of the Fascist party leader on the train bound for Cinecittà*

another tall one, extremely high, carries the powerful lights on it. There is the director of photography, Tonino Delli Colli, and Fellini is already at work with his assistants, when a small Japanese television crew, anticipating the interview scheduled for the next day, stalks the director in order to shoot everything and interview him.

The beginning of this "little movie", as Fellini calls it, is a dream that gives the sensation of flying as if the camera hovered over the sound stage, filming it from above. In the midst of megaphone problems, smoke and artificial lights, Fellini describes his dream: feeling about with his hands in deep darkness, he manages to take off and to recognize various tents and buildings.

It is morning, and, acting upon his advice, the Japanese are interviewing Fellini's trusted assistant director, Maurizio Mein, who shows them the tools of the trade, the whistle and the megaphone, explaining their roles. Meanwhile, Federico arrives, and the Japanese rush over to him while 'il Chiodo', a Roman and a nuisance who wants to work with the maestro, begins to stick his nose into everything, and will continue to do so for the rest of the movie. A young man has to be chosen for the part of Karl in *America*, based on the Kafka novel, and, among the tree-lined avenues, some commercials are being shot. Fellini confesses to the woman interviewer that the existence of Cinecittà is a comfort. Then he redirects her to Nadia, "the priestess of Cinecittà...", which is to say the custodian of the film library. Nadia is very busy: she has to go to the coffee bar, a place which is haunted by the Cinecittà workers, and pick chicory in the surrounding fields where the old remains of sets from *Ben Hur, Quo Vadis* and the naval battle of *Cleopatra* still fight against the ravages of time, and are now surrounded with horrid high-rise buildings.

Asked to recall his first visit to Cinecittà, Fellini points out the "Casa del passagero", a hotel for travelers, in front of which there was once the stop for the blue tram, the only transport into Rome. Mein's and the photographer's hunt for locations having produced nothing, they are now reconstructing the façade at the site of the old tram depot. When 'Peter' – Pietro Notarianni – the production director, arrives, Fellini explains that his relationship with the producers is one of "total mutual mistrust."

The old tram that ran in Via Tuscolana is being refurbished in a shed. Two exact replicas are being prepared for the filming, while the actor, Sergio Rubini, will play the part of Fellini as a reporter, who when very young went to interview Katia, the Neapolitan diva of 'Cinemagazzino'.

All made up with a pimple on his nose to make him feel even more ill at ease with the actress, Rubini/Fellini, together with the other passengers, board the tram. As there is no-one to play the part of the Fascist official, Fellini makes Notarianni portray the role, complete with uniform, medals and black boots.

At last the false tram with the crew, technicians, wardrobe and makeup personnel leave for Cinecittà, with the little processional from *The White Sheik* playing in the background. The music changes (ironically?) to the score from *Il Bidone* as soon as the Fascist officer says: "I am proud of this line. Ah yes, we built it in record time." The tram runs from Porta San Giovanni towards Via Appia Nuova, while a landscape of ancient ruins rolls past the tram windows. Young Fellini smiles at a girl with movie ambitions, and the Fascist officer recalls with pride that he too, and *he* most of all, had begun as a newspaper

confirms that travelling for him means stepping outside of Cinecittà.

In the middle of the night, some cars and a truck pass through the gates of Cinecittà. They begin preparing for the shooting of a Fellini movie. They mount the camera on a large crane, while

161

The journalist (Sergio Rubini) alias young Fellini, among the extras

Rubini and Antonella Ponziani, playing the part of an aspiring actress in a screen test

Youth, the past and La Dolce Vita *magically return on an improvised screen in Anita Ekberg's villa*

man. Two stops have to be made when a festive group of peasants offers fruit and grapes to the passengers, and when a donkey, like every morning, stops on the tram tracks.

The trip is resumed. A monk goes butterfly hunting, green meadows and waterfalls roll by until they arrive at a very narrow stretch of railway track and, as testimony to their approaching their destination and the truly adventurous nature of the trip to Cinecittà at the beginning of the Forties, as in Westerns, Indians appear and, soon after, elephants. They have arrived.

Once past the gate and the grumbling keeper, Rubini/Fellini finds himself among the avenues where he can see for the first time – and furthermore placing himself directly in the middle of the camera's sight line – the movies at work: the director, nervous and snappy; all kinds of tricks, scenes repeated, howling, confusion, elephants, actors, extras, technicians and workers running to and fro... Suddenly everything stops with the arrival of the beloved lunch boxes. The lead actor takes one and goes with the seamstress into the diva's trailer, after having watched the delicious scene in which a Roman house painter has a laugh three times over at the expense of his fellow worker, Cesare, while they are painting a big blue sky on the backdrop.

Meanwhile, Fellini is at Cinecittà, where he must choose the cast for *America* (a project never completed), and his alter ego interviews as best he can the beautiful and ignorant diva as she drinks a fresh egg and undergoes a lengthy makeup session. Once she has put on the Indian costume for her role, Katia presents herself on the exotic set where, amidst veils, fake elephants, Hindu temples, dancers and maharajas, smoke and small lakes, she discovers the extremely angry director: the shooting is not going well, and the actress is three hours late.

The Milanese producer also has his troubles, and ends up quarreling with the director who, in a total rage over the painted elephants, wants to abandon the movie.

Of course, it is a movie within a movie. Fellini interrupts Marra, the angry director, while the Japanese television crew, always alert and discrete, films everything as it happens. The journalist introduces the part dedicated to the casting.

The scene changes to the Rome subway. At the Cinecittà stop, the assistant Mein gets off with the photographer and eight Junoesque women he has picked up around town. Meanwhile, in the architects' studio, Mein and Gino Millozza are notified that a bomb has been hidden in Sound Stage 2. The police evacuate the premises, but find nothing.

The difficult job of choosing the faces for the movie resumes. An endless line of strange-looking characters file past Mein. In another room, Fellini, Delli Colli, Danilo Donati, Notarianni and Millozza study the photos and discuss economic problems, when a sudden gust of wind blows open the window and Marcello Mastroianni appears in a Mandrake costume for a commercial. Fellini, together with Rubini and Marcello, the Japanese crew and others, go and visit Anita Ekberg in her villa guarded by many dogs.

It is the ideal occasion for a plunge into memories of the good old *La Dolce Vita* days. With a tap of his magic wand, Marcello/Mandrake materializes the ball scene, and the Fontana di Trevi scene, on an improvised screen.

On Sound Stage 4, they are organizing the scenes and costumes for the rushes of *America*. Mein is explaining to the Japanese what it means to shoot rushes, and why one face is preferred to another, what

it means to be photogenic, and the secret of being photogenic. Fellini is at work: for the role of Karl, he tests the boys more than once, after which it is the turn of the curvaceous women and other scenes. Then the moment arrives to go outside for the exterior shots amidst the floodlights that mark the muddy road traversed by Karl in a carriage when taking his friend to the casino under a gray sky threatening rain.

The custodian of the film library complains, because there is no part for her as she had been promised, and then it starts raining hard. The floodlights are turned off because the water caused them to explode, and everyone takes shelter in the truck or under a providential plastic tent. Evening arrives, coffee is served, but the storm does not pass and, as the notes of 'Stormy Weather' are heard, lightening lights up the metal towers and the tall buildings in the background, until there is nothing more to be said or done.

At dawn, everyone is still under the cellophane – awaiting the imminent attack. A ball of fire starts the action. The Indians in war dress brandish television antennas instead of lances. Their chief gives the signal and the horses descend rapidly from the mountain on the plastic redoubt where the movie people defend themselves with rifle shots. Everyone halts at Fellini's command. He says that it is good, the scene is finished, and with it the picture. It is almost Christmas, everyone exchanges good wishes, bottles and Christmas cakes. The movie people get into their cars and leave a few at a time. The set is taken down, Mein greets Millozza, while the meadow and structures are left deserted and silent.

Against the backdrop of the images of the illuminated, empty studio, Fellini's voice says that the movie is truly finished – and without that shred of hope, that ray of sunshine that one of his old producers would have so much desired. The director now tries to furnish it. The silhouette of a camera, the ray of light from a spot aimed at the ground and a clap of the clapperboards – will they be enough?

The Fellini of *Eight and a Half* had to use his alter ego, Guido Anselmi, to live out his anguish at not being able to make a movie. In *Intervista*, it is the young Rubini – does that name have any connection with the journalist Marcello in *La Dolce Vita*? – who is Fellini's companion, now the victor over his old fears. At this point, if a secondary character has not been cast, one can take the production director to fill the role, if television is pushing to occupy the place of the movies with interviews and special reports on the set, or if commercials have arrived in the avenues of the city of cinema, Fellini does not have to limit himself to satires like *Ginger and Fred*, but, regaining a director's courage, he will have to make a 'director's resistance'. And, in fact, he resists in his own

Lunch break inside the stomach of the papier-mâché elephant, transformed into images and narrative when making movies within movies

personal way: politely accepting the Japanese crew, presenting Nadia, the priestess of movie history, as a character in *Fellini's Roma*, approaches life with detachment and considers the coffee-bar break to be work on a par with the bitter salad, the chicory that "like Roman people, seems to reject you while actually being very fond of you." In short, he invents a film to tell once again about his arrival at Cinecittà, to tell about how *he* made, and makes, movies, about how he casts faces, and how he behaves during the screen tests. And if it is not enough to resist as a director, he adds the extra force of Mastroianni, of Ekberg, of *La Dolce Vita*.

And then, if television still wants to invade cinema territory, understood literally as the film set, as happens in the finale, well there is the paradoxical clash between the antenna-bearing Indians and the movie people, which is expressed from the inside out, and is made into a single thing: not the commercials, not television, but the movies, which can only be ended by his conclusive command "stop!".

In portraying that cinema zoo of Fellini's, and his personal way of conceiving and making movies, there is room in *Intervista* for the parody of stars and sets, dedications to humble people, the Cinecittà workers with

their worn-out or clever faces, with their witty remarks and comic scenes like the incredible one of the two house painters. And perhaps it is precisely this latter event that is emblematic of how, for Fellini, the magic of the cinema is truly something that comes not only from invented memory, images from the unconscious, or the help of sorcerers, mediums and psychics, whom he compulsively frequented for a long time – Rol of Turin, for one – but also comes from the incomprehensible fusion of exaggeration with poetry, of high fantasy working on a trivial pretext – a fusion condensed in the phrase "A Ce'… Vattela a pia 'n der culo" (Hey, Cesare… go fuck yourself), spoken in front of that placid backdrop of a blue sky veined with a few light white clouds. It is a comforting image for the viewer after the catastrophic vision of *Orchestra Rehearsal*, of *And the Ship Sails On,* and with which Fellini, warding off his own and other people's intellectual temptations, imagining the freedom of wind and flight, already seems to be setting the scene of homage at his own death, which will occur on October 31, 1993 (when the world of cinema will gather in that exact location of Sound Stage 5, under that very same afflicting sky). At the same time, it inclines the viewer to

Just like a family photograph, Fellini poses with his young alter ego (Rubini, third from the left) on the set of the Neopolitan diva (Paola Liguori)

hear his final ethical and poetic cinematic utterance, *The Voice of the Moon.*

In fact, there is often a lot of sky during the journey of the hero Ivo and his companion Gonnella. In fact, one might say that the nourishment and stimuli that they continually receive into their 'lunatic' heads all come from a super-worldly, ethereal, suspended dimension. *The poem of the lunatics*, the strange, psychically almost "miniaturized" actions of the protagonists, beg Fellini to turn them into a movie, but as often happens to him before shooting, he repents, finds a myriad of dissuading reasons, and would like to back out, like Guido in *Eight and a Half*. It is almost as if, having already lived for a while with the eccentric characters of the story and created mental images of their colors, it is no longer so indispensable to give them body, form or meaning. This uncertainty of the repentant author, and of the protagonists in their confused peregrinations between the episodes in which they are both actors and spectators, fills the ambience of this movie, another nomadic voyage – the last – into the interior of man.

During one summer night, Ivo Salvini roams the countryside, illuminated by the full moon, because he hears the voices that call to him from the wells. The area appears deserted and silent, but in reality not everyone is asleep. For example, there is someone who, for a price, will allow his friends to spy on his aunt from his window while she undresses to the languid rhythm of the song 'Abat-jour'. Ivo joins the group and, as he does not have the money to pay, he recounts the story of the mythical birth of the Milky Way from the breast of Juno.

The cemetery caretaker arrives to make his nightly rounds and Ivo, keeping him company, confesses that, in spite of all his efforts, he cannot resist the night-time call from the wells. Guided by a watchman's light, the pair reach the gravestones, where Gertrude brings dinner to her husband, a crazed oboe player who has decided to live in a pavilion which is under construction.

There is also a newspaper man out hunting for news, and the oboe player tells him how and why he came to leave his house. When he practised, every time he played the sequence of four notes 'g', 'a', 'c', 'e', – the medieval 'diabolus' – the furniture moved of its own accord, the Great Eater laid waste to the refrigerator, and then three people, the neighborhood commission, suddenly appeared, seated in the living room. Not even burying the oboe in the garden had silenced the instrument, and the oboe player continued to hear its sound even when he was a long way from its burial place. Meanwhile, as the two guards imitate the raven's song in order to lure it down, as they do every evening, Ivo finds the headstone of his grandfather, Giacinto. He asks out loud where the dead go, and how is it that no-one ever gets any news, even though there must surely be a passage somewhere, a hole through which one can communicate with them. Raising his eyes, Ivo sees a hole in the ceiling, the raven arrives, and it starts to rain. The musician lays down to sleep, his wife complains that she has lost the heel of her shoe and goes away promising to bring mashed potatoes tomorrow for dinner.

Ivo takes shelter under a large tree from the pouring rain and the thunder, and remembers "God travelling in a coach" (with the face of the bearded man in the oboe player's living room), as his grandmother used to say when he was a child. And the woman immediately appears, calling him as she runs "Pinocchino! Pinocchino!" and hiding him under her big black skirt.

Then, in front of the fire before going to bed, Ivo/Pinnochino tells his amused grandmother how, in the morning, he changed into a poplar tree, complete with roots, branches and leaves. Hiding under the bed, he watches the fire spark, and asks himself, as he did about the dead and music when it stops playing, where the sparks go.

This is all due to the effect of the full moon, and that very night,

when the thunderstorm knocks out the electricity, Ivo goes to visit Aldina, whom he likes very much because she is blonde and light like the moon. With his sister's help, he stands there in ecstasy, watching his sleeping love by candle-light, but she wakes up and throws a shoe at him in a rage, causing him to run away.

By now it is two o'clock in the morning and, in the empty square of the village in the Po valley where the whole story takes place, only the ex-police chief Gonnella – another eccentric type – is walking around. Affected by a persecution complex, he imagines 'the others' plotting against him everywhere. The doctor follows him in his car, and leaves him at the door to his home. Upon entering his apartment, Gonnella suspiciously continues to closely watch every 'move' of the enemy, who could even be cunningly hiding among the elderly, innocuous neighbors on the same floor.

The next morning in the square, the travelling textile and clothes vendor arrives, together with a group of Japanese who take non-stop photos. Ivo, seated at the foot of the monument, seems to shake himself, and snaps a picture with the Polaroid of one of the tourists, because he wants to see the silver-plated rings surrounding the bells that are ringing. But he is disappointed when they are not to be seen in the snapshot.

The prefect Gonnella (Paolo Villaggio) and sincere Ivo Salvini (Roberto Benigni) play the lead roles in The Voice of the Moon, *the last of Fellini's masterpieces*

The Maestro with Benigni and Nadia Ottaviani, who plays the part of the beautiful, moonstruck Aldina, Ivo's unattainable love

Meanwhile, things begin to liven up. A truck unloads several white statues of the Madonna, the lawyer expounds his theory, which the parish priest contests: the little madonnas are a 'race' that always appear to be numerous to the ignorant but never to educated people.

A brief discussion with the ex-psychiatrist is interrupted because Ivo's attention is attracted by Giuanin Micheluzzi, the sewer worker who, in an incomprehensible dialect, laments about the moon (as his brother explains).

In the meantime, after separating from her husband Nestor, another likeable 'lunatic', Marisa, has almost finished moving out. The young woman leaves in tears with her new lover, a horsemeat butcher and the owner of a big motorcycle. Ivo recognizes Nestor on the balcony and goes up to join him.

The apartment is now empty except for the washing machine, of which Nestor is very fond. It looks out over the roof-tops, a place of great attraction for the timid little fellow, who immediately takes Ivo out there and recounts his recollections of how he met, married and was left by Marisa. A manicurist and pert little girl from Romagna, she becomes infatuated with his tapered fingers and causes him to become infatuated with her. After the lunch and the honeymoon, she forces him into intense, exhausting and unsustainable sexual activity which he manages, fantastically, to bring to an end by flying off. Pointing out the solar plexus that one must open like a flower in order to take off, Ivo recalls Aldina's silver shoe.

He immediately decides to return it, and travels along the roof-tops to reach the girl's house. But the people below think he is in danger, and Micheluzzi's crane, driven by one of the brothers, Terenzio, intervenes in order to bring him down to the ground. They inform him that, with a specially adapted machine, they intend to capture the moon when it is low over the houses, so that it cannot influence people any more.

It is evening, and among the bright shop windows and crowded streets downtown, Ivo meets Gonnella, with whom, after a few initial misunderstandings, he establishes a compassionate relationship. The confusion in their heads is transferred to the organization of the Gnoccata (dumpling festival), and the election of Miss Farina 1989, filmed in its entirety by the new television broadcaster.

The whole village joins in the festivities. There is a great *gnocchi* (dumpling) feast, and a ball in honor of the new queen, Aldina. At first, Ivo is trapped beneath the stage. Then, jealous of Gonnella's doctor who is dancing, he tips a big plate of spaghetti with sauce over the man's head.

The ex-police chief, for his part, follows at a distance, because he does not want to give 'them' the satisfaction of taking part in the festivities, and he makes his devoted, understanding wife keep at a distance too.

Under the brilliant flashes of the fireworks that end the *festa*, Ivo and Gonnella find themselves at the edge of the countryside. Ivo remembers that he began to hear the voices coming from the room adjacent to the room he had as a baby, while Gonnella insists that he is of noble blood just like his wife.

But as Gonnella continues to talk, Ivo has already moved on. He finds himself again coming out of a well into which he fell because of the voices that buzz around in his head like a swarm of bees. Ivo discourses a little on 'normal' people and 'others' like himself, and concludes with the idea that he was born in order to learn to understand these insistent voices and what happens to him.

Aldina's sister (Syusy Blady) sneaks Ivo into his beloved's bedroom so that he can watch her sleep

Helped by the farm workers and the Micheluzzi brothers, who assure him that the moon's days are numbered, Ivo is named as Gonnella's lieutenant. Gonnella shows him the boundaries of his imaginary police district, and the pair wander among the meadows bathed by the moonlight and a limpid, thinly veiled sky.

During their wanderings among the workers harvesting the fruit at night, and the Micheluzzis' machine for disinfesting the fields, the two lunatics find themselves in a place that Gonnella calls 'their den', whereas it is in reality a discotheque full of lights, loud music and many, many young people. The two night-time ramblers hug and wish each other good luck because they may never meet again, which will in fact be the case. Inside the club, Ivo looks for the princess missing a silver shoe, and finally realizes that all the women are only one woman – the Aldina of his desires.

The police chief tries to occupy the DJ's platform, in order to chase away the 'enemy' – the destroyer of good music – but he is pushed back under the big tent. Here he dances romantic Strauss waltzes with his wife, a delicate and very brief moment usurped by the hammering rhythm of modern music.

In his old room on the floor above, there is a picture of the poet Giacomo Leopardi and a great wooden Pinocchio. Ivo cannot resist opening the door of the empty room: seated at the window, Nestor tells him that they have finally done it. All of the people, even those

from nearby villages, are going to the square to see the moon captured by the Micheluzzi brothers and tied down with strong ropes.

In fact, many, many people are converging on the square, where there is the television broadcaster, various civil and religious authorities, and all the important people seated on the platform. The two enormous television screens at the sides show live pictures of the Micheluzzi brothers, who comment on the operation, with Giuanin in tears because he misses the presence of the moon up in the sky.

Finally, the heavenly body appears on screen, while the authorities, each in his own way, comment upon the extraordinary event. The politician says everything possible has been done very rationally, while the monsignor maintains that there is nothing to reveal because, for the Church, everything has already been revealed, the parish priest is saddled with the question of paradise, about which nothing has been said for so long, and he does not know how to reassure his parishioners of its real existence.

A man from amongst the crowd first wants clear answers about the meaning of life, and the purpose of man on this earth, and then, when he does not get them, he shoots at the moon, hitting it right in the center.

Panic breaks out, and amidst the general rushing around, the illustrious guests are hastily spirited away, including the police chief Gonnella, who has illicitly taken refuge in the politician's car and is roughly forced out.

The lights and the screens are turned off, the square is silent and deserted. Only the wild rock fan, Rossella, remains dancing with her new boyfriend, Angelino. Somewhere around, there is also Ivo.

Pinocchietto looks up at the full moon, which is telling him how lucky he is not to understand the voices that are ceaselessly resounding in his head. Ivo Salvini does not need to understand, he must only stay still and listen to those voices. The moon, which speaks with a Neapolitan accent, must interrupt its discourse, however, because it is time to say, as they do on television, the magic word: "Com-mer-cials!".

To the accompaniment of frogs and crickets, with the moon lighting the background, Ivo approaches one of his speaking wells for the last time. He has understood that, in order to understand anything about himself and the world , the only thing he and others can do is to keep silent. He approaches the well and looks down into it, while the final image is dissolved into blackness.

For Fellini, two positive, appropriate conditions are, as is well known, shipwreck and confusion, which he alchemically reproduces in *The Voice of the Moon* (1990), according to an ideal sequence. In the grip of an inner tempest, Fellini found something to hold onto in the movies themselves, a desert island as a gift that he could populate with an entire imaginary universe. The 'shipwrecked' Fellini, Robinson Crusoe of the cinema, fills the barren sound stages of Cinecittà like Robinson's island, with the sensitivity of Pascoli's *fanciullino*, a sort of eternal child to whom destiny concedes flights of fantasy, leaps from earth to heaven. By dint of that privileged talent, he can even manage to see heaven and earth united, and so looks from one side to the other, breathing and filming "that atmosphere surrounding things" which he attributed to Rossellini.

And the air, in this movie, is an element which still has some useful information: the director's desire to do something different, but also a return to childhood memories of the countryside around Gambettola – reinvented, on the threshold of his seventieth year, by filtering it through Ermanno Cavazzoni's atmospheric novel – going back to Mario Tobino's *Le Libere Donne di Magliano* and his psychiatric experiences, and then the immersion, in an irrational key, of those fears of the worst, hinted at in *And the Ship Sails On*. A fear of catastrophe which was not put to rest in the image of the rhinoceros, a symbol more of the circus than of the fish monstrosity of *La Dolce Vita*.

Between heaven and earth, or between Fellini's water and air, the 'rhinoceros' is the theme of madness, the symbol of the 'lunatics', the sublime new clowns of contemporary reality in the circus of life. A circus that it would be superfluous to identify once again with the cinema, a presentiment perceived by way of *confusion*. This is the extraordinary excuse and trick behind which Fellini has always hidden himself because, while everyone on the set is agitatedly running around, 'activated' by the *deus ex machina*, the demiurge itself can direct and *think*.

Portrayed by Roberto Benigni and Paolo Villaggio – two different faces of the clown – both of whom have permitted Fellini to run the "course that began in darkness and continued in darkness." Villaggio, having abandoned the grotesque mask of the character Fantozzi, puts on the fearful one of old age and paranoia of the ex-police chief Gonnella, who roams about at night, staring at people and reality with the confidence of the functionary, of one who, the director recalls, "personifies order, authority, hierarchy, ceremony, officialdom and for whom the discotheque and its raging music are the empire of evil, perdition, today's collective madness."

Benigni plays the part of Ivo Salvini, or "Leopocchio" as he calls him, a personage half way between the 'moon poet' Giacomo Leopardi and Collodi's puppet Pinocchio – a mask of mosaics, "a Shakespearian will-o'-the-wisp, a kind of Puck from *The Midsummer Night's Dream,* or a kind of Thyler, De Coster's character. He is a figure out of Grimm's fairy tales, a Pierrot." Salvini has the astonishment, the ingenuousness and the unpredictability of the imagination, and the joy of living that the director and magic piper

A scene from the festival which highlights the interesting variety of faces that the director has picked out

The nightclub, in the ex-prefect Gonnella's opinion, is a true representation of hell

wanted to instil in his mad encounters with the other characters, which are much closer to the daydreams, the disordered visions of mental creativity, the fugitive reinterpretations of memory, than they are to real life happenings.

"Imagination is a place where the rain pours in," says Calvino in the fourth of his *Lezioni americane* ("Visibility"), repeating a verse from Dante's *Purgatory* – "*Poi piovve dentro a l'alta fantasia*" ('Then the rain poured right into the imagination'), and *The Voice of the Moon* is completely flooded with fantasy images, starting with the spell of the wells, and of the voices that continue to call to Ivo in order to impart important things to him which he will never

understand, distracted as he is by what happens to him and by the surrounding air – the same air that, for the poet Tonino Guerra, is "that light substance that circles around your head and becomes brighter when you laugh." Bright as the moon. The men who pay to watch the 'home-made' strip-tease from the window, the tales of Nestor and of the oboe player who sleeps at the cemetery, the roaring moon voices that fill Ivo's head, incessantly confounding him but also making him think of lovers' things. And Ivo himself, enamoured of life and the spectacle it offers, is also in love with Aldina/Miss Farina, whom he likes because she is candid and lunar – his own personal moon. But the girl knows nothing of the silver moon and how it can strike the hearts of men; she is not like the Micheluzzi brothers who can neutralize it, capture it, and show it on television.

This final well without beginning or end does not resemble in the least the hole that Ivo is seeking for the dead, the sparks, or the music, which provide communication between heaven and earth. It is only a container for distant, strident voices, such as the authorities who were interviewed, a screen-moon that, like Miss Farina, acts like Miss Commercial. Fellini opportunely uses this in order to ironically portray this phenomenon, as he had already done in *Ginger and Fred* and *Intervista*. (He had thought of having Silvio Berlusconi, the owner of Italy's most important commercial televison network, launch this appeal to consumerism).

If, however, moon sickness makes men suffer and go mad, increases Ivo's confusion and Gonnella's insanity, the babel of television at least has this unwitting merit of putting the

Paolo Villaggio portrays the acute suffering of his character in his encounters with a world that he does not understand, almost like the relationship between the modern world of movies with its special effects and Federico Fellini

moon back in the sky where it can give one last piece of advice, not about what to buy this time, but to rectify all those who, like Ivo, want to understand: "You must not understand. Woe to those who understand. You must only listen." And, in fact, the serious buffoon Leopocchio, sublimating the innate incomprehensibility of television, bends over the well to *listen* with new ears to the words which, until now, he had only grasped in fragments, an incomprehensible babel. Not, however, before leaving the spectator with a snapshot of the contemporary crisis, that which the director prescribes for us all to do at the end of the millennium in order to battle against the Great Disorientation: "I believe that if there were a bit of silence, if everyone were to be a little silent, we might understand something."

And, in the face of these words, one cannot help feeling a shiver run down one's back when thinking about the characters in his films, at the broken dialogues, at the digressions from the tales, at the unforeseeable coherence or incoherence bestowed by the editing, at the modest reticence, at what has not been said as a part of the fantastic 'whole', to be shown or intimated, disappear, falsify, dance with the camera, laugh and be moved in the mind as well as the gut.

By inventing everything, including memory, Fellini has truly left deep traces in contemporary world cinema and if, as he said, his was the assassin syndrome, that is to say to hide and cause every last trace of his past to disappear. In so doing, he has left cinematic art of this century a unique ironic and political testament. And so, a shiver of pleasure.

The same shiver that, as a child, one feels at the circus when the trapeze artists fly without a net under the big top. The Sorcerer never wanted this sort of protection either for himself or his movies, which he always filmed with great determination, talent and freedom. And even in the period between his last movie and his passing away, when he was sanctified and forgotten by the producers, he still found a way to employ his creative imagination: in collaboration with Milo Manara and Vincenzo Mollica, he 'directs' two comic strips, the transformation of old projects into images (*Viaggio a Tulum* by Carlos Castaneda and *Il viaggio di G. Mastorna detto Fernet*).

And then, contrary to the endings of his movies, where the words 'The End' never appear, his moment will arrive with dignity, indomitable creativity and courage – he wanted to tell the story of two clowns after they suffered a stroke. Because Fellini knew and taught us that, within his images, death does not exist, it is only an event of normal reality, always conquered by the power of imagination. In his movies, death is a mask with many aspects. Death for Fellini is the prince of clowns, crying and laughing while staring at the audience.

Filmography

Variety Lights *(Luci del varietà)*
Directors: Alberto Lattuada and Federico Fellini; *From a story by:* Federico Fellini; *Screenplay*: Federico Fellini, Alberto Lattuada, Tullio Pinelli, Ennio Flaiano; *Photography*: Otello Martelli; *Cameraman*: Luciano Trasatti; *Music*: Felice Lattuada; *Sets* and *costumes*: Aldo Buzzi; *Editor*: Mario Bonotti; *Assistant director*: Angelo D'Alessandro; *Cast*: Carla Del Poggio (Liliana 'Lilly' Antonelli), Peppino De Filippo (Checco Dalmonte), Giulietta Masina (Melina Amour), Folco Lulli (Adelmo Conti), Franca Valeri (the Hungarian choreographer), Carlo Romano (Enzo La Rosa, the lawyer), John Kitzmiller (John), Silvio Bagolini (Bruno Antonini, the journalist), Dante May (Remo, the comedian), Alberto Bonucci and Vittorio Caprioli (the duet), Giulio Calì, Mario De Angelis (the conductor), Checco Durante (the theater owner), Joe Fallotta (Bill), Giacomo Furia (Duke), Renato Malavasi (the hotel keeper), Fanny Marchiò (a soubrette), Gina Mascetti (Valeria Del Sole), Vania Orico (Gypsy singer*), Enrico Piergentili (Melina's father), Marco Tulli (the speactator), Alberto Lattuada (man in the theater); *Producers:* Alberto Lattuada and Federico Fellini; *Production director*: Bianca Lattuada; *General organizer:* Mario Ingrami; *Prodution*: Capitolium Film; *Country*: Italy (date of censor's permit: November 18, 1950); *Distribution in Italy*: Fincine; *Duration*: 100'.

The White Sheik *(Lo sceicco bianco)*
Director: Federico Fellini; *From a story by:* Federico Fellini and Tullio Pinelli, based on an idea by Michelangelo Antonioni; *Screenplay*: Federico Fellini, Tullio Pinelli, Ennio Flaiano; *Photography*: Arturo Gallea; *Cameraman*: Antonio Belviso; *Music*: Nino Rota, directed by Fernando Previtali; *Sets*: Raffaello Tolfo; *Editor*: Rolando Benedetti; *Assistont director*: Stefano Ubezio; *Sound*: Armando Grilli, Walfredo Traversari; *Makeup*: Franco Titi; *Production secretary*: Moraldo Rossi; *Still photography*: Osvaldo Civirani; *Cast*: Alberto Sordi (Fernando Rivoli, 'the White Sheik'), Brunella Bovo (Wanda Cavalli), Leopoldo Trieste (Ivan Cavalli), Giulietta Masina (Cabiria), Lilia Landi (Felga), Ernesto Almirante (the director of the 'White Sheik'), Fanny Marchiò (Marilena Vellardi, the newspaper editor), Gina Mascetti (Fernando Rivoli's wife), Giulio Moreschi (the hotel concierge), Ugo Attanasio (Ivan's uncle), Jole Silvani (Cabiria's prostitute friend), Enzo May (the hotel bell-boy), Antonio Acqua (the police officer), Anna Primula, Nino Billi, Armando Libianchi, the comedian Aroldino, Elettra Zago, Giorgio Savioni, Carlo Mazzoni, Rino Leandri, Piero Antonucci, Guglielmo Leoncini; *Producer*: Luigi Rovere; *Production*: P.D.C.-O.F.I.; *Country*: Italy (date of censor's permit: April 7, 1952); *Distribution*: P.D.C.; *Duration*: 86'.

I Vitelloni
Director: Federico Fellini; *From a story by:* Federico Fellini, Ennio Flaiano, Tullio Pinelli, based on an idea by Tullio Pinelli; *Screenplay*: Federico Fellini, Ennio Flaiano; *Photography*: Otello Martelli, Luciano Trasatti, Carlo Carlini; *Cameramen*: Roberto Girardi, Franco Villa; *Music*: Nino Rota, directed by Franco Ferrara; *Sets*: Mario Chiari; *Costumes*: Margherita Marinari Bomarzi; *Editor*: Rolando Benedetti; *Cast*: Franco Interlenghi (Moraldo), Alberto Sordi (Alberto), Franco Fabrizi (Fausto), Leopoldo Trieste (Leopoldo), Riccardo Fellini (Riccardo), Eleonora Ruffo (Sandra, Moraldo's sister), Jean Brochard (Fausto's father), Claude Farell (Alberto's sister), Carlo Romano (Michele, the antiquarian), Lida Baarova (Giulia, Michele's wife), Enrico Viarisio (Moraldo's father), Paola Borboni (Moraldo's mother), Arlette Sauvage (woman in the cinema), Vira Silenti (Leopoldo's date), Maja Nipora (the soubrette), Achille Majeroni (the comedian), Silvio Bagolini (Giudizio), Franca Gandolfi (ballerina), Giovanna Galli, Gondrano Trucchi (the waiter), Guido Martufi, Milvia Chianelli, Gustavo De Nardo, Graziella de Roc; *Production manager*: Luigi Giacosi; *Production supervisor*: Danilo Fallani; *Production secretary*: Ugo Benvenuti; *Production*: Peg Film (Rome), Cité Film (Paris); *Country*: Italy and France (date of censor's permit: September 17, 1953); *Distribution in Italy*: ENIC; *Duration*: 104'.
Leone d'argento at the Venice Film Festival, 1953.
Nastro d'argento, 1954.

Love in the City – Marriage Agency (*L'amore in città – Agenzia matrimoniale*)

Director: Federico Fellini; *From a story by*: Federico Fellini; *Screenplay*: Federico Fellini, Tullio Pinelli; *Photography*: Gianni Di Venanzo; *Music*: Mario Nascimbene; *Sets*: Gianni Polidori; *Set decor*: Giovanni Checchi; *Assistant director*: Luigi Vanzi; *Editor*: Eraldo Da Roma; *Cast*: Antonio Cifariello (the journalist), and non-professional actors; *Producer*: Cesare Zavattini; *Production*: Faro Film; *Country*: Italy (date of censor's permit: November 13, 1953); *Distribution in Italy*: D.C.N.; *Duration*: 32′ (of all six episodes: 104′).

Matrimonial Agency is the fourth of six episodes that make up *Love in the City*. The others are, in order of presentation: *Paid Love (L'amore che si paga)*, directed by Carlo Lizzani; *Paradise Four Hours (Paradiso per quattro ore)*, directed by Dino Risi; *Attempted Suicide (Tentato suicidio)*, directed by Michelangelo Antonioni; *Story of Caterina (Storia di Caterina)*, directed by Francesco Maselli and Cesare Zavattini; *Italian Stare (Gli italiani si voltano)*, directed by Alberto Lattuada.

La Strada

Director: Federico Fellini; *From a story by*: Federico Fellini, Tullio Pinelli; *Screenplay*: Federico Fellini, Tullio Pinelli, Ennio Flaiano; *Dialogue*: Ennio Flaiano; *Artistic collaboration*: Brunello Rondi; *Photography*: Otello Martelli; *Cameraman*: Roberto Girardi; *Music*: Nino Rota, directed by Franco Ferrara; *Sets*: Mario Ravasco; *Costumes*: Margherita Marinari Bomarzi; *Editor*: Leo Catozzo; *Assistant editor*: Lina Caterini; *Sound*: A. Calpini; *Assistant director*: Moraldo Rossi; *Director's assistant*: Paolo Nuzzi; *Makeup*: Eligio Trani; *Continuity*: Narcisio Vicari; *Still photography*: A. Piatti; *Cast*: Giulietta Masina (Gelsomina Di Costanzo), Anthony Quinn (Zampanò), Richard Basehart (il Matto), Aldo Silvani (the circus owner), Marcella Rovere (the widow), Livia Venturini (the nun), Mario Passante (the waiter), Yami Kamadeva, Anna Primula; *Production*: Dino De Laurentiis, Carlo Ponti; *Country*: Italy (date of censor's permit: September 18, 1954); *Duration*: 107′.

Leone d'argento at the Venice Film Festival, 1954.
Nastro d'argento, 1955.
Oscar for best foreign film, 1956.

Il Bidone

Director: Federico Fellini; *Story and Screenplay*: Federico Fellini, Ennio Flaiano, Tullio Pinelli, from an idea by Federico Fellini; *Artistic collaboration*: Brunello Rondi; *Photography*: Otello Martelli; *Cameraman*: Roberto Gerardi; *Assistant cameraman*: Arturo Zavattini; *Music*: Nino Rota, directed by Franco Ferrara; *Sets and Costumes*: Dario Cecchi; *Editor*: Mario Serandrei, Giuseppe Vari; *Sound*: Giovanni Rossi; *Assistant director*: Moraldo Rossi, Narciso Vicario; *Director's assistant*: Dominique Delouche, Paolo Nuzzi;

Makeup: Eligio Trani; *Wigs*: Fiamma Rocchetti; *Continuity*: Nada Delle Piane; *Set decor*: Massimiliano Capriccioli; *Still photography*: G.B. Poletto; *Cast*: Broderick Crawford (Augusto, voice dubbed by Arnoldo Foà), Richard Basehart (Picasso, voice dubbed by Enrico Maria Salerno), Franco Fabrizi (Roberto), Giulietta Masina (Iris), Giacomo Gabrielli ('Baron' Vargas), Alberto De Amicis (Rinaldo), Sue Ellen Blake (Susanna), Lorella De Luca (Patrizia), Mara Werlen (the dancer), Irene Cefaro (Marisa), Riccardo Garrone (Riccardo), Xenia Walderi, Mario Passante (the monsignor's secretary), Paul Grenter, Emilio Manfredi, Lucetta Muratori, Sara Simoni, Maria Zanoli, Ettore Bevilacqua, Ada Colangeli, Amedeo Trilli, Tiziano Cortini, Gino Buzzanca, Barbara Varenna, Rosanna Fabrizi, Yami Kamadeva, Gustavo De Nardo, Gianna Cobelli, Tullio Tomadoni, Grazia Carini, Giuliana Manoni; *Production manager*: Giuseppe Colizzi; *Production supervisor*: Antonio Negri; *Production secretary*: Manolo Bolognini; *Administration secretary*: Ezio Rodi; *Production*: Titanus (Rome), S.G.C. (Paris); *Country*: Italy and France (date of censor's permit: October 4, 1955); *Distribution in Italy*: Titanus; *Duration*: 104′.

The Nights of Cabiria (*Le notti di Cabiria*)

Director: Federico Fellini; *Story and Screenplay*: Federico Fellini, Ennio Flaiano, Tullio Pinelli, from an idea by Federico Fellini; *Additional dialogue*: Pier Paolo Pasolini; *Artistic consultant*: Brunello Rondi; *Photography*: Aldo Tonti; *Music*: Nino Rota, conducted by Franco Ferrara; *Sets and Costumes*: Piero Gherardi; *Editor*: Leo Catozzo; *Assistant editor*: Adriana Olasio; *Sound*: Roy Mangano; *Assistant directors*: Moraldo Rossi, Dominique Delouche; *Press secretary*: Narciso Vicario; *Makeup*: Eligio Trani; *Cast*: Giulietta Masina (Maria Ceccarelli, Cabiria), François Périer (Oscar D'Onofrio), Franca Marzi (Wanda), Dorian Gray (Jessy), Amedeo Nazzari (Alberto Lazzari), Aldo Silvani (the hypnotist), Mario Passante (the cripple), Pina Gualandri (Matilda), Polidor (the monk), Ennio Girolami (Amleto, the 'pimp'), Riccardo Fellini, Giovanna Gattinoni, Christian Tassou, Jean Molier, Maria Luisa Rolando, Amedeo Girard, Loretta Capitoli; *Production*: Dino De Laurentiis (Rome), Les Films Marceau (Paris); *Production manager*: Luigi De Laurentiis; *Country*: Italy and France (date of censor's permit: March 15, 1957); *Distribution in Italy*: Paramount; *Duration*: 110′.

Oscar for best foreign film, 1957.
Grand Prize to Giulietta Masina for best actress at the Cannes Festival, 1957.

La Dolce Vita

Director: Federico Fellini; *From a story by*: Federico Fellini, Tullio Pinelli, Ennio Flaiano, from an idea by Federico Fellini; *Screenplay*: Federico Fellini, Tullio Pinelli, Ennio

Flaiano, with Brunello Rondi; *Photography*: Otello Martelli; *Cameraman*: Arturo Zavattini; *Assistant cameraman*: Ennio Guarnieri; *Music*: Nino Rota, directed by Franco Ferrara; *Singers*: 'I Campanino' and Adriano Celentano; *Sets and costumes*: Piero Gherardi; *Set assistants*: Giorgio Giovannini, Lucia Mirisola, Vito Anzalone; *Editor*: Leo Catozzo; *Editor's assistants*: Adriana and Wanda Olasio; *Assistant director*: Guidarino Guidi, Paolo Nuzzi, Dominique Delouche; *Director's assistants*: Giancarlo Romani, Gianfranco Mingozzi, Lilli Veenman; *Artistic collaboration*: Brunello Rondi; *Sound*: Agostino Moretti; *Continuity*: Isa Mari; *Makeup*: Otello Fava; *Hair*: Renata Magnanti; *Cast*: Marcello Mastroianni (Marcello Rubini), Anouk Aimée (Maddalena), Anita Ekberg (Sylvia), Walter Santesso (Paparazzo), Giulio Paradisi (second photographer), Enzo Cerusico (third photographer), Enzo Doria (fourth photographer), Yvonne Fourneaux (Emma), Magali Noël (Fanny), Alain Cuny (Steiner), Carlo Di May (Totò Scalise, the producer), Annibale Ninchi (Marcello's father), Mino Doro (Nadia's lover), Nadia Gray (Nadia), Jacques Sernas (matinée idol), Laura Betti (Laura, the blonde actress/singer), Riccardo Garrone (Riccardo, master of the house), Lex Barker (Robert), Gio Staiano (effeminate youth), Valeria Ciangottini (Paola), Umberto Orsini (boy who helps Nadia undress), Gianfranco Mingozzi (the young priest), Leonida Repaci, Anna Salvatore, Letizia Spadini, Iris Tree, Margherita Russo, Winnie Vagliani, Desmond O'Grady (guests at the Steiners'), Polidor (clown), Adriano Celentano (rock 'n' roll singer), Cesare Miceli Picardi (irritated man at the nightclub), Donatella Esparmer, Maria Pia Serafini (lady with the irritated man), Adriana Moneta, Anna Maria Salerno (prostitutes), Oscar Ghiglia, Gino Marturano (two pimps), Thomas Torres (hospital journalist), Carlo Mariotti (male nurse), Leonardo Botta (doctor), Francesco Luzi (radio news broadcaster), Francesco Consalvo (producer's assistant), Guglielmo Leoncini (producer's secretary), Alessandro [Sandy] Von Norman (interpreter at the press conference), Tiziano Cortini (newsreel cameraman), Maurizio Guelfi (journalist at the press conference), Gondrano Trucci (waiter at 'Caracalla's'), Archie Savage (black dancer), Alain Dijon (Frankie Stout), Paolo Labia (waiter at Maddalena's house), Giacomo Gabrielli (Maddalena's father), Alfredo Rizzo (television director), Alex Messoyedoff (the miracle priest), Rina Franchetti and Aurelio Nardi (mother and uncle of the fake miracle children), Marianne Leibl (woman with Emma at the miracle), Giovanna and Massimo (the two miracle children), Renée Longarini (Steiner's wife), Nello Meniconi (angry mam on Via Veneto), Massimo Busetti (gossip-monger in Via Veneto), Lilly Granado (Lucy), Gloria Jones (Gloria), Nico Otzak (sophisticated girl in Via Veneto),

Prince Vadim Volkonsky (Prince Mascalchi), Giulio Questi (Don Giulio Mascalchi), Ida Galli (débutante of the year), Mario De Grenet (tired boy with dog), Franco Rossellini (the handsome rider), Maria Marigliano (Massimilla), Loretta Ramaciotti (possessed woman at the séance), Giuseppe Addobbati (doctor), Paolo Fadda (vice-commissioner), Vando Tres (police commissioner), Franco Giacobini (jounalist on the telephone), Giuliana Lojodice (Steiners' maid), Federika André (Steiners' lodger), Giancarlo Romano (carabiniere), Antonio Jaconi, Carlo Musto ('transvestites'), Tino Buzzo (hulking thug), Sandra Lee (Spoleto dancer), Leontine Von Strein (matinée idol's mistress), Leo Coleman (black dancer), Daniela Calvino (Daniela), Christine Denise (woman with chicken); *Producer*: Giuseppe Amato; *Executive producer*: Franco Magli; *Production director*: Manlio M. Moretti, Nello Meniconi; *Production supervisor*: Alessandro Von Norman; *Production secretaries*: Mario Basile, Mario de Biase, Osvaldo de Micheli; *Production*: Riama Film (Roma), Pathé Consortium Cinéma (Paris); *Country*: Italy and France (date of censor's permit: January 21, 1960); *Distribution in Italy*: Cineriz; *Duration*: 178'.
Palme d'ore at the Cannes Festival, 1960.

Boccaccio '70 – The Temptations of Doctor Antonio (Boccaccio '70 – *Le tentazioni del dottor Antonio*)

A joke in four acts, from an idea by Cesare Zavattini.
Act II: *The Temptations of Doctor Antonio* .
Director: Federico Fellini; *From a story by*: Federico Fellini; *Screenplay*: Federico Fellini, Tullio Pinelli, Ennio Flaiano; *in collaboration with*: Brunello Rondi, Goffredo Parise; *Photography* (Technicolor): Otello Martelli; *Cameraman*: Arturo Zavattini; *Music*: Nino Rota; *Sets*: Piero Zuffi; *Editor*: Leo Catozzo; *Cast*: Peppino De Filippo (Dr. Antonio Mazzuolo), Anita Ekberg (woman on the billboard), Antonio Acqua (the head of the moralists), Eleonora Nagy (the child), Donatella Della Nora (Dr. Antonio's sister), Dante May, Giacomo Furia, Alfredo Rizzo, Alberto Sorrentino, Polidor, Silvio Bagolini (some workers), Achille Majeroni, Enrico Ribulsi, Mario Passante, Giulio Paradisi, Gesa Meiken, Gondrano Trucchi, Ciccio Bardi, Monique Berger; *Producer*: Carlo Ponti; *Production*: Concordia Compagnia Cinematografica and Cineriz (Roma), Francinex and Gray Films (Paris); *Country*: Italy and France (date of censor's permit: February 6, 1962); *Duration*: 60'.
The other episodes of the film are: Act I: *Renzo and Luciana (Renzo e Luciana)*, directed by Mario Monicelli; Act III: *The Job (Il lavoro)*, directed by Luchino Visconti; Act IV: *The Raffle (La riffa)*, directed by Vittorio De Sica.

Eight and a Half *(Otto e mezzo)*

Director: Federico Fellini; *From a story by*: Federico Fellini, Ennio Flaiano, from an idea by Federico Fellini; *Screenplay*: Federico Fellini, Tullio Pinelli, Ennio Flaiano, Brunello Rondi; *Artistic collaboration*: Brunello Rondi; *Photography*: Gianni Di Venanzo; *Cameraman*: Pasquale De Santis; *Music*: Nino Rota; *Sets and costumes*: Piero Gherardi; *Assistant set designers*: Luciano Riccieri, Vito Anzalone, Orietta Nasalli Rocca; *Editor*: Leo Catozzo; *Assistant editor*: Adriana Olasio; *Assistant directors*: Guidarino Guidi, Giulio Paradisi, Francesco Aluigi; *Continuity*: Mirella Comacchio; *Makeup*: Otello Fava; *Hairstyles*: Renata Magnanti; *Still photography*: Tazio Secchiaroli; *Cast*: Marcello Mastroianni (Guido Anselmi), Anouk Aimée (Luisa), Sandra Milo (Carla), Claudia Cardinale (Claudia), Rossella Falk (Rossella), Barbara Steele (Gloria, Mezzabotta's mistress), Guido Alberti (Pace, the producer), Madeleine Lebeau (French actress), Jean Rougeul (the intellectual), Caterina Boratto (the lady at the spa), Annibale Ninchi (Guido's father), Giuditta Rissone (Guido's mother), Edra Gale (Saraghina), Mario Conocchia (production manager), Cesarino Miceli Picardi (production supervisor), Tito Masini (the cardinal), Mario Pisu (Mezzabotta), Polidor (a clown), Jacqueline Bonbon (Yvonne, the soubrette), Jan Dallas (Maurice, the telepathic man), Georgia Simmons (Guido's grandmother), Edy Vessel (Edy, fashion model), Annie Gorassini (Pace's girlfriend), Rossella Como (Luisa's girlfriend), Gilda Dahlberg (wife of the American journalist), Olimpia Cavalli (Olimpia), Hazel Rogers (black girl), Bruno Agostini (production secretary), A. Cini (a cardinal), Mario Tedeschi (boarding school director), Elisabetta Catalano (Luisa's sister), Sebastiano De Leandro (a priest), Frazier Rippy (the cardinal's lay secretary), Roberta Valli (a child), Eva Gioia and Dina De Santis (the production supervisor's girls), Roby Nicolosi (a spa doctor), Neil Robinson (French actress's agent), Mino Doro (Claudia's agent), Mario Tarchetti (Claudia's press agent), Eugène Walter (American journalist), Mary Indovino (Maurice's partner), John Stacy (cashier), Mark Herron (Luisa's timid suitor), Francesco Rigamonti, Matilde Calman (other girlfriends of Luisa), Alfredo De Lafeld (cardinal's secgretary), Maria Colomber and Maria Raimondi (Guido's aunts), Nadine Sanders (hostess), Riccardo Guglielmi (Guido as a child), Marco Gemini (Guido as a boarding school student), Giulio Calì; *Producer*: Federico Fellini, Angelo Rizzoli; *Production manager*: Nello Meniconi; *General organization*: Clemente Fracassi, Alessandro Von Norman; *Production supervisor*: Mario Basili; *Production secretary*: Albino Morandin; *Production*: Cineriz (Rome), Francinex (Paris); *Country*: Italy (date of censor's permit: February 6, 1963); *Distribution in Italy*: Cineriz; *Duration*: 114'.

Oscar for best foreign film, 1963.
Grand Prize at the Moscow Festival, 1963.
Nastro d'argento, 1964.

Juliet of the Spirits *(Giulietta degli spiriti)*

Director: Federico Fellini; *From a story by*: Federico Fellini, Tullio Pinelli, from an idea by Federico Fellini; *Screenplay*: Federico Fellini, Tullio Pinelli, Ennio Flaiano; *Collaboration on the screenplay*: Brunello Rondi; *Photography* (Technicolor): Gianni Di Venanzo; *Cameraman*: Pasquale De Santis; *Music*: Nino Rota, directed by Carlo Savina; *Sets and costumes*: Piero Gherardi; *Assistant set designers*: Luciano Ricceri, E. Benazzi Taglietti, Giantito Burchiellaro; *Assistants to costume designer*: Bruna Parmesan, Alda Marussig; *Set decor*: Vito Anzalone; *Assistant set decor*: Franco Cuppini; *Assistant directors*: Francesco Aluigi, Liliana Betti, Rosalba Zavoli; *Sound*: Mario Faraoni, Mario Morici; *Continuity*: Eschilo Tarquini; *Makeup*: Otello Fava, Eligio Trani; *Hairstyles*: Renata Magnanti, Marisa Fraticelli; *Editor*: Ruggero Mastroianni; *Assistant editor*: Adriana Olasio; *Cast*: Giulietta Masina (Giulietta Boldrini), Mario Pisu (Giorgio, her husband), Sandra Milo (Susy, Iris, Fanny), Valentina Cortese (Valentina), Caterina Boratto (Juliet's mother), Lou Gilbert (Juliet's grandfather), Sylva Koscina (Sylva, Juliet's sister), Luisa Della Noce (Adele, Juliet's second sister), José De Villalonga (José, the romantic cavalier), Valeska Gert (Nhishma, the fortune-teller), Silvana Jachino (Dolores), Fred Williams (Arab prince), Milena Vukotic (domestic and the 'Santa'), Genius (Genius), Dany Paris (Susy's desperate friend), Alberto Plebani ('Occhio di lince', the dream detective), Yvonne Casadei (maid at Susy's court), Mario Conocchia (family lawyer), Cesarino Miceli Picardi (friend of Giorgio), Felice Fulchignoni (Dr. Raffaele), Lia Pistis (beach friend), Alba Cancellieri (Juliet as a child), Guido Alberti, Mino Doro; *Producer*: Angelo Rizzoli; *Production directors*: Mario Basili, Alessandro Von Norman; *General organization*: Clemente Fracassi; *Production supervisor*: Walter Benelli; *Production secretary*: Renato Fiè, Ennio Onorati; *Production*: Federiz (Rome), Francoriz (Paris); *Country*: Italy and France (date of censor's permit: September 23, 1965); *Distribution in Italy*: Cineriz; *Duration*: 129'.

The Spirits of the Dead – Toby Dammit *(Tre Passi nel Delirio – Toby Dammit)*

Film in three episodes: *Metzengerstein*, directed by Roger Vadim; *William Wilson*, directed by Louis Malle and *Toby Dammit*.
Director: Federico Fellini; Freely adapted from the story *Never Bet the Devil Your Head* by Edgar Allan Poe; *Screenplay*: Federico Fellini, Bernardino Zapponi; *Photography* (Technicolor-Eastmancolor): Giuseppe Rotunno; *Cameraman*: Giuseppe Maccari; *Music*: Nino Rota; *Song*: "Ruby" by Mitchell Parish

(lyrics) and Heinz Römheld (Music), sung by Ray Charles; *Sets and costumes*: Piero Tosi; *Editor*: Ruggero Mastroianni; *Special effects*: Joseph Natanson; *Set decor*: Carlo Leva; *Assistants to the director*: Eschilo Tarquini, Francesco Aluigi, Liliana Betti; *Assistants to the editor*: Adriana and Wanda Olasio; *Cast*: Terence Stamp (Toby Dammit), Salvo Randone (Father Spagna), Antonia Pietrosi (actress), Polidor (old actor), Anne Tonietti (television commentator), Fabrizio Angeli (first director), Ernesto Colli (second director), Aleardo Ward (first interviewer), Paul Cooper (second interviewer), Marisa Traversi, Rick Boyd, Mimmo Poli (party guests), Marina Yaru (child), Brigitte (the tall girl); *Producers*: Alberto Grimaldi, Raymond Eger; *Production manager*: Tommaso Sagone; *General organization*: Enzo Provenzale; *Production*: PEA (Rome), Les Films Marceau and Cocinor (Paris); *Country*: Italy and France (date of censor's permit: July 24, 1968); *Distribution in Italy*: PEA; *Duration*: 37' (all three episodes: 121').

Fellini: a Director's Notebook (*Bloc-notes di un regista*)

Director: Federico Fellini; *Screenplay*: Federico Fellini, Bernardino Zapponi; *Photography*: Pasquale De Santis; *Music*: Nino Rota; *Editor*: Ruggero Mastroianni; *Assistant directors*: Maurizio Mein, Liliana Betti; *Continuity*: Norma Giacchero; *Assistant editor*: Adriana Olasio; *Dialogue director*: Christopher Cruise; *English dialogue*: Eugène Walter; *Series unit manager*: Joseph Nash; *Cast*: Federico Fellini, Giulietta Masina, Marcello Mastroianni, Caterina Boratto, Marina Boratto, David Maumsell, Prof. Genius, Cesarino, Gasparino, Bernardino Zapponi, Lina Alberti (playing themselves), and non-professional actors; *Producer*: Peter Goldfarb; *General organization*: Lamberto Pippia; *Production*: N.B.C.; *Country*: USA, 1969; *Duration*: 60'.

Fellini's Satyricon (*Fellini-Satyricon*)

Director: Federico Fellini; Freely based on Petronius Arbiter; *Screenplay*: Federico Fellini, Bernardino Zapponi; *Photography* (Technicolor-Panavision): Giuseppe Rotunno; *Cameraman*: Giuseppe Maccari; *Special effectsi*: Joseph Natanson; *Music*: Nino Rota; *Music assistants*: Ilhan Mimaroglu, Tod Docksader, Andrew Rudin; *Ideas for the sets*: Federico Fellini; *Sets*: Danilo Donati, Luigi Scaccianoce; *Costumes and set decor*: Danilo Donati; *Assistant for the sets*: Dante Ferretti, Carlo Agate; *Assistants for the costumes*: Franco Antonelli, Renzo Bronchi, Dafne Cirrocchi; *Consultants for the paintings*: Rino Scordia; *Head of paintings*: Italo Tomassi; *Architect*: Giorgio Giovannini; *Editor*: Ruggero Mastroianni; *Assistant editor*: Adriana Olasio; *Edition*: Enzo Ocone; *Continuity*: Norma Giacchero; *Assistant director*: Maurizio Mein; *Assistants to the director*: Liliana Betti, Lia Consalvo; *Makeup*: Rino Carboni; *Hairstyles*: Luciano Vito; *Latin language consultant*: Luca Canali; *Still photography*:

Mimmo Cattarinich; *Cast*: Martin Potter (Encolpio), Hiram Keller (Ascilto), Max Born (Gitone), Salvo Randone (Eumolpo), Mario Romagnoli (Trimalchio), Magali Noël (Fortunata), Capucine (Trifena), Alain Cuny (Lica), Fanfulla (Vernacchio), Danika La Loggia (Scintilla), Giuseppe Sanvitale (Abinna), Genius (rich ex-slave), Lucia Bosè (suicidal woman), Joseph Wheeler (suicidal man), Hylette Adolphe (slave-girl), Elisa Mainardi (Arianna), Gordon Mitchell (the predator), Tania Lopert (the emperor), Luigi Montefiori (Minotaur), Marcello Di Falco (Proconsel), Donyale Luna (Enotea), Carlo Giordana (ship's capitain), Pasquale Baldassarre (hermaphrodyte), Lina Alberti (the golden idol *[part cut by the editor]*); *Producer*: Alberto Grimaldi; *Production manager*: Roberto Cocco; *General organization*: Enzo Provenzale; *Production supervisors*: Lamberto Pippia, Gilberto Scarpellini, Fernando Rossi; *Production secretary*: Michele Pesce; *Production*: PEA (Rome), Les Productions Artistes Associés (Paris); *Country*: Italy and France (date of censor's permit: September 3, 1969); *Distribution in Italy*: PEA; *Duration*: 138'.

The Clowns (*I clowns*)

Director: Federico Fellini; *Story and screenplay*: Federico Fellini, Bernardino Zapponi; *Photography* (Technicolor): Dario Di Palma; *Cameraman*: Blasco Giurato; *Music*: Nino Rota, directed by Carlo Savina; *Sets and set decor*: Renzo Gronchi; *Costumes*: Danilo Donati; *Editor*: Ruggero Mastroianni; *Assistant editor*: Adriana Olasio; *Assistant director*: Maurizio Mein; *Director's assistant*: Liliana Betti; *Continuity*: Norma Giacchero; *Makeup*: Rino Carboni; *Special effects*: Adriano Pischiutta; *Hairstyles*: Paolo Franceschi; *Mixage*: Alberto Bartolomei; *Cast*: Liana, Rinaldo, Nando Orfei, Franco Migliorini, Anita Ekberg (playing themselves), Billi, Scotti, Fanfulla, Reder, Valentini, Merli, Rizzo, Pistoni, Furia, Sbarra, Carini, Terzo, Vingelli, Fumagalli, Zerbinati, The 4 Colombaioni, The Martana, May, Janigro, Sorrentino, Maunsell, Peverello, Valdemaro, Bevilacqua (the clowns); Maya Morin, Lina Alberti, Alvaro Vitali, Gasparino (the troupe), Alex, Bario, Père Loriot, Ludo, Charlie Rivel, Maïss, Nino (the French clowns), Pierre Etaix, Victor Fratellini, Annie Fratellini, Baptiste, Tristan Rémy (circus historian), Pipo and Rhum, the ex-animal tamer Buglioni, the ex-director of the Hugue Circus; *Producers*: Elio Scardamaglia, Ugo Guerra; *Production manager*: Lamberto Pippia; *Production*: Rai (Radiotelevisione Italiana) and Compagnia Leone Cinematografica (Italy), O.R.T.F. (France), Bavaria Film (R.F.T.); *Country*: Italy and France-R.F.T. (date of censor's permit: October 17, 1970); *Duration*: 93'.

Fellini's Roma (*Roma*)

Director: Federico Fellini; *Story and screenplay*: Federico Fellini, Bernardino Zapponi; *Photography* (Technicolor): Giuseppe

Rotunno; *Cameraman*: Giuseppe Maccari; *Assistant cameramen*: Pietro Servo, Roberto Aristarco, Michele Picciaredda; *Music*: Nino Rota, directed by Carlo Savina; *Ideas for sets*: Federico Fellini; *Sets and costumes*: Danilo Donati; *Assistants for the sets*: Giorgio Giovannini, Ferdinando Giovannoni; *Set decor*: Andrea Fantacci; *Assistants for the costumes*: Romano Massara, Rita Giacchero; *Frescoes and portraits*: Giuliano Geleng, Rinaldo Antonelli; *Editor*: Ruggero Mastroianni; *Assistant to the editor*: Adriana Olasio; *Assistant editor*: Leda Bellini; *Assistant director*: Maurizio Mein; *Assistants to the director*: Paolo Pietrangeli, Tonino Antonucci; *Special effects*: Adriano Pischiutta; *Makeup*: Rino Carboni; *Hairstyles*: Amalia Paoletti; *Continuity*: Norma Giacchero; *Mixage*: Renato Cadueri; *Choreography*: Gino Landi; *Cast*: Peter Gonzales (Fellini at 18), Fiona Florence (Dolores, young prostitute), Marne Maitland (guide to the catacombs), Pia De Doses (Princess), Dante Cleri (a father), Mimmo Poli (a customer), Galliano Sbarra (vaudeville host), Alvaro Vitali (tap-dancer at the Jovinelli Theater), Norma Giacchero (Mastroianni's interviewer), Federico Fellini (himself), Britta Barnes, Renato Giovannoli, Elisa Mainardi, Paule Rout, Paola Natale, Marcelle Ginette Bron, Mario Del Vago, Alfredo Adami, Stefano Mayore, Gudrun Mardou Khiess, Giovanni Serboli, Angela De Leo, Libero Frissi; *Interviews with*: Marcello Mastroianni, Anna Magnani, Gore Vidal, John Francis Lane, Alberto Sordi; *General organization*: Danilo Marciani; *Production manager*: Lamberto Pippia; *Production supervisors*: Alessandro Gori, Fernando Rossi, Alessandro Sarti; *Production*: Ultra Film (Rome) Les Productions Artistes Associés (Paris); *Country*: Italy and France, 1972; *Distribution in Italy*: Italnoleggio; *Duration*: 119'.

Amarcord

Director: Federico Fellini; *Story and screenplay*: Federico Fellini, Tonino Guerra, from an idea by Federico Fellini; *Photography* (Technicolor): Giuseppe Rotunno; *Cameraman*: Giuseppe Maccari; *Assistant cameramen*: Massimo Di Venanzo, Roberto Aristarco; *Music*: Nino Rota, directed by Carlo Savina; *Ideas for sets*: Federico Fellini; *Sets and costumes*: Danilo Donati; *Architect*: Giorgio Giovannini; *Set assistant*: Antonello Massimo Geleng; *Costume assistants*: Mario Ambrosino, Rita Giacchero, Aldo Giuliani; *Editor*: Ruggero Mastroianni; *Assistant editor*: Adriana Olasio; *Sound*: Oscar De Arcangelis; *Continuity*: Norma Giacchero; *Assistant director*: Maurizio Mein; *Assistants to the director*: Liliana Betti, Gerard Morin, Mario Garriba; *Makeup*: Rino Carboni; *Special effects*: Adriano Pischiutta; *Hairstyles*: Amalia Paoletti; *Set decor*: Andrea Fantacci; *Scene painter*: Italo Tomassi; *Cast*: Bruno Zanin (Titta Biondi), Pupella May (Miranda, Titta's mother), Armando Brancia (Aurelio, Titta's father), Stefano Proietti (Oliva, Titta's brother), Giuseppe Ianigro (Titta's grandfather),

Nandino Orfei ('il Pataca', Titta's uncle), Ciccio Ingrassia (Teo, the crazy uncle), Carla Mora (Gina, the housemaid), Magali Noël ('Gradisca', the hairdresser Ninola), Luigi Rossi (the lawyer), Maria Antonietta Beluzzi (the tobacco lady), Josiane Tanzilli (la 'Volpina'), Domenico Pertica (the blind man of Cantarel), Antonino Faà di Bruno (the count of Lovignano), Carmela Eusepi (the count's daughter), Gennaro Ombra (Biscein), Gianfilippo Carcano (Don Balosa), Francesco Maselli (Bongioanni, science teacher), Dina Adorni (Miss De Leonardis, maths teacher), Francesco Vona (Candela), Bruno Lenzi (Gigliozzi), Lino Patruno (Bobo), Armando Villella (Fighetta, professor of Greek), Francesco Magno (the principal 'Zeus'), Gianfranco Marrocco (the young count Poltavo), Fausto Signoretti (the coach driver, Madonna), Donatella Gambini (Aldina Cordini), Fides Stagni (arts teacher), Fredo Pistoni (Colonia), Ferruccio Brembilla (party leader), Mauro Misul (philosophy teacher), Antonio Spaccatini (party secretary), Aristide Caporale (Giudizio), Marcello Di Falco (the prince), Bruno Scagnetti (Ovo), Alvaro Vitali (Naso), Ferdinando De Felice (Ciccio), Mario Silvestri (Italian teacher), Dante Cleri (history teacher), Mario Liberati (owner of the Fulgor cinema), Marina Trovalusci, Fiorella Magalotti (Gradisca's sister), Vincenzo Caldarola (beggar), Mario Milo (photographer), Cesare Martignoni (barber), Mario Jovinelli (another barber), Costantino Serraino (Gigino Penna Bianca), Amerigo Castrichella, Dario Giacomelli (friends of 'Pataca'), Giuseppe Papaleo (dandy), Mario Nebolini (town secretary), Bruno Bartocci (the *carabiniere* Matteo, Gradisca's husband), Clemente Baccherini (owner of the Café Commercio), Torindo Bernardo (priest), Marcello Bonini Olas (gym teacher), Marco Laurentino (mutilated war veteran), Riccardo Satta (broker); *Producer*: Franco Cristaldi; *Production manager*: Lamberto Pippia; *Production supervisors*: Alessandro Gori, Gilberto Scarpellini; *Production secretaries*: Fernando Rossi, Giuseppe Bruno Bossio; *Production*: F.C. Produzioni (Rome), P.E.C.F. (Paris); *Country*: Italy and France (date of censor's permit: December 15, 1973); *Distribution in Italy*: Dear International; *Duration*: 127'.
Oscar for best foreign film, 1974.
Nastro d'argento, 1974.

Fellini's Casanova
(*Il Casanova di Federico Fellini*)
Director: Federico Fellini; *Story*: freely based on *Storie della Mia Vita* by Giacomo Casanova; *Screenplay*: Federico Fellini, Bernardino Zapponi; *Photography* (Technicolor): Giuseppe Rotunno; *Cameraman*: Massimo Di Venanzo; *Assistant cameramen*: Wolfango Soldati, Bruno Garbuglia; *Music*: Nino Rota, directed by Carlo Savina; *Songs*: "La grande Mouna" by Tonino Guerra, "La mantide religiosa" by Antonio Amurri, "Il cacciatore di Würtemberg" by Carl A. Walken, verses in

Venetian dialect by Andrea Zanzotto; *Ideas for sets*: Federico Fellini; *Sets and costumes*: Danilo Donati; *Costume assistants*: Gloria Mussetta, Raimonda Gaetani, Rita Giacchero; *Architects*: Giantito Burchiellaro; Giorgio Giovannini; *Assistant art director*: Antonello Massimo Geleng; *Set decor*: Emilio D'Andria; *Choreographer*: Gino Landi; *Assistant choreographer*: Mirella Aguyaro; *Sound*: Oscar De Arcangelis; *Assistant sound technicians*: Franco and Massimo De Angelis; *Editor*: Ruggero Mastroianni; *Assistant editors*: Adriana and Marcello Olasio, Ugo De Rossi; *Continuity*: Norma Giacchero; *Makeup*: Rino Carboni; *Donald Sutherland's makeup*: Giannetto De Rossi; *Hairstyles*: VItalyna Patacca; *Assistant hairstylists*: Gabriella Borzelli, Paolo Borzelli, Vincenzo Cardella; *Special effects*: Adriano Pischiutta; *Assistant director*: Maurizio Mein, Liliana Betti, Gerard Morin; *Cast*: Donald Sutherland (Giacomo Casanova), Tina Aumont (Henriette), Cicely Browne (Madame d'Urfé), Carmen Scarpitta and Diane Kourys (the Mistresses Charpillon), Clara Algranti (Marcolina), Daniela Gatti (Giselda), Margaret Clementi (Sister Maddalena), Mario Cencelli (Dr. Mœbius, the entomologist), Olimpia Carlisi (Isabella, the entomologist's daughter), Silvana Fusacchia (the entomologist's second daughter), Chesty Morgan (Barberina), Adele Angela Lojodice (Rosalba, the mechanical doll), Sandra Elaine Allen (the giantess), Clarissa Mary Roll (Anna Maria), Alessandra Belloni (the princess), Marika Rivera (Astrodi), Angelica Hansen (the hunchback actress), Marjorie Belle (Countess of Waldenstein), Marie Marquet (Casanova's mother), Daniel Emilfork-Berenstein (Du Bois), Luigi Zerbinati (the father); *Producer*: Alberto Grimaldi; *General organization*: Giorgio Morra; *Production manager*: Lamberto Pippia; *Production assistants*: Alessandro Von Norman, Maria Di Biase; *Production secretaries*: Titti Pesaro, Luciano Bonomi; *Production*: P.A.N.D.A.; *Country*: Italy (date of censor's permit: December 1, 1976); *Distribution in Italy*: Titanus; *Duration*: 170'.

Orchestra Rehearsal *(Prova d'orchestra)*

Director: Federico Fellini; *Story*: Federico Fellini; *Screenplay*: Federico Fellini, Brunello Rondi; *Photography* (Technicolor): Giuseppe Rotunno; *Cameraman*: Gianni Fiore; *Music*: Nino Rota, directed by Carlo Savina; *Musical consultant*: Carlo Savina; *Sets*: Dante Ferretti; *Set decor*: Nazzareno Piana; *Costumes*: Gabriella Pescucci; *Editor*: Ruggero Mastroianni; *Assistant editor*: Adriana Olasio; *Special effects*: Adriano Pischiutta; *Assistant director*: Maurizio Mein; *Assistants to the director*: Christa Reeh, Giovanna Bentivoglio; *Dubbing director*: Carlo Baccarini; *Cast*: Baldwin Baas (conductor), Clara Colosimo (harpist), Elisabeth Labi (pianist), Ronaldo Bonacchi (double bassoon player), Ferdinando Villella (violoncellist), Giovanni Javarone (tuba player), David Mauhsell (first violinist), Francesco Aluigi (second violinist),

Andy Miller (oboe player), Sibyl Mostert (flutist), Franco Mazzieri (trumpet player), Daniele Pagani (trombonist), Luigi Uzzo (violinist), Cesare Martignoni (clarinet player), Umberto Zuanelli (copyist), Filippo Trincia (orchestra manager), Claudio Ciocca (union representative), Angelica Hansen, Heinz Kreuger (violinists), Federico Fellini (the interviewer's voice); *General organization*: Lamberto Pippia; *Rai production representative*: Fabio Storelli; *Production*: Daime Cinematografica SpA and Rai-TV (Rome), Albatros Produktion GmbH (Munich); *Country*: Italy and Germany (date of censor's permit: February 19, 1979); *Distribution in Italy*: Gaumont-Italy; *Duration*: 70'.

City of Women *(La città delle donne)*

Director: Federico Fellini; *Story and screenplay*: Federico Fellini, Bernardino Zapponi, Brunello Rondi; *Photography* (Technicolor): Giuseppe Rotunno; *Cameraman*: Gianni Fiore; *Music*: Luis Bacalov, directed by Gianfranco Plenizio; *Songs*: "Una donna senza uomo è" (words and music: Mary Francolao), "Donna addio" (lyrics: Antonio Amurri); *Ballet*: Mirella Aguiaro; *Consultant to the choreographer*: Leonetta Bentivoglio; *Ideas for sets*: Federico Fellini; *Sets*: Dante Ferretti; *Set assistants*: Claude Chevant; *Architect*: Giorgio Giovannini; *Set decor*: Bruno Casari, Carlo Gervasi; *Set technician*: Italo Tomassi; *Assistant architect*: Nazzareno Piana; *Sculptures*: Giovanni Chianese; *Paintings and frescoes*: Rinaldo and Giuliano Geleng; *Costumes*: Gabriella Pescucci; *Costume assistants*: Maurizio Millenotti; Marcella De Marchis; *Mastroianni's wardrobe*: Piattelli; *Assistant director*: Maurizio Mein; *Assistants to the director*: Giovanni Bentivoglio, Franco Amurri; *2nd unit assistant director*: Jean-Louis Godfroy; *Editor*: Ruggero Mastroianni; *Assistant editors*: Bruno Sarandrea, Roberto Puglisi; *Assistant editor*: Adriana Olasio; *Special effects*: Adriano Pischiutta; *Sound*: Tommaso Quattrini, Pierre Paul Marie Lorrain; *Makeup*: Rino Carboni; *Cast*: Marcello Mastroianni (Snaporaz), Anna Prucnal (Elena, his wife *[dubbed by Valeria Moriconi]*), Bernice Stegers (woman on the train), Ettore Manni (Dr. Sante Katzone), Jole Silvani (the fireman/motorcyclist), Donatella Damiani (Donatella, soubrette), Fiammetta Baralla ('Ollio'), Helene G. Calzarelli, Catherine Carrel, Marcello Di Falco (homosexuals at Katzone's party), Gabriella Giorgelli (the fish seller), Rosaria Tafuri (Sara, second soubrette), Sylvie Wacrenier, Carla Terlizzi (a feminist), Jill and Viviane Lucas (the twins), Mara Ciukleva (old woman), Mimmo Poli (guest at Katzone's party), Nello Pazzafini, Armando Paracino, Umberto Zuanelli, Pietro Fumagalli (the three old magicians), Alessandra Panelli (housewife holding a baby), Helene G. Calzarelli, Catherine Carrel, Silvana Fusacchia, Dominique Labourier, Stephane Emilfork, Sylvie Mayer, Meerberger Nahyr, Sibilla Sedat, Katren Gebelein, Nadia Vasil, Loredana

Solfizi, Fiorella Molinari; *Producer and executive producer*: Franco Rossellini; *General organization*: Lamberto Pippia; *2nd unit production manager*: Philippe Lorain Bernard; *Production*: Opera Film Production (Rome), Gaumont (Paris); *Distribution in Italy*: Gaumont-Italy; *Country*: Italy and France (date of censor's permit: March 27, 1980); *Duration*: 145'.

And the Ship Sails On *(E la nave va)*

Director: Federico Fellini; *Story and screenplay*: Federico Fellini, Tonino Guerra (opera texts by Andrea Zanzotto); *Photography* (Technicolor): Giuseppe Rotunno; *Cameraman*: Gianni Fiore; *Assistant cameramen*: Gian Maria Majorana, Luigi Bernardini; *Music*: Gianfranco Plenizio, directed by the author; *Orchestra and chorus*: Rai (Radiotelevisione Italiana); *Chorus master*: Ines Meisters; *Assistant conductor*: Elvio Monti; *Sets*: Dante Ferretti; *Costumes*: Maurizio Millenotti; *Costume assistant*: Barbara Mastroianni; *Architects*: Nazzareno Piana, Massimo Razzi; *Set decor*: Massimo Tavazzi, Francesca Lo Schiavo; *Choreographer*: Leonetta Bentivoglio; *Paintings and frescoes*: Rinaldo and Giuliano Geleng; *Scene painter*: Italo Tomassi; *Special effects*: Adriano Pischiutta; *Sculptures*: Giovanni Gianese; *Editor*: Ruggero Mastroianni; *Assistant editors*: Adriana Olasio, Leda Bellini, Rosanna Landi; *Assistant director*: Giovanni Arduino; *Assistant to the director*: Andrea De Carlo; *Continuity*: Norma Giacchero; *Dubbing director*: Riccardo Cucciolla; *Mixage*: Fausto Ancillai; *Studios*: Cinecittà; *French troupe*: Catherine Breillat (Screenplay), Therry Nahon (Assistant director), George Dybman (Production manager), Willy Ramau (Production supervisor); *Adaptation of Italian dialogue*: Roberto De Leonardis; *Cast*: Freddie Jones (Orlando), Barbara Jefford (Ildebranda Cuffari), Victor Poletti (Aureliano Fuciletto), Peter Cellier (Sir Reginald Dongby), Elisa Mainardi (Teresa Valegnani), Norma West (Lady Violet Dongby), Paolo Paoloni (Maestro Albertini), Sara Jane Varley (Dorotea), Fiorenzo Serra (Grand Duke of Herzog), Pina Bausch (Princess Lherimia), Pasquale Zito (Count of Bassano), Janet Suzman (Edmea Tetua), Linda Polan (Ines Ruffo Saltini), Phillip Loche (the Prime Minister), Jonathan Cecil (Ricotin), Maurice Barrier (Ziloev), Fred Williams (Sabatino Lepori), Elizabeth Kaza (producer), Colin Higgins (police chief), Umberto Zuanelli (Maestro Rubetti 1), Vittorio Zarfati (Maestro Rubetti 2), Ugo Frangareggi (head waiter), Claudio Ciocca, Antonio Vezza, Alessandro Partexano, Domenica Pertica, Christian Fremont, Marielle Duvelle, Helen Stirling; *Singers' voices*: Mara Zampieri (Ildebranda Cuffari), Elizabeth Norberg Schulz (Ines Ruffo Saltini and first Serbian soprano), Nucci Condò (Teresa Valegnani), Giovanni Bavaglio (Aureliano Fuciletto), Carlo Di Giacomo (Sabatino Lepori), Boris Carmeli (Ziloev), Bernadette Lucarini (second Serbian soprano), Bruno Beccaria (Serbian tenor); *Producer and executive producer*:

Franco Cristaldi; *Associate producer*: Aldo Nemni (SIM); *General organization*: Pietro Notarianni; *Production manager*: Lucio Orlandini; *Production supervisors*: Roberto Mannoni, Massimo Cristaldi; *Production*: Rai (Radiotelevisione Italiana) and Franco Cristaldi Vides (Italy), Gaumont (France); *Country*: Italy and France, 1983; *Duration*: 132'.

Ginger and Fred *(Ginger e Fred)*

Director: Federico Fellini; *Story*: Federico Fellini, Tonino Guerra; *Screenplay*: Federico Fellini, Tonino Guerra, Tullio Pinelli; *Photography* (technicolor): Tonino Delli Colli, Ennio Guarnieri; *Cameramen*: Aldo Marchiori, Carlo Tafani, Giovanni Fiore; *Assistant cameramen*: Gianfranco Torinti, Antonio Scaramuzza, Marco Sperduti, Luca Luparini; *Music*: Nicola Piovani, directed by the composer; *Sets*: Dante Ferretti; *Set assistant*: Franco Ceraolo; *Special effects*: Adriano Pischiutta; *Costumes*: Danilo Donati; *Set decor*: Gian Franco Fumagalli; *Architect*: Nazzareno Piana; *Costume assistant*: Rosanna Andreoni; *Paintings*: Rinaldo and Giuliano Geleng; *Choreographer*: Tony Ventura; *Editor*: Nino Baragli, Ugo De Rossi, Ruggero Mastroianni; *Assistant editor*: Marcello Olasio; *Continuity*: Norma Giacchero Del Pace; *Assistant director*: Gianni Arduini; *Assistants to the director*: Filippo Ascione, Daniela Barbiani, Eugenio Cappuccio, Anke Zindler; *Makeup*: Rino Carboni, Alfredo Tiberi; *Wigs*: Aldo Signorelli, Rosa Luciani, Giancarlo Marin; *Dubbing director*: Mario Maldesi; *Mixage*: Fausto Ancillai; *Studio*: Cinecittà; *Cast*: Giulietta Masina (Ginger), Marcello Mastroianni (Fred), Franco Fabrizi (television host *[dubbed by Alberto Lionello]*), Frederick Ledenburg (admiral), Martin Maria Blau (assistant director), Frederick Thun (kidnapped man), Jacques Henri Lartigue (flying monk), Toto Mignone (Toto), Antoine Saint Jean (assistant), Augusto Pederosi (transvestite), Antonio Iuorio (television supervisor), Nando Pucci Negri (director's assistant), Ezio Marano (intellectual), Laurentina Guidotti (production secretary) Elena Cantarone (nurse), Elisabetta Flumeri (journalist), Antonio Lorio (television supervisor), Barbara Scoppa (journalist), Salvatore Billa (Clark Gable), Ginestra Spinola (mother, voices of the deceased), Stefania Marini (television secretary), Francesco Casale (*mafioso*), Gianfranco Alpestre (lawyer), Filippo Ascione (pianist), Elena Cantarone (nurse), Cosimo Chiusoli (ex-priest's wife), Claudio Ciocca (cameraman), Sergio Ciulli (son, voices of the deceased), Federica Paccosi (ballerina), Alessandro Partexano (sailor), Tiziana Bucarella (photographer), Leonardo Petrillo (Marcel Proust), Renato Grilli (Franz Kafka), Daniele Aldrovandi (Marty Feldman), Barbara Montanari (Bette Davis), Barbara Golinska (Marlene Dietrich), Luigi Duca (Adriano Celentano), Eolo Capritti (Kojak), Nadia Giallorenzo (Queen Elizabeth), Carlo Di Placido (President Reagan), Fabrizio Libralesco (Woody

Allen), Elena Magola (literary critic), Mauro Misul (editor), Luigi Rossi (medal winner), Franco Trevisi (*carabinieri* captain), Narcisio Vicario (television station president), Vittorio De Bisogno, Roberto De Sandro, Fabrizio Fontana, Laurentina Guidotti, Giorgio Iovine, Danika La Loggia, Isabelle-Thérèse La Porte, Luigi Leoni, Luciano Lombardo, Marielle Loreley, Franco Marino, Jurgen Morhofer, Pippo Negri, Antonietta Patriarca, Nando Pucci Negri, Patty Vailati, Hermann Weiskoff; *Producer*: Alberto Grimaldi; *General organization*: Luigi Millozza; *Production manager*: Walter Massi, Gianfranco Coduti, Roberto Mannoni, Raymond Leplont; *Production supervisors*: Tullio Lullo, Fernando Rossi, Vieri Spadoni, Franco Marino; *Production secretaries*: Alessandro Mancini, Lyda Garozzo, Carla Ferroni, Maurizio Pigna, Filippo Spolentini, Marcello Mancini; *Production*: P.E.A. (Rome), Revcom Films in association with Les Films Arianne, FR3 Film Productions (Paris), Stella Film in association with Anthea (Munich), in collaboration with Rai Uno; *Country*: Italy, France and Germany (date of censor's permit: October 30, 1985); *International distribution*: Sacis; *Distribution in Italy*: Istituto Luce, Italnoleggio Cinematografico; *Duration*: 125'.
In 1985, at the Venice Film Festival, Federico Fellini was awarded the Leone d'oro for his career.

Intervista

Director: Federico Fellini; *Story and screenplay*: Federico Fellini; *Collaboration on the screenplay*: Gianfranco Angelucci; *Photography* (Eastmancolor – Dolby stereo): Tonino Delli Colli; *Music*: Nicola Piovani, with homage to Nino Rota; *Music recording*: Dolby Spectar Recording; *Sets and costumes*: Danilo Donati; *Editor*: Nino Baragli; *Assistants to the editor*: Patrizia Ceresani, Rita Mauro; *Assistant director*: Maurizio Mein; *Assistants to the director*: Daniela Barbiani, Filippo Ascione; *Casting assistant*: Fiammetta Profili; *Continuity*: Norma Giacchero Del Pace; *Dubbing director*: Carlo Baccarini; *Sound effects*: Luciano and Massimo Anzellotti; *Mixage*: Romano Pampaloni; *Cast*: Federico Fellini (himself), Sergio Rubini (the journalist), Paola Liguori (the diva), Maurizio Mein (director's assistant), Nadia Ottaviani (the Vestal), Lara Wendel (the bride), Antonella Ponziani (the girl), Pietro Notarianni (the Fascist leader), Anita Ekberg (herself), Marcello Mastroianni (himself), Maria Teresa Battaglia, Antonio Cantafora, Roberta Carlucci, Ettore Geri, Eva Grimandi, Armando Marra, Lionello Pio di Savoia, Germana Dominici, Adriana Facchetti, Mario Miyakawa, Patrizia Sacchi, Antonello Zanini, 'Il Chiodo' and the entire troupe; *General organization*: Gino Millozza; *Production manager*: Roberto Mannoni; *Executive producer*: Fernlyn; *Production supervisor*: Michele Janczreck; *Post-production*: Lillo Capoano; *RAI production representative*: Silvio Specchio;

Production secretary: Mario Mearelli; *Production*: Aljosha Productions (Ibrahim Moussa), with the collaboration of Cinecittà and Rai Uno; *Country*: Italy and France, 1987; *Distribution in Italy*: Academy; *Duration*: 113'.
Grand Prize of the XV Moscow International Film Festival.
Prize of the XL Anniversary of the Cannes Festival.

The Voice of the Moon (*La voce della luna*)

Director: Federico Fellini; *Story and Screenplay*: Federico Fellini, freely based on the novel *Il poema dei lunatici* by Ermanno Cavazzoni; *Collaborators on the screenplay*: Tullio Pinelli, Ermanno Cavazzoni; *Photography* (Technicolor): Tonino Delli Colli; *Cameraman*: Marco Sperduti; *Assistant cameramen*: Massimo Intoppa, Roberto De Franceschi; *Color*: Carlo La Bella; *Music*: Nicola Piovani; *Sets*: Dante Ferretti; *Architects*: Massimo Razzi, Nazzareno Piana; *Costumes*: Maurizio Millenotti; *Costume assistants*: Alfonsina Lettieri, Carlo Poggioli; *Set decor*: Francesco Lo Schiavo; *Choreographer*: Mirella Aguyaro; *Editor*: Nino Baragli; *Assistant director*: Gianni Arduini; *Assistants to the Director*: Daniela Barbiani, Marco Polimeni; *Sound*: Tommaso Quattrini; *Cast*: Roberto Benigni (Ivo Salvini), Paolo Villaggio (Gonnella), Nadia Ottaviani (Aldina Ferruzzi), Marisa Tomasi (Marisa, 'la vaporiera'), Angelo Orlando (Nestore), Sim (oboe player), Syusy Blady (Aldina's sister), Dario Ghirardi (journalist), Dominique Chevalier (Tazio, first Micheluzzi brother), Nigel Harris (Giuanin, second Micheluzzi brother), Vito (third Micheluzzi brother), Eraldo Turra (lawyer), Giordano Falzoni (professor), Ferruccio Brembilla (doctor), Giovanni Javarone (the grave-digger), Lorose Keller (the Duchess), Patrizio Roversi (the prefect Gonnella's son), Uta Schmidt (grandmother), Daniela Airoldi, Stefano Antonucci, Eric André Averlant, Stefano Cedrati, Giampaolo Cocchi, Roberto Corbiletto, Mario Falcione, Francesco Gabriele, Fabio Gaetani, Ettore Geri, Arrigo Mozzo, Pippo Negri, Angela Parmigiani, Carmine Ponticiello, Roberto Russoniello, Concetta Sferrazza, Giorgio Soffritti, Massimo Speroni, Silvana Strocchi, Arturo Vacquer; *Producer*: Mario and Vittorio Cecchi Gori; *Executive producers*: Bruno Altissimi, Claudio Saraceni; *Production manager*: Roberto Mannoni; *General organization*: Pietro Notarianni, Maurizio Pastrovich; *Production supervisors*: Piero Spadoni, Nicola Mastrolilli; *Production*: C.G. Group, Tiger Cinematografica and Cinemax, with the collaboration of Rai (Radiotelevisione Italiana); *Studios*: Stabilimenti Cinematografici Pontini SpA; *Distribution in Italy*: Penta Distribution in Italy; *Country*: Italy and France (date of censor's permit: February 1, 1990); *Duration*: 118'.
In 1993, in Los Angeles, Fellini received a special Oscar for his career.

Bibliography

Screenplays:

Luci del Varietà, Rome, V. Ferri 1950.

Moraldo in Città, "Cinema" (new series), Milan, August-December 1954.

La Strada, Rome, Bianco and Nero 1955.

Il Bidone, Rome, Seat 1955.

La Strada. Un film de Federico Fellini, edited by François-Régis Bastide, Juliette Caputo and Chris Marker, Paris, Editions du Seuil 1956.

Il Bidone, Paris, Flammarion 1956.

Cabiria, edited by Lino Dal Fra, Bologna, Cappelli 1957.

La Dolce Vita, edited by Tullio Kezich, Bologna, Cappelli 1960.

La Douceur de Vivre, Paris, Julliard 1960.

La Dolce Vita, edited by Hollis Alpert, New York, Ballantine Books 1961.

Boccaccio '70, edited by Carlo Di Carlo and Gaio Fratini, Bologna, Cappelli 1962.

Otto and mezzo, edited by Camilla Cederna, Bologna, Cappelli 1963.

Huit et Demi, "L'Avant-Scène Cinéma", 63, Paris 1964.

Giulietta degli Spiriti, edited by Tullio Kezich, Bologna, Cappelli 1965.

Julia und die Geister, Hamburg, Von Schroeder 1966.

Tre Passi nel Delirio, with Louis Malle and Roger Vadim, edited by Liliana Betti, Ornella Volta and Bernardino Zapponi, Bologna, Cappelli 1968.

Il Primo Fellini (*Lo Sceicco Bianco, I Vitelloni, La Strada, Il Bidone*), edited by Renzo Renzi, Bologna, Cappelli 1969.

Fellini-Satyricon, edited by Dario Zanelli, Bologna, Cappelli 1969 (American translation: *Fellini's Satyricon*, New York, Ballantine Books 1970).

Fellini: La Strada (il *découpage*), "L'Avant-Scène Cinéma", 102, April 1970.

Three screenplays: I Vitelloni, Il Bidone, The Temptations of Doctor Antonio, New York, Orion Press 1970.

Early screenplays: Variety Lights, The White Sheik, New York, Grossman Publishers 1971.

Fellini TV: Block-notes di un regista. I Clowns, edited by Renzo Renzi, Bologna, Cappelli 1972.

Roma, edited by Bernardino Zapponi, Bologna, Cappelli 1972.

Roma, "L'Avant-Scène Cinéma", 129, Paris 1972.

Amarcord, Milan, Rizzoli 1973.

Quattro film (*I Vitelloni, La Dolce Vita, Otto e Mezzo, Giulietta degli Spiriti*), with Ennio Flaiano and Tullio Pinelli, Turin, Einaudi 1974.

Das süße Leben (La Dolce Vita), Zürich, Diogenes 1974.

8 1/2, Zürich, Diogenes 1974.

Julia und die Geister, Zürich, Diogenes 1974.

Amarcord, with Tonino Guerra, edited by Gianfranco Angelucci and Liliana Betti, Bologna, Cappelli 1974.

Amarcord, with Tonino Guerra, Paris, Seghers 1974.

Amarcord, je me souviens, Paris, Gallimard 1974.

Amarcord, with Tonino Guerra, Milan, Rizzoli 1975.

Il Casanova di Fellini, with Bernardino Zapponi, Turin, Einaudi 1976.

Il Casanova di Federico Fellini, with Bernardino Zapponi, edited by Gianfranco Angelucci and Liliana Betti, Bologna, Cappelli 1977.

Die Müssiggänger (I Vitelloni), Zürich, Diogenes 1977.

Das Lied der Strasse (La Strada), Zürich, Diogenes 1977.

Die Nächte der Cabiria, Zürich, Diogenes 1977.

Le Casanova de Fellini, Paris, Albin Michel 1977.

Casanova: Drehbuch, edited by Christian Strich, Zürich, Diogenes 1977.

I Clowns, Bologna, Cappelli 1978.

Prova d'Orchestra, edited by Anna Buresi, Paris, Albatros 1979.

Orchesterprobe (Orchestra Rehearsal), Zürich, Diogenes 1979.

8 and 1/2, Paris, Albatros 1980.

Prova d'Orchestra, Milan, Garzanti 1980.

Lo Sceicco Bianco, edited by Oreste Del Buono, Milan, Garzanti 1980.

La Città delle Donne, edited by Liliana Betti, Milan, Garzanti 1980.

La Cité des Femmes, edited by Anna Buresi, Paris, Albatros 1980.

Die Stadt der Frauen (City of Women), Zürich, Diogenes 1980.
Le Notti di Cabiria, Milan, Garzanti 1981.
La Dolce Vita, Milan, Garzanti 1981.
E La Nave Va, edited by Gianfranco Angelucci, Milan, Longanesi 1983.
Moraldo in Città and *A Journey with Anita*, edited by John C. Stubbs, Urbana, University of Illinois Press 1983.
E La Nave Va, Zürich, Diogenes 1984.
Ginger and Fred, edited by Mino Guerrini, Milan, Longanesi 1986.
Viaggio a Tulum, in 'Corriere della Sera', May 1986 (in five editions).
La Strada, New Brunswich, Rutgers University Press 1987.
8 1/2, edited by Charles Affron, New Brunswich, Rutgers University Press 1987.
Intervista, Zürich, Diogenes 1987.
Bloc-notes di un regista, Milan, Longanesi 1988.
Die weisse Scheich (The White Sheik), Zürich, Diogenes 1988.
Der Gauner (Il Bidone), Zürich, Diogenes 1988.
I Clowns. Un viaggio nell'ombra, edited by Renzo Renzi, Bologna, Cappelli 1988.
La Strada, "L'Avant-Scène Cinéma", 381, May 1989.
I Vitelloni, La Strada, with Tullio Pinelli and Ennio Flaiano, Milan, Longanesi 1989.
La Dolce Vita, with Gian Luigi Rondi, edited by Gianfranco Angelucci, Rome, EdItaly 1989.
La Voce della Luna, edited by A. Luppi, Turin, Einaudi 1990.
La Voce della Luna, edited by Lietta Tornabuoni, Florence, La nuova Italia 1990.
Die Stimme des Mondes (The Voice of the Moon), Zürich, Diogenes 1990.
Il Viaggio di G. Mastorna, Milan, Bompiani 1995.
Die Reise des G. Mastorna (Il Viaggio di G. Mastorna), Zürich, Diogenes 1995.
La Strada, edited by Alberto Cattini, Mantova, Provincia di Mantova 1995.
Text from several unedited volumes, various *Lettere*, a selection of captioned images from his dream diary, *Libro dei sogni,* and two *Film-Fumetto* (comic-strips) designed by the author – *Viaggio a Tulum* and *Il viaggio di G. Mastorna* – can be found in the catalogue entitled *Federico Fellini*, edited by Lietta Tornabuoni, Milan, Rizzoli 1995, put together for the Exhibition and Convention held in Rome, January-March 1995.

Books and Essays about the Director and his Films:

Geneviève Agel, *Federico Fellini*, Brussels, Club du livre du cinéma 1954.
Geneviève Agel, *Les Chemins de Fellini*, Paris, Editions du Cerf 1956.
Renzo Renzi, *Federico Fellini*, Parma, Guanda 1956.
Giulio Cesare Castello, *Federico Fellini*, Monza, Circolo Monzese del Cinema 1958.
M. Sclappner, *Von Rossellini zu Fellini. Das Menschenbild im italienischen Neo-Realismus*, Zürich, Origo Verlag 1958.
Enrico Baragli, *Dopo la Dolce Vita*, Rome, La Civiltà Cattolica 1960.
Leonida Repaci, *Compagni di Strada*, Rome, Edizioni Moderne Canesi 1960.
Angelo Solmi, *Storia di Federico Fellini*, Milan, Rizzoli 1962 (English translation: *Fellini*, London, Merlin 1967).
Michel Estève (edited by), *Federico Fellini. 8 1/2*, "Études Cinématographiques", 28-29, Paris 1963.
Ercole Sega, *Federico Fellini amico e regista*, Bologna 1963.
Mario y Stelio Cro, *La Tematica de Fellini y La Poetica de "Ocho y Medio"*, Mar del Plata 1963.
Gilbert Salachas, *Federico Fellini*, "Cinéma d'aujourd'hui", 13, Paris, Seghers 1963.
Giuseppe Baldini, *Fellini Minerale*, Padova, Marsilio 1964.
Giulia Contri, *L'individualismo neorealistico di Federico Fellini*, Milan, Quaderni del CUCMI, 6, 1964.
O. Pinkas, *Federico Fellini*, Praha, Film a Doba 1964.
Oreste Del Buono, *Federico Fellini*, Monza, Circolo Monzese del Cinema 1965.
Fernaldo Di Giammatteo, *Federico Fellini*, 57-58, Venice, La Biennale di Venezia 1965.
Brunello Rondi, *Il Cinema di Fellini*, Rome, Edizioni di Bianco and Nero 1965.
David Grimberg, *Federico Fellini*, Tel Aviv Omanut Hakolnoa 1966.
Suzanne Rudgen, *Fellini*, London, British Film Institute 1966.
G. Boghemskij (edited by), *Federico Fellini*, Moscow, Iskusstvo kino 1968.
Gilbert Salachas, *Federico Fellini*, New York, Crown 1969.
Liliana Betti, *Federico A.C.*, Milan, Milano Libri 1970.
AA.VV., *Fellini*, "L'Arc", 45, Paris 1971.
Michele Grisolia, *Federico Fellini*, Dossier du Cinéma, Cinéastes III, Brussels, Casterman 1971.
Eileen Lanouette Hughes, *On the set of "Fellini Satyricon"*, New York, Morrow 1971.
AA.VV., *Federico Fellini*, "Kultura Filmowa", 7-8, Warsavia 1972.
Maria Kowatowska, *Federico Fellini*, Warsavia, Waif 1972.
Roger Ortmayer, *Fellini's Film Journey*, in *Three European Directors: François Truffaut, Federico Fellini, Luis Buñuel*, Grand Rapids, Eerdmans, James M. Wall 1973.
Luis Trelles Plazaola, *El Cine de Federico Fellini*, Rio Piedras, Editorial Universitaria 1973.
Pietro Angelini, *Controfellini: il fellinismo tra restaurazione e magia bianca*, Milan, Ottaviano 1974.
Albert E. Benderson, *Critical Approaches to Federico Fellini's "8 1/2"*, New York, Arno Press 1974.

Oreste Del Buono, Liliana Betti, *Federcord, Disegni Amarcord di Federico Fellini*, Milan, Milano Libri 1974.

Peter Harcourt, *Six European Directors: Eisenstein, Renoir, Buñuel,* London Penguin Books 1974.

Anna Keel, Christian Strich (edited by), *Aufsätze und Notizen*, Zürich, Diogenes 1974.

Franco Pecori, *Fellini*, Florence, La Nuova Italy 1974.

Liliana Betti, Gianfranco Angelucci (edited by), *Casanova. Rendez-vous con Federico Fellini*, Milan, Bompiani 1975.

Andrea Zanzotto, *Filo. Per il "Casanova" di Fellini*, Venice, Edizioni del Ruzante 1976 (and Mondadori 1988).

Charles B. Ketcham, *Federico Fellini: The Search for a New Mythology*, New York, Paulist Press 1976.

Edward Murray, *Fellini, The Artist*, New York, F. Ungar Publishing Co. 1976 and 1985 (Isle of Wight, ed. BCW 1977).

Stuart Rosenthal, *The Cinema of Federico Fellini*, South Brunswick, A.S. Barnes & Co. 1976.

Theodore Price, *Fellini's Penance: The Meaning of "Amarcord"*, Old Bridge, N.J., Boetius Press 1977.

Gilbert Salachas, *Federico Fellini*, Grenoble, Jacques Glénat 1977 (American translation: New York, Crown Publishers 1979).

Bernardino Zapponi, *Casanova: in un Romanzo la Storia del Film di Fellini*, Milan, Mondadori 1977.

Peter Bondanella (edited by), *Federico Fellini, Essay in Criticism*, New York, Oxford University Press 1978.

Michael Buchwal (edited by), *Fellini handkoloreret: en billed- og ord antologi*, Copenhagen 1978.

L'Officina del Casanova: Disegni e Bozzetti per il Film di Federico Fellini, Pisa, Istituto di Storia dell'arte dell'Università di Pisa 1978.

Tullio Kezich, *Il Dolce Cinema. Fellini & Altri*, Milan, Bompiani 1978.

Barbara Anne Price, Theodore Price, *Federico Fellini: an Annotated International Bibliography*, Matuchen, N.J., Scarecrow Press 1978.

John Caldwell Stubbs, Constance D. Markey, Marc Lenzini, *Federico Fellini. A Guide to References and Resources*, Boston, G.K. Hall 1978.

Liliana Betti, *Federico Fellini*, Boston Little Brown 1979.

Liliana Betti, *Fellini, un Portrait*, Paris, Albin Michel 1980.

Sonia Schoonejans, *Fellini*, Rome, Lato Side 1980.

Carlos Colon, *Rota-Fellini: la Music en las Peliculas de Federico Fellini*, Seville, Universidad de Sevilla 1981.

Michel Estève (edited by), *Federico Fellini aux Sources de l'Imaginaire*, "Études Cinématographiques", 127-130, Paris 1981.

Ennio Bispuri, *Federico Fellini, il Sentimento Latino della Vita*, Rome, Il Ventaglio 1981.

Raffaele Monti, *Bottega Fellini. La Città delle Donne: Progetto, Lavorazione, Film*, Rome, De Luca 1981.

Sandra Milo, *Caro Federico*, Milan, Rizzoli 1982.

Donald P. Costello, *Fellini's Road*, Notre Dame (Indiana), University of Notre Dame Press 1983.

Esther De Miro, Mario Guaraldi (edited by), *Fellini della Memoria*, Florence, La Casa Usher 1983.

Andrea Zanzotto, *Cori per il Film "E la Nave Va"*, Milan, Milano Libri 1983.

Frank Burke, *Federico Fellini: from "Variety Lights" to "La Dolce Vita"*, Boston, Twayne 1984.

Raffaele Monti and Pier Marco De Santi, *L'Invenzione Consapevole: Disegni e Materiali di Federico Fellini per il Film "E la Nave Va"*, Florence, Artificio 1984.

Jorge Grau, *Fellini desde Barcelona*, Barcelona, Ambit Servicios Editoriales 1985.

Hollis Alpert, *Fellini: a Life*, New York, Atheneum 1986.

Paolo Pillitteri, *Appunti su Fellini*, Milan, Cooperativa Libraria IULM 1986 (and Franco Angeli 1990).

Tullio Kezich, *Fellini*, Milan, Camunia 1987 (and Rizzoli 1988).

Dario Zanelli, *Nel Mondo di Federico: Fellini di Fronte al Suo Cinema (ed a quello degli altri)*, Turin, Nuova ERI 1987.

Michel Ciment, *Federico Fellini*, Paris, Rivages 1988.

Franco Pinna, *I Set di Fellini*, Rome, Essegi 1988.

Pier Marco De Santi, *Federico Fellini dai Disegni ai Film*, Rome, Giardini 1989.

Michael Toeteberg, *Federico Fellini*, Reinbek bei Hamburg, Rowhlt 1989.

Zdenek Zaoral, *Federico Fellini*, Praha, Filmovy klub-osobnosti 1989.

Jean Collet, *La Création selon Fellini*, Paris, José Corti 1990.

Jacqueline Risset, *Fellini, Le Cheik Blanc: L'Annonce Faite à Federico*, Paris, A. Biro 1990.

Claudio G. Fava, Aldo Viganò, *I Film di Fellini*, Rome, Gremese 1992 [2] (1981); (American translation: *The Films of Federico Fellini*, Secaucus, Citadel Press 1985; German translation: *Federico Fellini. Seine Filme – sein Leben*, Munich, Übersetzung 1989).

Harald Schleicher, *Film-Reflexionen: autothematische von Wim Wenders, Jean-Luc Godard und Federico Fellini*, Tübingen, Niemeyer 1991.

Maddalena Fellini, *Storia in Briciole d'una Casalinga Straripata: Autoritratto Tragicomico di una Coppia Riminese dalla Guerra a Oggi*, Rimini, Guaraldi 1992.

Peter Bondanella, *The Cinema of Federico Fellini*, Princeton, N.J., Princeton University Press 1992 (Italian translation: *Il Cinema di Federico Fellini*, Rimini, Guaraldi 1994).

Peter Bondanella, Cristina Degli Esposti (edited by), *Perspectives on Federico Fellini*, New York, Maxwell Macmillan International 1993.

Matilde Passa (edited by), *Fellini! Le Parole di un Sognatore da Oscar*, Rome, L'Unità 1993.

AA.VV., *Federico Fellini*, Rome, Gruppo Prospettive 1994.

AA.VV., *Fellini: I Costumes e Le Mode*, Milan, Charta 1994.

John Baxter, *Fellini: The Biography*, New York, St. Martin's Press 1994.

Ennio Cavalli, *10 Fellini 1/2: Raccontando Ricordi*, Rimini, Guaraldi 1994.

Max Evans, *Bluefeather Fellini in the Sacred Realm*, Niwot (Colorado), University Press of Colorado 1994.

Bertrand Lavergeois, *Fellini Curriculum. Fellini, La Dolce Vita du Maestro*, Paris, Arsenal 1994.

Mario Verdone, *Federico Fellini*, Rome, Il Castoro Cinema 1994.

Renzo Renzi, *L'Ombra di Fellini*, Bari, Dedalo 1994.

Charlotte Chandler, *Moi, Fellini. Treize Ans de Confidences*, Paris 1994.

José Luis de Villalonga, *Fellini*, Paris, Michel Lafont 1994.

Lietta Tornabuoni (edited by), *Federico Fellini*, Milan, Rizzoli 1995 (German translation *Federico Fellini*, Potsdam, Diogenes 1995).

Andrea Zanzotto, *La Veillée (Filo) pour "Casanova" de Fellini*, Chambéry, Comp'Act 1995.

Bernardino Zapponi, *Il Mio Fellini*, Venice, Marsilio 1995.

Manuela Gieri, *Contemporary Italian Filmaking*, Toronto, Toronto University Press 1995.

Tullio Kezich, on *La Dolce Vita* with Federico Fellini, Venice, Marsilio 1996 (new edition of *Dolce cinema*, cit.).

Writings and Interviews:

Entretiens avec Fellini, "Cahiers PTB", Brussels, Radio-télévision belge 1962.

La Mia Rimini, Bologna, Cappelli 1967.

Fellini TV, Bologna, Cappelli 1972.

Aufsätze und Notizen, edited by Anna Keel and Christian Strich, Zürich, Diogenes 1974.

Fare un Film, Turin, Einaudi 1974.

Fellini on Fellini, edited by Anna Keel and Christian Strich, London, Methuen (and New York, Delacorte Press/S. Lawrence) 1976.

Propos, Paris, Buchet-Chastel 1980.

Fellini. Intervista sul Cinema, edited by Giovanni Grazzini, Rome-Bari, Laterza 1983.

Un Regista a Cinecittà, Milan, Mondadori 1988 (English translation: London, Studio Vista 1989).

La Mia Rimini, edited by Renzo Renzi, Bologna, Cappelli 1987[2].

Federico Fellini. Dossier Positif-Rivages, Paris-Marseille, Rivages 1988.

iMago. Appunti di un Visionario, edited by Toni Maraini, Rome, Semar 1994.

Il Mestiere di Regista, edited by Rita Cirio, Milan, Garzanti 1994.

Je Suis un Grand Menteur, edited by Damien Pettigrew, Paris, L'Arche 1994.

Giulietta, Genova, Il Melangolo 1994.

Ich, Fellini, edited by Charlotte Chandler, Munich, Herbig Verlagsbuchhandlung 1994 (French translation: *Moi Fellini. Treize Ans de Confidences*, Paris, Robert Laffont 1994; Italian translation: *Io, Federico Fellini*, Milan, Mondadori 1995; American translation: New York, Random House 1995).

Conversations avec Federico Fellini, Paris, Éditions Denoël 1995 (Italian translation: *Fellini. Raccontando di Me*, edited by Costanzo Costantini, Rome, Editori Riuniti 1996).

Il Mio Amico Pasqualino, Rimini, Fondazione Federico Fellini 1997 (anastatic printing of Edizioni dell'Ippocampo, s.d.).

Comic Strips:

Viaggio a Tulum, edited by Vincenzo Mollica; Milan, Milano Libri-RCS 1990; second edition, *Viaggio a Tulum. Milo Manara. Da un Book di Federico Fellini per un Film da Fare*, Rome, Editori del Grifo 1991.

Il viaggio di G. Mastorna detto Fernet, edited by di Vincenzo Mollica, "Il Grifo" 1992.

Iconographic Material:

Federico Fellini: Dessins, with preface by Topor, Paris, Albin Michel 1977.

Christian Strich (edited by), *Fellini's Filme: die vierhundert schoensten Bilder aus Federico Fellini's fünfzehneinhalb Filmen*, Zürich, Diogenes 1976 (American translation: *Fellini's Films: the Four Hundred Most Memorable Stills from Federico Fellini's Fifteen and a Half films*, New York, Putnam 1977 and Holt, Rinehart and Winston 1982; Italian translation: *Federico Fellini. Le Più Belle Fotografie dei Quindici Film e Mezzo di Federico Fellini*, preface by Georges Simenon, Rome, Gremese 1979).

Christian Strich (edited by), *Fellini's Faces: Vierhundertachtzehn Bilder aus Federico Fellini's Fotoarchiv*, Zürich, Diogenes 1981.

Pier Marco De Santi (edited by), *I Disegni di Fellini*, Rome-Bari, Laterza 1982.

Index of names